From Telling to Selling

Language at work for Key Stage 4

Sarah Matthews

and

Huw Parker

Stanley Thornes (Publishers) Ltd

First published in 1998 by:
Stanley Thornes (Publishers) Ltd
Ellenborough House
Wellington Street
CHELTENHAM GL50 1YW
England

98 99 00 01 02 / 10 9 8 7 6 5 4 3 2 1

A catalogue record for this book is available from the British Library

ISBN 0-7487-2979-8

Printed and bound in Great Britain by Scotprint Ltd, Musselburgh, Scotland

Typeset by Tech Set Ltd, Gateshead, Tyne & Wear

Acknowledgements

With thanks to the following for permission to reproduce copyright material in this book:

Airtours Holidays Ltd for a page from their holiday brochure; Art of Memory (Interactive) Ltd for frames from CD Rom on *Twelfth Night*; Bantam Press, a division of Transworld Publishers Ltd, for material from Stephen Hawking, *A Brief History of Time*. Copyright © Space Time Publications 1988; BBC Worldwide Ltd for 'Going Out in a Blaze of Glory', *Radio Times*, 21-23 October 1996; Cambridge University Press for material from David Crystal, *The Cambridge Encyclopedia of Language*, 1987, p. 247; The Controller of Her Majesty's Stationary Office for material from the leaflets, 'Drugs and Solvents: A Young Person's Guide' and 'Solvents: A Parent's Guide'; Guardian News Service Ltd for Zygmunt Bauman, 'The haunted house', *New Internationalist*, April (1997). Copyright © New Internationalist; review by Andy Bodle, 'Caroline in The City', *The Guardian*, 14.9.96. Copyright © The Guardian; Linda Grant, 'Violent Anxiety', *The Guardian*, 28.9.96. Copyright © The Guardian; Linda Grant, 'Children of the Eighties', *The Guardian*, 6.1.96. Copyright © The Guardian; interview of Helen Mirren by Ian Katz, *The Guardian*, 4.1.97. Copyright © The Guardian; Phil Hogan, 'Him indoors', *The Observer*, 'Life' section, p. 86. Copyright © The Observer; review by Philip French, 'A Time to Kill', *The Observer*, 15.9.96. Copyright © The Observer; Fourth Estate Ltd for material from Harriet Blodgett, ed., *The Englishwoman's Diary*. Copyright © 1991 by the Rector and Visitors of the University of Virginia; The Heath School for material from their prospectuses; Hello Ltd for an interview with Ian Botham by Ian Woodward, *Hello*, 1997. Copyright © Hello! Magazine; Just Seventeen for material from 'Life Sucks', *Just Seventeen*, May 1997; Northern Examinations and Assessment Board for 'Coursework Marking', NEAB English Syllabus 1998; Penguin UK for material from Maxim Gorky, *My Childhood*, trans. Ronald Wilks, Penguin Classics, 1966, pp. 13-5. Copyright © Ronald Wilks 1966; and David Willets, *Why Vote Conservative?* Penguin Books, 1997, pp. 1-3. Copyright © David Willets 1997; Peters Fraser & Dunlop Group Ltd on behalf of the author for material from Redmond O'Hanlon, *Into the Heart of Borneo*, Picador; Plan International UK for advertising material; Random House UK for extracts from Marcel Junod, *Warrior Without Weapons*, trans. Edward Fitzgerald, 1951, Jonathan Cape; and Gertrude Bell, *Amurath to Amurath*, William Heinemann, 1911; The Rough Guides for material from Richard Trillo, *The Rough Guide to Kenya*, 5th revised edition, Rough Guides/Penguin. 1996; Virago Press Ltd for material from Maya Angelou, *I Know Why the Caged Bird Sings*, 1969, pp. 11-4; Walker Books Ltd for material from Nicholas Fisk, *Pig Ignorant*, pp. 7-9. Copyright © 1992 Nicholas Fisk; Which? Ltd for material from the assured shorthold tenancy agreement in Peter Wilde, *The Which? Guide to Renting and Letting*, 1996.

The Reward of Merit boardgame on page 4 is reproduced by courtesy of the Trustees of the Victoria and Albert Museum, London.

Every effort has been made to contact copyright holders. The publishers apologise to anyone whose rights have been inadvertently overlooked, and will be happy to rectify any errors or omissions.

Contents

Introduction

This book has two main aims: to make non-fiction comprehensible, and to make it accessible and enjoyable. It is our hope that, after using this book, students will be in a position to read and react to any non-fiction text with confidence, whether in the examination room or in the world at large.

What is non-fiction? All human life is there, from the driest legal text to the most passionate propaganda. It is an area as wide and diverse as society itself. One of the problems we found in teaching non-fiction texts was the fragmented nature of the experience from the students' point of view – one day a passage from a diary, the next a leaflet on environmental issues – with no apparent link between the different kinds of texts studied or the tasks set. In order to enable the students to form a picture of the whole area, which would both enable them to make links between the different texts and also put them in a position to tackle any non-fiction text they encountered, we have developed the notion of a non-fiction continuum, based upon the purpose for which the text was written and the reaction it seeks from its readership. Each genre of non-fiction writing in the book is sited along this continuum.

In this book we therefore provide:

- **A coherent vision.** All non-fiction can be seen as having a place at some point along the continuum from 'information' to 'persuasion', depending upon its function and on the author's intention. By describing the continuum and clearly situating each text at the appropriate point along it, how to read, react to and reproduce that text and others like it will be made clear. The continuum is described further below and, although it recognises that not all non-fiction can be easily categorised, it does offer a clear framework for understanding.

- **A single source for the whole range of texts.** The following types of texts are included:

Autobiography	*Instructional writing*	*Promotional writing*
Biography	*Interviews*	*Reportage*
Diaries	*Legal writing*	*Reviews*
Electronic texts	*Letters*	*Social commentary*
Essays	*Philosophical writing*	*Travel writing*
Information writing	*Polemic*	

- **Differentiated texts and tasks to cater for all levels of ability.** Texts and tasks are arranged in a rising order of difficulty and complexity. This enables teachers to select texts for students and guide them towards appropriate tasks.

- **A range of cultures.** As well as drawing upon the British repertoire of non-fiction and non-literary texts, the book reflects the increasingly international character of the information network by drawing on a world-wide range of non-fiction texts written in or translated into English.

- **A range of periods.** While being predominantly contemporary, texts are also drawn from different moments in history, including some influential texts in

translation (such as Plato, Plutarch and Montaigne). This also provides a
context for recent developments in non-fiction.

- **Cross-curricular links.** Activities make clear how the reading and writing skills
fostered in the books are transferable across the whole curriculum.

- **Mutuality.** Activities make clear how the skills of reading, writing, speaking and
listening required in the English curriculum are mutually supportive, and how
they in turn support learning across the curriculum.

- **An understanding of how language works.** Knowledge about language no
longer features as a discrete section of the English National Curriculum. It
features heavily, however, in both the programmes of study and level
descriptions (for example, 'how authors achieve their effects through the use of
linguistic, structural and presentational devices') and remains an essential
component in every aspect of English teaching. The activities enable students to
develop close reading skills which in turn develop awareness of how language
works.

- **Information skills.** Many activities focus on and foster the ability to understand
and apply the information process of locating, reading, selecting, retrieving and
reproducing information.

- **Stimulating materials for reluctant readers.** Materials and activities cater for
and extend the understanding of those readers, both able and less able, who are
less confident with reading fiction texts, and who prefer reading non-fiction.

- **Links with GNVQ communication skills.** The skills required in the core
element of communication include taking part in discussions, producing written
material, reading and responding to written material and using images.
Students need to be clear about such issues as purpose, audience, situation,
convention and format. They will also need to demonstrate the ability to
retrieve and summarise information. This book affords ample opportunity to
address these requirements of GNVQs.

THE INFORMATION–PERSUASION CONTINUUM

Our aim in this textbook is to provide students with a strategy for reading,
understanding, responding appropriately and being in a position to replicate the
whole spread of non-literary texts. In order that they can do so, they need to be
able to identify what the text is there for, what the writer of the text is seeking to
achieve and what is the desired response from the reader.

All texts, whether literary or non-literary, are written for a purpose, even if that
purpose is only clarifying things for oneself. It might appear that the purpose of
non-literary writing is consistently open and clear – an instruction booklet is there
to tell the reader what to do in a particular set of circumstances, a political
manifesto is there to persuade the reader to accede to a particular set of beliefs or
to vote in a particular way. The intention appears obvious, and thus the
appropriate response to the text also appears obvious – follow the instructions,
agree, or disagree, with the content of the manifesto. But what of reviews,
biographies, travel writing? What of texts such as Swift's *A Modest Proposal*, where
apparent intention and actual intention are at odds with each other? In order to

be in a position to respond appropriately and to replicate accurately, the student needs to be able to decipher the authorial intention behind each and every text that they are faced with.

In order to facilitate that understanding, we have identified seventeen genres of non-literary texts and located them along a continuum which runs from straightforward instruction writing at the one end, where the aim of the writing is to be as transparent and unambiguous as possible, to enable the reader to take appropriate and successful action, to polemic at the other end, where the aim of the writing is to persuade the reader of the rightness of a cause or of a particular set of beliefs. The enfranchised reader and effective writer is one who can distinguish the intention of each text along this continuum, and act appropriately towards it.

The full continuum, set out below, is also reproduced at the beginning of each section, so that the specific genre under consideration can be located appropriately. Of course, there will be variations as to the locations of particular texts within a genre – some autobiographies are more obviously written to justify the author than others – and one activity that teachers could usefully do throughout the book is to ask the student how they would locate the text they have studied along the continuum.

Two of our selected genres are treated slightly differently in relation to the continuum. Letters, depending on the intention of the writer, may clearly be located at any point along it, while electronic texts, being a new way of *publishing* rather than a new way of *writing*, may include any of the genres we have identified.

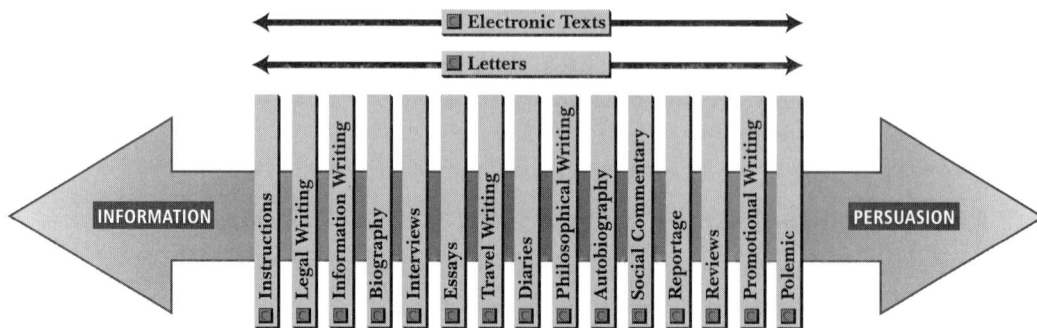

List of Texts Used

To the Student

This book is designed to help you get to grips with the whole range of non-fiction texts which you encounter every day, in school and out. Each category, or genre, of text has been placed along a continuum from information to persuasion, depending on why it was written and what kind of action or reaction is expected from the reader (see the diagram on page vi).

The continuum runs from straightforward instruction writing at the one end, where the aim of the writing is to be as clear and precise as possible so that the reader can take the appropriate action, to polemic at the other end, where the aim of the writing is to persuade the reader of the rightness of a cause or of a set of beliefs.

Of course, individual texts within a genre may vary in their locations along the continuum. Some autobiographies, for example, are written more to justify the author than others. As you work on the book, and tackle the individual texts, see whether you think that text does belong exactly where its category has been placed, or whether you would place it closer to information or nearer to persuasion.

Doing this with any text you encounter will help you to be clear what kind of text you are dealing with, and how to react to it.

INFORMATION

Instructions
Legal Writing
Information Writing
Biography
Interviews
Essays
Travel Writing
Diaries
Philosophical Writing
Autobiography
Social Commentary
Reportage
Reviews
Promotional Writing
Polemic

PERSUASION

1
Instructions

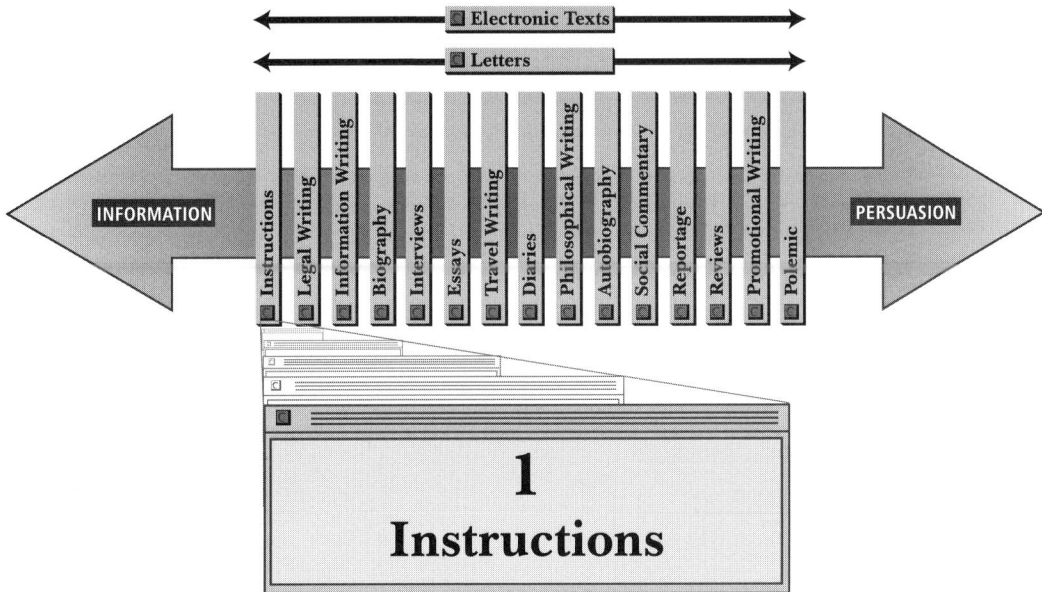

Instructions are both the simplest and, when you're writing them, the most difficult kind of writing that there is. In order to be reliable, instructions have to be absolutely clear, and it is not always easy to write in such a way that the language you use is simple and unambiguous. That is why instructions are often accompanied by illustrations, so that the text and pictures together can give a precise idea of the action that needs to be taken.

In the passages that follow you will find a range of different instructions aimed at getting the reader to take different kinds of action. One question you might like to ask yourself as you are reading is, are they always as clear as they need to be, and, if not, why not?

1 Coursework marking

All examination syllabuses come with descriptions and instructions, to ensure that the candidates for the examination are properly prepared. The extract below is taken from the Northern Examinations and Assessment Board's (NEAB) instructions to teachers on how to mark the candidates' coursework folders in the 1998 GCSE English examination.

(Some words are highlighted in the text. You will find further information about these words at the end of the passage.)

10 Coursework Marking

10.1   *Mark Schemes*

Three marks are required for coursework, one for Speaking and Listening (En1), Reading (En2) and Writing (En3). These marks must be **allocated** using the mark schemes in Appendix 6.

These mark schemes are provided to enable both final assessment of the candidates' complete submission at the end of the course, and the assessment of individual coursework responses. In allocating marks there must be a focus on the particular **assessment objectives** addressed by each response as well as on the general qualities expected in any mark range.

Details of penalties incurred by candidates who fail to make a complete submission are in para. 10.4.

10.2   *Internal Standardisation*

Centres must ensure that **internal standardisation** takes place across different teaching groups prior to the submission of coursework marks. A declaration to this effect must be made in Section C of the Coursework Cover Sheet by the teacher responsible for internal standardising.

10.3   *Mark Submission*

Coursework must be submitted by *30 April* in the year of the examination, using the mark form supplied by the NEAB. Marks submitted to the NEAB are confidential and must not be relayed to candidates prior to the publication of results.

10.4   *Incomplete Folders*

Where a candidate fails to present a complete En2 or En3 submission for assessment, or fails to take part in sufficient En1 activities to allow three assessments to be made, an initial mark should be awarded (using the appropriate mark schemes in Appendix 6) which reflects the overall achievement of the candidate **irrespective** of the number of responses submitted. This mark should then be reduced ***pro rata*** to the nearest whole number, i.e. by one third for each missing En1 assessment or En2 response or by one half for each missing En3 response.

From Syllabus 1202 English paper, NEAB, 1988

DICTIONARY

allocated awarded, given

assessment objectives skills being examined

internal standardisation a process of checking to ensure that all teachers in a department are marking to the same level

irrespective without taking into account

pro rata proportionately

CLOSER READING

1 The mark schemes provided by the Board apply to two different things. Look through the extract again, and note down the two things for which the mark schemes are to be used.

2 Look through and note down whether or not candidates may told their coursework marks before they have sat the examinations.

3 Re-read 10.4, the section on incomplete folders, and write down in your own words how a mark is given to a folder where there is a piece of written work missing.

4 Look through the whole extract again, and check to see whether there are any areas to do with marking which have not been covered. If you find any, write down extra instructions to cover them, using the same tone and language as the original.

2 | Hot cross buns

In the recipe below, the author has two main things to communicate to the reader – what to use, and how to use them. These are often broken down into two sections, *ingredients* and *method*. One question you might like to ask yourself as you read through is just how much specialist knowledge is still assumed, even though the instructions appear very clear.

HOT CROSS BUNS
Ingredients

30g (1oz) fresh yeast, or 15g ($\frac{1}{2}$oz)
  dried yeast
5 tablespoons lukewarm water
150ml ($\frac{1}{4}$ pint) lukewarm milk
450g (1lb) strong plain flour
85g (3oz) caster sugar
1 level teaspoon salt
2 level teaspoons mixed spice

60g (2oz) butter, softened
85g (3oz) currants
30g (1oz) mixed peel (chopped)
1 egg, beaten
85g (3oz) plain flour
1 teaspoon vegetable oil
2–3 tablespoons water
2 tablespoons each milk and water,
  for glaze

Preparation time: 45 minutes
Rising time: 1$\frac{1}{2}$ hours
Cooking time: 20 minutes
Makes 12 buns

Method

If using fresh yeast, mix the water and milk, add the yeast and stir until dissolved.

If using dried yeast, add to 4oz of the strong flour and sift into a bowl. Stir in 1 teaspoon of caster sugar.

If using fresh yeast, pour in the yeast liquid at this stage, and beat until smooth. Cover and leave in a warm place for 15 minutes, until frothy.

Sift the salt, mixed spice and remaining strong flour into a bowl and rub in the butter. Stir in the currants, peel and 60g (2oz) of the remaining caster sugar. Make a well in the centre and add the yeast mixture and the egg. Mix to a soft dough, then knead it on a lightly floured board for 10 minutes until smooth and elastic. Put the dough into a lightly oiled bowl, cover well and leave in a warm place for about an hour or until doubled in size.

Reknead and shape the dough into 12 smooth balls. Place, spread slightly apart, on a greased baking sheet, cover with lightly oiled cling-film and leave in a warm place for 30 minutes or until doubled in size.

Meanwhile, preheat the oven to 190°C (375°F, Gas mark 5). To make the crosses, sift the plain flour into a bowl then stir in the oil and enough water to make a smooth paste which will hold its shape when piped. Spoon into a small, paper piping bag, cut a hole in the bottom, and pipe a cross on the top of each bun. Bake for 20 minutes or until the buns are golden brown and sound hollow when tapped on the bottom.

Meanwhile, heat the remaining sugar in the milk and water until dissolved. Keep hot, and brush over the buns immediately they are removed from the oven. Cool on wire racks.

CLOSER READING

1 Read through the Method again, putting a number against each stage of the instructions. (You should end up with about ten.)
2 Draw a small illustration for each numbered stage.
3 Write a short caption for each of your illustrations. The first one might look something like this.

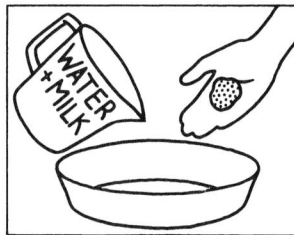

1. If using fresh yeast, add it to the water and milk mixture, and mix together.

3 Assembling the MSR XGK II™ Shaker Jet Stove

The instructions on page 5 are for putting together a camping stove. As the stove generates a very high temperature flame, it is important that the instructions are clear if the user of the stove is not to have a serious accident.

MSR XGK II ™ Shaker Jet Stove

⚠️ **WARNING:** TO AVOID INJURY, read, understand and follow all instructions and warnings in this manual before using the stove.

Use ONLY MSR Fuel Bottles with this stove. Non-MSR Fuel Bottles may result in fuel leakage and/or separation from the Pump. Fuel may ignite possibly resulting in injury or death.

DO NOT light or use indoors, in a tent, vehicle or other enclosed areas. A fire or carbon monoxide poisoning could cause injury or death.

ALWAYS check for spilled fuel and fuel leaks before lighting stove. If leaks are found, DO NOT USE STOVE. Repair it or send it to MSR retailer or MSR Product Service Center for repairs.

NEVER put your head or body above stove when priming, lighting or burning. Keep clothing and other materials that may catch fire away from stove.

NEVER unlock the Catch Arm or disconnect the stove, Pump or Fuel Bottle when the stove is lit, warm from recent use or near any flame or heat source. Leaking fuel can cause a serious fire hazard.

DO NOT relight a warm stove. Warm stove parts may vaporize liquid fuel and cause a dangerous "fireball" when relighting.

DO NOT shake a stove in operation.

Below about -24° C (-10° F) O-Rings may become stiff and can leak or break causing a fire.

DO NOT place heavy or large capacity cookware on the stove (Maximum weight: 8 lbs, maximum pot diameter: 9").

Before taking the stove on a trip, check for fuel leaks and practice using and maintaining it.

NEVER leave a burning or hot stove unattended. NEVER allow children to use stoves. ALWAYS SUPERVISE CHILDREN IN THE VICINITY OF THE STOVE.

DO NOT use the stove in any way other than as described in these instructions. DO NOT alter the stove or use non-MSR parts. DO NOT disassemble beyond what is described in these instructions.

FAILURE TO FOLLOW THESE WARNINGS AND INSTRUCTIONS COULD RESULT IN SERIOUS INJURY OR DEATH!

XGK II Fuels & Stove Performance

SG-Jet Fuels

- White gas is typically the fuel of choice for the XGK II. Also called "pressure appliance fuel," common brands include MSR® White Gas, Goleman® Fuel and CampLite®. Good quality white gas burns clean and leaves few deposits in the Fuel Line.
- Automobile gasoline is very volatile and contains additives that leave more deposits in the Fuel Line than white gas or kerosene.
- Piston engine airplane fuel or aviation (AV) gas has additives that clog the stove.

SK-Jet Fuels

- Kerosene is inexpensive and readily available worldwide, but it burns with more soot, is more difficult to prime, and can cause frequent cleaning.
- Commercial jet fuel or "Jet-A" is similar to a high quality kerosene. It can be a good alternative fuel source when travelling internationally.
- Diesel fuel creates a lot of soot, is hard to prime, and requires frequent cleaning.

Before Assembling the Stove

Ensure the correct Shaker Jet is installed:

Use the SG Jet for white gas, automobile gasoline [1] and aviation (AV) gas. The SG Jet is pre-installed in the stove.

Use the SK Jet for kerosene, jet fuel and diesel. The SK Jet is contained in the Parts Kit included with your stove. To change Jets, see "Burner Maintenance."

Assembling the Stove

1. Fill an MSR Fuel Bottle to the 2 inch Fill Line.
2. Screw the Pump snugly into the Fuel Bottle.
3. Pump the Plunger 15-20 strokes. If the Fuel Bottle is half full, pump Plunger 40-55 pump strokes, or until firm resistance is felt when you push down on the Plunger. *The less fuel in the Fuel Bottle, the more Pump strokes needed to pressurize it for proper stove operation.*
4. Lubricate the end of the Fuel Line lightly with MSR Pump Cup Oil (saliva or other mineral-based lubricant), then insert it into the Fuel Tube Bushing on the Pump (Figure 1).
5. Snap the Catch Arm securely into the slot on the Pump Body (Figure 2).
6. Put the Heat Reflector over the burner and push down to the rim of the Enclosure.
7. Insert the lower and upper Panwires firmly into the slots in the Enclosure (Figure 3).

[1] Automobile gasoline is very volatile and contains additives that leave more deposits in the Fuel Line than white gas or kerosene.

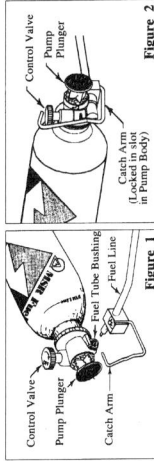

Figure 1

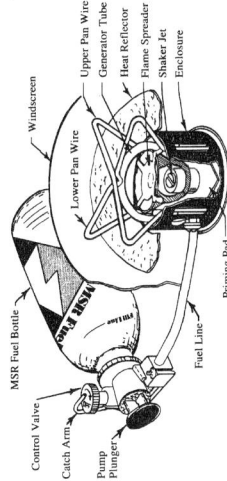

Figure 2

Figure 3

Operating the Stove

Before lighting the stove check that:

- Stove assembly has no fuel leaks.
- Catch Arm is locked and stove is properly assembled.
- Area is clear of flammable material and spilled fuel.
- Correct Jet is installed.

Priming

To pre-heat the stove, the priming flame must contact the Generator Tube. Insufficient priming may result in flare-up.

1. Open the Control Valve until fuel flows through the Jet and wets the Priming Pad.
2. **Turn the Control Valve off.**
3. Check for leaks at the Control Valve, Pump, Jet and Fuel Line. If leaks are found, DO NOT USE STOVE (See "Troubleshooting").
4. Light the Priming Pad.
5. Place the Windscreen around the stove, then fold the ends together to keep it securely in place.

Turning the Stove On

1. As the priming flame gets smaller, slowly open the Control Valve. DO NOT force the Control Valve past the Stop Nut, since this can strip the threads of the Pump.
2. If the stove:
   - Goes out, turn the Control Valve off. After the stove cools return to "Priming."
   - Burns with erratic yellow flames, but the Priming Cup flame is still burning, turn the Control Valve off and pre-heat longer.
   - Burns with a blue flame, wait 1 minute then adjust to the desired setting. *There is a delay between turning the Control Valve and changes in the amount of flame.*
3. To maintain stove performance, pump the Plunger 3 - 5 strokes as needed to keep enough pressure in the Fuel Bottle. You should feel firm resistance when you pump down on the Plunger. The less fuel in the Fuel Bottle, the more Pump strokes needed to pressurize it for proper stove operation. Do not over-pressurize. Fuel Bottle pressure that is too high causes erratic flames. Fuel Bottle pressure that is too low causes low flames and very slow burn times.
4. To simmer, operate the stove at low Fuel Bottle pressure. Turn the Control Valve down until the flame becomes unsteady, then open Control Valve until the flame stabilizes.

Turning the Stove Off

1. Turn the Control Valve off. The flame will take a few seconds to die out. WAIT for the stove to cool before disassembling.
2. To depressurize the Fuel Bottle: unlock the Catch Arm and pull the Fuel Line out of the Pump/Fuel Bottle assembly. Away from heat, sparks or flame, hold the Fuel Bottle upright, keep the Pump/Fuel Bottle away from you, and unscrew the Pump to release pressure.
3. For transporting or storing: keep the Pump assembled in the Fuel Bottle or, to be sure the Control Valve does not open by mistake, remove the Pump and replace it with the Fuel Bottle Cap.

CLOSER READING

1 Look again at the Warning section, and note down in your own words:
   - the two items that are specifically stated as being the possible causes of injury or death;
   - the items that may result in a fire;
   - the item that may cause a fireball.
2 Re-read the section on fuels, and list in order of preference the fuels that are recommended for use, starting with the cleanest and ending with the one most likely to clog up the stove.
3 Look again at the section entitled Turning the Stove On, and re-write it as a conversation between an experienced user of the stove giving advice to somebody who has never used the stove before. Remember to use speech punctuation accurately.

4 | The Reward of Merit

The extract below is from the instructions to a board game first published in 1801, just in time for the Christmas market. As well as being a game, it is also intended as moral instruction, with good behaviour being rewarded and bad behaviour, such as truanting, being punished. The player who finally wins through to the end is shown receiving a clock as 'the reward of merit'.

(Some words are highlighted in the text. You will find further information about these words at the end of the passage.)

A NEW, MORAL AND ENTERTAINING GAME OF THE REWARD OF MERIT

Explanation of the game

This Game must be played with a **Teetotum,** and any number of Persons may play it. The Teetotum must have six faces, and be numbered from one to six. Every Player must be **furnished** with a Dozen Counters, the value of which to be agreed on; and also with another Counter, bearing the Initial of his Name, to be called a Mark. Each Person must then stake two Counters into the Pool. One person must be appointed to store all the Marks, and that Person to be entitled to the first Spin for his trouble. When he has spun twice, he must place his Mark under the number corresponding with the Amount of the numbers he has Spun and act as they are directed. When all the rest have regularly done the same, he must Spin again and add the amount of the numbers Spun to the number which his Mark occupies and to their total he must advance his Mark. Each Player in his turn must proceed in the same manner, till some Person wins the game by arriving at (37) The Reward of Merit.

Rules of the Game

1. Whoever is confined in the Dungeon cannot be released till some other Person is sent there and when released must begin the game again.

2. When two come together the last Spinner must take possession of the place he comes to; the other Person must return to the place from whence he came, and must receive a Stake from the Person who takes his place as a compensation for being thrown back.

3. Should the Pool at any time become empty or not contain a sufficient number of Stakes to satisfy a player's demands, each Person must stake two Counters into it, as at the beginning of the game; the Claimant then to receive his proper number of Stakes.

4. Whoever exceeds the number (37) must begin the game again.

5. Whoever arrives at (37) The Reward of Merit wins the game and is entitled to the contents of the Pool.

DICTIONARY

Teetotum a small disk or die having an initial letter or number written on each of its sides, and a spindle passing down through it by which it could be twirled or spun with the fingers like a small top, the letter or number which lay uppermost, when it fell, deciding the fortune of the player

furnished provided

CLOSER READING

1 Re-read the instructions for starting the game, and re-write them in your own words, making them as clear as possible. You may wish to break them down into numbered sections.

2 Look through the Rules of the Game again, and put them into your own words.

3 Take the two passages which you have written, and swap them with a partner. Read each other's passages, to see how clear they are. Suggest any changes you think necessary.

4 Read through the changes your partner has suggested, and make any changes necessary.

FURTHER ACTIVITIES

1 The Jumper Game

- You will need to work in groups of five or six, and will need a jumper and a blindfold for each group.

- Select two players, Player 1 to be the person following the instructions, and Player 2 to be the instructor. The instructor needs to be securely blindfolded so that they can genuinely not see at all.

- Player 2 stands or sits and tells Player 1 how to put on the jumper. It is important that Player 1 does exactly what they are told, and does not do anything that they are not told to do. For instance, if the instructor says, 'Take hold of the end of the sleeve and put your arm through it,' Player 1 may put their arm through either end of the sleeve, and must not release their hold unless told to do so.

- The other members of the group should watch and observe, then each in turn become instructors and the person following instructions.

- When everybody has had a turn, discuss as a group which instructions worked best.

- On your own, write instructions for putting on a jumper. You may include illustrations if you wish.

2 Opening a Door

- Working with a partner, observe and note down the different stages you need to go through in order to open, go through and close a door.

- With your partner, draw up a flow-chart of all the actions you need to take, in the order you need to take them. Your flow-chart might begin like the one on page 9.

1. With right hand, grasp door handle

↓

2. Turn door handle to left

↓

3. Pull door towards you

- On your own, using the flow-chart as a basis, write a set of instructions for opening and going through a door. You may not include illustrations.

3 Surviving School

- On your own, invent and make a board game called 'Surviving School'. You will need to draw up instructions and a set of rules.
- In groups of three or four, test out each other's games, and make notes of any improvements that could be made.
- On your own, write a report for a games manufacturer on the best game in the group, saying how it works and why it is effective.

INFORMATION ←——————————→ PERSUASION

Electronic Texts

Letters

Instructions · Legal Writing · Information Writing · Biography · Interviews · Essays · Travel Writing · Diaries · Philosophical Writing · Autobiography · Social Commentary · Reportage · Reviews · Promotional Writing · Polemic

2
Legal Writing

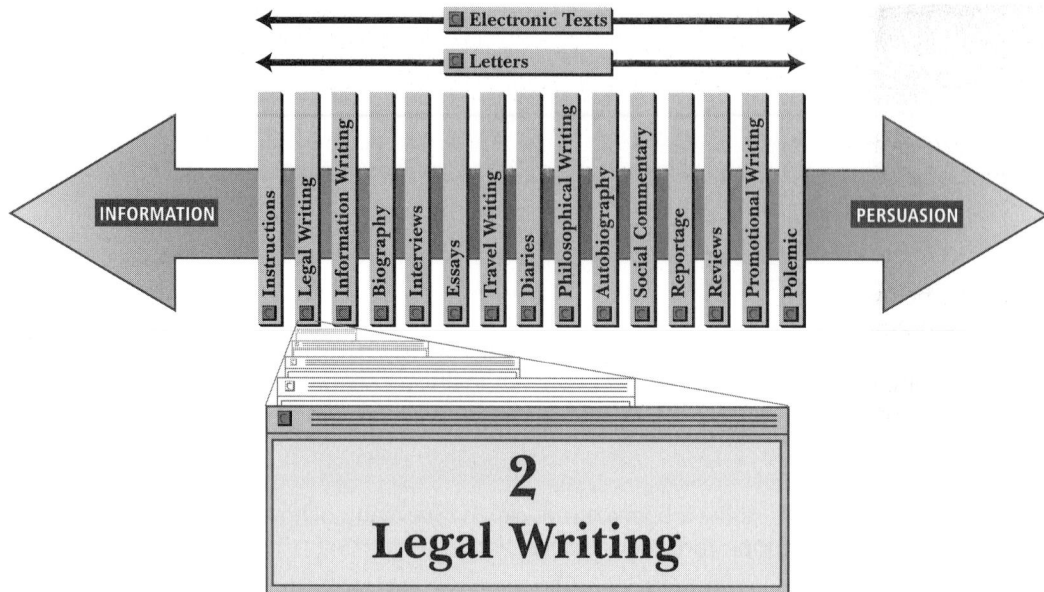

The aim of legal writing is to be completely clear and unambiguous, so that there is no doubt as to what has been agreed. Because of this need for clarity, both the use of language and the use of punctuation are extremely important. A word that can be misinterpreted may lead to a dispute, while a comma in the wrong place can completely change the meaning of a sentence, so that the wrong action is taken.

The most important legal documents that the majority of people come across are agreements, wills and contracts, while the most important legal writing that affects us is the writing of the laws that govern our behaviour as citizens.

1 Powers of police to stop and search

This is an extract from the Criminal Justice and Public Order Act 1994. The Act forms part of a continuing process of change and reform, in which politicians have sought to regulate what people may and may not do, in order to establish a safe and peaceful society.

The passage below, taken from Section 60 of the Act, deals with the powers given to the police to stop and search people.

(Some words are highlighted in the text. You will find further information about these words at the end of the passage.)

POWERS TO STOP AND SEARCH IN **ANTICIPATION** OF VIOLENCE

(1)   Where a police officer of or above the rank of superintendent reasonably believes that—
   (a) incidents involving serious violence may take place in any **locality** in his area, and
   (b) it is **expedient** to do so to prevent their occurrence,
   he may give an authorisation that the powers to stop and search persons or vehicles conferred by this section shall be exercisable at any place within that locality for a period not **exceeding** twenty four hours.

(2)   The power **conferred** by subsection (1) above may be exercised by a chief inspector or inspector if he reasonably believes that incidents involving serious violence are **imminent** and no superintendent is available.

(3)   If it appears to the officer who gave the authorisation or to a superintendent that it is expedient to do so, having regard to offences which have, or are reasonably suspected to have, been committed in connection with any incident falling within the authorisation, he may direct that the authorisation shall continue in being for a further six hours.

(4)   This section confers on any constable in uniform power—
   (a) to stop any pedestrian and search him or anything carried by him for offensive weapons or dangerous instruments;
   (b) to stop any vehicle and search the vehicle, its driver and any passenger for offensive or dangerous instruments.

(5)   A constable may, in the exercise of those powers, stop any person or vehicle and make any search he thinks fit whether or not he has any grounds for suspecting that the person or vehicle is carrying weapons or articles of that kind.

(6)   If in the course of a search under this section a constable discovers a dangerous instrument or an article which he has reasonable grounds for suspecting to be an offensive weapon, he may seize it.

(7)   This section applies (with the necessary modifications) to ships, aircraft and hovercraft as it applies to vehicles.

(8)   A person who fails to stop or (as the case may be) to stop the vehicle when required to do so by a constable in the exercise of his powers under this section shall be liable on summary conviction to imprisonment for a term not exceeding one month or to a fine not exceeding level 3 on the standard scale or both.

(9)   Any authorisation under this section shall be in writing signed by the officer giving it and shall specify the locality in which and the period during which the powers conferred by this section are exercisable and a direction under subsection (3) above shall also be given in writing or, where that is not practicable, recorded in writing as soon as it is practicable to do so.

(10)   Where a vehicle is stopped by a constable under this section, the driver shall be entitled to obtain a written statement that the vehicle was stopped under the powers conferred by this section if he applies for such a statement not later than the end of the period of twelve months from the day on which the vehicle was stopped and similarly as respects a pedestrian who is stopped and searched under this section.

(11)   In this section—
'dangerous instruments' means instruments which have a blade or are sharply pointed;
'offensive weapon' has the meaning given by section 1(9) of the Police and Criminal Evidence Act 1984; and
'vehicle' includes a caravan as defined in section 29(1) of the Caravan Sites and Control of Development Act 1960.

(12)   The powers conferred by this section are in addition to and not in **derogation** of, any powers otherwise conferred.

From the Criminal Justice and Public Order Act 1994

DICTIONARY

anticipation action taken in order to stop another possible action taking place
locality place, location
expedient useful
exceeding more than
conferred given
imminent likely to happen soon
derogation lessening, diminishing

CLOSER READING

1 Look again at subsections 1 and 2. Summarise in your own words what needs to happen for this part of the Act to come into effect, and who has the power to decide to enforce it.

2 Re-read subsections 4, 5 and 6. Summarise in your own words what these subsections permit a constable to do.

3 List all the vehicles to which this section of the Act applies. Note down any that you think have been left out.

4 There are two mentions of the need to put things in writing in this section of the Act. Note down what these two instances are, and then put them in your own words.

2 | Two wills

In order to avoid disputes arising after somebody has died, their will has to be drawn up according to a very precise formula, using particular forms of words, and recorded in a specific way.

Extract A below gives an example of a modern-day will, while extract B is a transcript of parts of the will left by William Shakespeare.

(Some words are highlighted in the text. You will find further information about these words at the end of the passages.)

A

THIS IS THE LAST WILL AND TESTAMENT
of me Elizabeth Joan Sadler
of 79 Markham Square, London, SW3

I hereby **revoke** all previous wills and **codicils** I have made. This is my last Will.

As **executor**(s) of this my will, I appoint: my husband Stephen Mark Sadler, of 79 Markham Square, London, SW3 and my daughter Mrs Carol Anne Spearpoint, of 17 Marsh Drive, Upper Stanton, Oxfordshire.

I direct that all my debts and funeral and **testamentary expenses** be paid as soon as is convenient after my death.

1. I leave my collection of stamps and of books on stamps and stamp-collecting to my grandson Angus Spearpoint, of 17 Marsh Drive, Upper Stanton, Oxfordshire, in the hope that it will remind him of the importance of letters.

2. I leave all the mirrors I possess, of whatever size, to my granddaughter Eleanor Spearpoint, of 17 Marsh Drive, Upper Stanton, Oxfordshire, so that she can remember me as frequently as she looks at herself.

3. I leave my knife-sharpener to my son-in-law James Griffith Spearpoint, of 17 Marsh Drive, Upper Stanton, Oxfordshire, in case his tongue ever loses its edge.

4. I leave all the jars of jam and honey remaining in my house at my death to my daughter Mrs Carol Anne Spearpoint, of 17 Marsh Drive, Upper Stanton, Oxfordshire, so that she may learn the importance of not only being sweet on the outside.

5.   I leave a framed photograph of myself to the landlord of the Dog and Duck public house, King's Road, London, SW3, to be hung up over the bar, so that my husband may see me more often after I am dead than ever he did when I was alive.

6.   I leave the remainder of my estate to Michael Ernest Donoghue, of 17 Maplethorpe Drive, Piddinghoe, East Sussex, who, until his recent retirement on grounds of exhaustion, was the cream of milkmen, and who was always there for me, whatever the weather.

Dated this 17th day March 1997

Signed

....

....   (1st witness)

of

....
....
....   (2nd witness)

of

....
....

Signed by the **testatrix** in our presence and by us in hers.

B

In the name of god Amen I William Shackspeare [being] in perfect health and memorie god be praysed doe make & **Ordayne** this my last will and testament in manner and forme followeing. That ys to saye ffirst I Comend my Soule into the handes of god my Creator hoping & assuredlie beleeving through **thonelie** merittes of Jesu Christe my Saviour to be made **partaker** of lyfe everlastinge, And my bodye to the Earth whereof yt ys made ... Item I gyve unto my **wief** my second best bed with the furniture ... All the Rest of my goodes **Chattels** Leases plate Jewels & household stuffe whatsoever after my dettes and Legasies are paied and my funerall expences discharged I hereby gyve and bequeathe to my Sonne in Law John Hall and to my Daughter Susanna.

From Shakespeare's last will and testament, 25 March 1616, PRO

DICTIONARY

revoke cancel

codicils supplement to the main part of a will

executor person appointed to see that the provisions of the will are carried out

testamentary expenses expenses incurred in carrying out the provisions of the will

testatrix woman making the will

DICTIONARY

Ordayne ordain, order, lay down
thonelie the only
partaker sharer
wief wife
Chattels possessions

CLOSER READING

1 Re-read extract A, and then draw up two columns, one headed Legally Required, the other Personal Wishes. List in the first column all the wording that seems to you be legally required, and in the second column note down everything that seems to be the wishes of the person making the will. Your table may start something like this.

Legally Required	Personal Wishes
I hereby revoke all previous wills and codicils	my husband Stephen Mark Sadler

2 Look again at Extract B, and draw up the same sort of table as you have already noted down for Extract A.

3 Compare your two tables, and note down anything that seems to you very different and anything that seems to you very much the same.

4 Write a Plain Guide to Writing Your Will, setting out the legal requirements in a way that is clear and straightforward.

3 | A credit card agreement

Credit card agreements are some of the commonest legal documents signed by people the world over. The passage below deals with the terms and conditions of payment.

(Some words are highlighted in the text. You will find further information about these words at the end of the passage.)

10   PAYMENTS

10.1   You will be personally **liable** to pay us the amount of all Transactions and all interest and other charges due under the Agreement (except as mentioned in condition 11.3), even if:

(a) the Account balance exceeds the credit limit;

(b) the Card, Card number, Cheque or PIN is used in a way that is not authorised by this Agreement; or

(c) production, despatch or delivery of the statement is prevented or delayed.

10.2 Any payment to us will take effect when credited to the Account.

10.3 Any amount credited to the Account will be applied in this order:

(a) the premium for optional payment protection insurance; charges under condition 14.1;

(b) interest on Cash Advances or on handling charges;

(c) interest on **Retail Transactions** or on charges under condition 14.1;

(d) handling charges; Cash Advances shown on any statement;

(e) Retail Transactions shown on any statement;

(f) Cash Advances not yet shown on any statement; and

(g) Retail Transactions not yet shown on any statement

10.4 You must not withhold or set off payment under this Agreement because of any dispute between a Cardholder and another person about a Transaction, unless you have a legal right to do this.

10.5 You must pay us immediately:

(a) any amount by which the Account exceeds the credit limit;

(b) the amount of any Transaction made in breach of this Agreement;

(c) the amount of any arrears under this Agreement.

10.6 All amounts outstanding on this Agreement will be payable on demand if:

(a) this Agreement ends;

(b) you fail to make a payment in full on or before its due date;

(c) you commit any serious or repeated breach of this Agreement and, if the breach is remediable, it has not been remedied;

(d) a **bankruptcy order** is made against you, or you make a voluntary agreement with your creditors; or

(e) you die.

10.7 Before we demand payment under condition 10.6 we will carry out any procedures required by law. If we demand payment under 10.6 we will inform you immediately of our reason.

DICTIONARY

liable legally responsible
Retail Transactions the buying of goods
bankruptcy order declared unable to pay your debts

CLOSER READING

1 Re-read section 10.1, and note down in your own words the conditions under which the cardholder will have to pay all the money owed to the credit card company.

2 Look again at section 10.6, and list in your own words the occasions when the credit card company can demand repayment of all the money owed to it.

3 Re-write section 10.4 in your own words, making the meaning of this section as clear as possible.

4 Section 10.3 lists the order in which any amount paid to the credit card company will reduce the cardholder's debt. Look through the list, and say in your own words why you think the credit card company has decided on that order of repayment.

4 A shorthold tenancy agreement

We all have to have somewhere to live, and so, in the short or long term, we are likely to have to enter into an agreement for buying or renting a property. It is crucially important for a person to be sure just what their rights and responsibilities are with regard to the property they are going to live in. The passage below is an extract from an assured shorthold tenancy agreement.

(Some words are highlighted in the text. You will find further information about these words at the end of the passage.)

THIS AGREEMENT is made on the fifteenth of November 1997
BETWEEN
(1) The Landlord, James Cricket, and
(2) The Tenant, Humphrey Dumpty.

IT IS AGREED as follows:
The Landlord lets and the Tenant takes the premises being The Heights, Wall Street, Worcester, Worcestershire …

(7) The Tenant agrees with the Landlord as follows:

1. (a) to pay the rent (and **sums recoverable as rent**) according to the terms of this Agreement
    (b) in the event of any instalment of rent or any other money payable under this Agreement remaining unpaid after it has become due, then it will carry interest at the rate of 5 per cent **per annum** above the base rate of Moneymakers Bank plc from time to time in force from the date upon which the money became due until the date of payment.

2. To keep the interior of the Premises and the **Fixtures and Fittings** in good repair and condition throughout the Term (excepting only those installations which the Landlord is obliged to repair under Section 11 of the Landlord and Tenant Act 1985).

3. To **make good** (or, if required by the Landlord, to pay for) all damage to the Premises howsoever caused and to the Building caused by the act of omission of the Tenant or of any other person residing with or visiting the Tenant.

4. To make good or replace (or, if required by the Landlord, to pay for) all items of the Fixtures and Fittings which may, from whatsoever cause, be lost, stolen, broken, damaged or destroyed during the Term.

5. Upon not less than two days' notice (except in an emergency) to permit the Landlord and the Landlord's agents and any other persons authorised by the Landlord to enter the Premises (with or without workmen and with all necessary equipment) for any or all of the following purposes:
    (a) to examine the condition of the Premises or the Building or any adjoining or neighbouring property
    (b) to repair, maintain, alter, improve or rebuild the Premises or the Building or any adjoining or neighbouring property
    (c) to examine or to repair, maintain or replace the Fixtures and Fittings
    (d) to comply with any obligation imposed on the Landlord by law.

6. Not to do or **omit** to do anything:
    (a) which causes any policy of insurance on the Premises or the Building or the Fixtures and Fittings to be or to become **void** or voidable
    (b) which causes the rate of **premium** on any policy of insurance to be increased.

From P. Wilde, *The Which? Guide to Renting and Letting*, Which? Books, 1996

DICTIONARY

sums recoverable as rent money which can set against any rent due
per annum each year
Fixtures and Fittings objects such as light sockets which are attached to the premises
make good repair
omit fail
void invalid, no longer legally binding
premium the amount agreed on, in an insurance policy, to be paid to the insurers

C)LOSER READING

1 Re-read paragraph 2. Describe what areas of the property the tenant is responsible for, and which are the responsibility of the landlord.

2 Look again at paragraph 4. Imagine an event in which a fixture or fitting becomes broken, and write a letter to the landlord explaining what has happened.

3 Re-read paragraph 5, and re-write it in your own words, to make the meaning as clear as possible.

4 Imagine that you are a lawyer, explaining this agreement to your client. Look through the whole extract, and make a list in your own words of all the things the tenant is agreeing to.

FURTHER ACTIVITIES

1
- On your own, re-read Text no. 2, the two wills, and the notes that you have made on them.
- Choose a character from a Shakespeare play that you have read (for instance, Romeo, Juliet, Macbeth ...). Think of the kind of person they are, and what they care about most.
- Draw up their will, basing your language and layout on the examples that you have on pages 13–15. Make sure that the legal requirements and your character's personal wishes are both equally clear.

2
- For this activity, you need to begin by working in fairly large groups of eight or nine. Divide your group in two: one group will be representing the school governors and school management, the other will be representing the students.
- In the group representing the school governors and management, decide on a list of five items you think reasonable to set out as being the central part of your job with regard to the students, and then five basic requirements that follow from these. You might, for instance, see your main job as providing a broad education for all the students attending the school. This would then entail that all students attend all the classes provided for them.
- In the group representing the students, draw up a list of five expectations you have of the school – what you want the school to do for you, and then five results of these expectations – what you would need to do in order to make it possible for the school to meet your expectations. You might, for instance, see it as part of the school's job to prepare you for the world of work, and that one requirement of this preparation would be to give you a fair measure of responsibility for organising your own studies in the way that best suits you.
- Once you have worked out your lists of aims and requirements in each group, appoint a spokesperson to put your point of view, and then negotiate with the other half of your group until you have reached a common list of five aims and five requirements which you all consider reasonable. Each member of the group needs to note these down.
- On your own, draw these aims and requirements up into a contract between the school and the students attending the school. Use Text no. 3 and Text no. 4 for the kind of language and layout you will need to use. Make your wording as clear as possible, so that each party to the contract knows what their obligations are.
- In pairs, swap your contract with somebody who has worked in a different group. Check your partner's contract for clarity – would you know what was required of you if you signed that contract? Note down any points that seem to you to need clarifying, and then pass the contract and your notes back to your partner.
- On your own, re-draft your contract, making any changes necessary.

- As a final phase of this activity, you might like to invite a member of the school's senior management team into your classroom to discuss your contracts with you, and to give their comments on the workability of your ideas in a real school environment.

3

- On your own, re-read Text no. 1, the extract from the Criminal Justice and Public Order Act 1994, and the notes you made in response to the Closer Reading questions. Make sure you are entirely clear in your own mind what this part of the Act is saying. Note down any parts you are unsure about.

- As a class, discuss this part of the Act, and ask any questions you may have about it, until you are confident that you understand every provision, or clause, of this part of the Act.

- In pairs, choose one aspect of this part of the Act which interests you, and write a short drama script setting out an incident covered by the Act and how the police may act in that situation.

- As a class, watch each other's play scenes, and note down anything that strikes you about the way the Act appears to work in practice. Take particular notice of the way in which the good of society as a whole and the freedom of the individual are dealt with.

- On your own, imagine that you are a Member of Parliament. You are writing a speech which you are going to give before the House of Commons, either in support of some part of the Act or against it. Argue your case, using examples drawn from the play scenes you have watched.

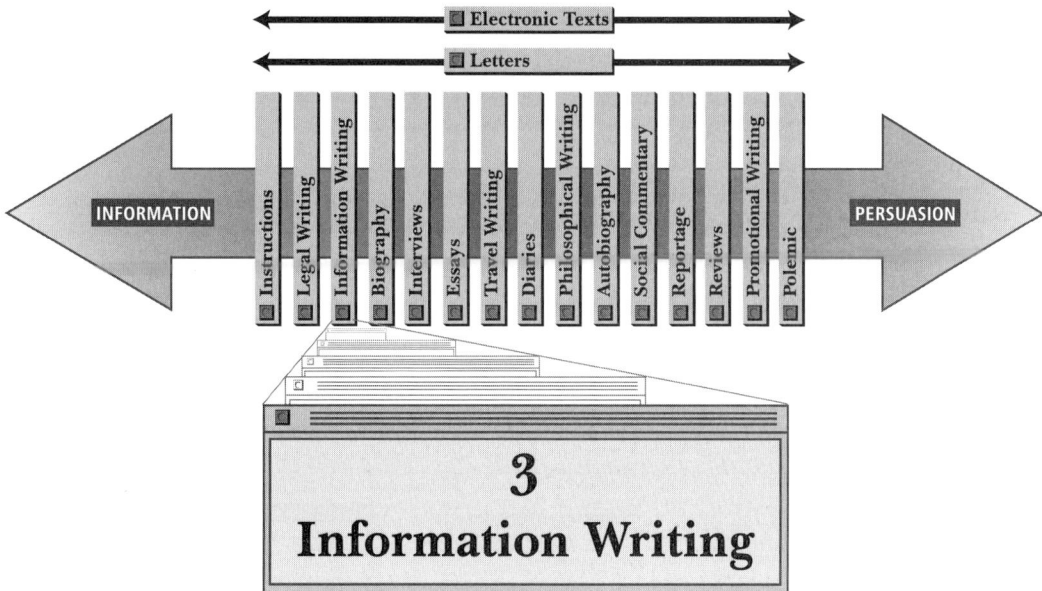

Electronic Texts

Letters

INFORMATION ← Instructions | Legal Writing | Information Writing | Biography | Interviews | Essays | Travel Writing | Diaries | Philosophical Writing | Autobiography | Social Commentary | Reportage | Reviews | Promotional Writing | Polemic → PERSUASION

3
Information Writing

Much of what you read on a day to day basis is *informative*. Its purpose is to set out factual information which will help you to act in a particular way, rather than to persuade you to take a particular course of action. It is usually in the form of instructions or guidance. (For instructions, see chapter 1, pages 1–9.)

The most important factor that needs to be considered by the writer of information is the people for whom it is written. This will influence choices about *content, language* and *layout*. In any piece of information writing the aim will be to include the content that is appropriate for the audience. A book that is for people beginning to learn a new sport, for example, will contain more basic information than one that is for people who are experienced. Because information writing aims to explain things, it is important that the language used is clear, precise and appropriate for the intended audience. For example, the vocabulary used in a leaflet about under-age drinking would be different depending on whether it was being written for teenagers or parents. Finally, to make their writing easy to read and attractive, writers may set out the information by using sub-headings, boxes and illustrations, as well as highlighting important words and using numbers or bullet points.

1 & 2 Health advice

These two extracts from leaflets on the same issue – drug and solvent abuse – were designed for two different audiences. They were both produced a few years ago, by the government of the time, using an approach that was then regarded as effective. One extract is from *Drugs and Solvents: A Young Person's Guide*, and the other from *Solvents: A Parent's Guide*. It should be fairly obvious which is which!

(You will find further information about some of the words in Extract 1 on page 25.)

If you think that sniffing has 'gone out of fashion', think again – there are over 100 deaths each year from solvent sniffing, and most of those who die are teenagers. Some youngsters who sniff have accidents while they are intoxicated and some suffer damage to their health.

This booklet has been written to help you understand more about solvent misuse and to suggest ways in which you can help your children, whether they are sniffing or not.

Solvent misuse related deaths 1971–1990

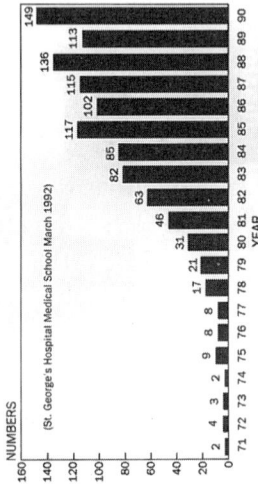

(St. George's Hospital Medical School March 1992)

YEAR	NUMBERS
71	2
72	4
73	3
74	2
75	8
76	8
77	17
78	21
79	31
80	46
81	63
82	82
83	85
84	117
85	102
86	115
87	136
88	113
89	149
90	

How many young people sniff?

Only about one in ten secondary school children try sniffing, and most of these will only experiment; they won't sniff for very long. But a few may become heavy and frequent solvent misusers. The number of youngsters sniffing varies from place to place and at different times. Some people say there is more sniffing in the summer, but perhaps it's just more obvious in the long summer evenings. Sniffing will vary from school to school, from youth club to youth club and from one residential children's home to another. It can be quite a craze in a neighbourhood for a while and then almost disappear. Most young people will never try sniffing. And most of

What is solvent sniffing?

Solvent sniffing usually means getting 'high' by breathing in the fumes from butane, aerosols, glues or other products found around most people's houses or which are easily available from shops. The most common term for this is 'glue sniffing', but there are many other products that can be sniffed:

■ butane gas (in cigarette lighters and refill canisters. Butane is also used as a propellant in many aerosols)
■ aerosol sprays (virtually any aerosol may be used; hairsprays and pain-relieving sprays are common)
■ solvent-based glues (such as Evo-Stik)
■ correcting fluids (such as Tipp-Ex)
■ dry-cleaning fluids
■ the contents of some types of fire extinguishers
■ thinners
■ petrol

In the average home there are over thirty sniffable products.

1

Who sniffs?

those who do will only try it once or a few times. A few youngsters may go on sniffing for a while – perhaps regularly with their friends. A very few will carry on, sometimes very heavily, for a number of years.

[Proportions]
- Only tried it. [7%]
- Sniffed for a few weeks or months. [2%]
- Long term users. [1%]

Never Sniffed

It can be anyone. Children from any social class and from 'good' homes may try sniffing. This does not necessarily mean that their parents have failed or brought them up badly. It's more likely to be one of the 'disobedient' and sometimes risky things that youngsters do. Not many children try solvents before the age of 11, and it seems that the peak age for experimenting is around 13 or 14 years. Girls sniff too, although perhaps a slightly smaller proportion than boys. More children in inner city areas try solvents.

How do they do it?

Because there is such a wide range of substances there are many ways they can be misused. Butane gas and aerosols may be sniffed from bags, but are sometimes sprayed directly into the mouth. Glue is generally sniffed from bags, often freezer or crisp bags. Sniffing is not really the right word because the vapours are inhaled through the nose and mouth; some users call it 'huffing'. There are other methods as well. Thinners such as Tipp-Ex may be sniffed from a cloth or a coatsleeve. Some may put their heads inside a plastic bag.

Where do they do it?

Sniffable products are widely available and they are portable. So people can sniff while walking around, they can sniff in school or anywhere around their home. They may sniff in bed, using the bedcovers as a tent to contain the fumes. Some solvent misusers may absorb the product onto a rag (which they carry in their pocket) or onto a piece of their clothing. Some may go to out-of-the-way places to sniff which can add to the dangers.

What are the effects?

The effects of sniffing are similar to being drunk on alcohol. But people get the effects more quickly from sniffing because the substances enter the blood-stream from the lungs instead of the stomach. This can take new users by surprise – they become intoxicated before they realise it. But the effects of sniffing wear off quickly, too. To keep 'high' it is necessary to keep sniffing, so if the solvent is taken away, the sniffer will soon 'sober up'.

What are the dangers?

Sniffing these substances can be lethal or cause long-term damage.

■ sniffing can have an effect on the heart, so if it is followed by exertion or fright, death may result

■ if butane gas or aerosols are sprayed directly into the mouth, they may cool the throat tissues causing swelling and perhaps suffocation

■ most sniffable products are a mixture of chemicals and the manufacturers may change their formulation. This makes it hard to assess the dangers of particular products

■ some solvents contain poisonous substances such as lead in some petrol or n-hexane in some glues

■ since many of these products are inflammable there is a fire risk, especially when youngsters combine sniffing and smoking

■ using solvents with other drugs, like alcohol, may add to the dangers

■ getting intoxicated is always potentially dangerous: people may become more reckless than usual and be less able to deal with danger

■ young and inexperienced users run greater risks

■ some youngsters have died at their first sniffing session

■ some solvent misusers may do bizarre and possibly dangerous things in response to their 'hallucinations'

■ if solvent misusers use large plastic bags, they may suffocate themselves

■ if solvent misusers become unconscious they may choke on their own vomit

■ because solvent misusers often sniff in out-of-the-way places (such as on railway embankments, near canals and in derelict buildings) they may face hazards in these dangerous environments.

■ some solvent misusers sniff on their own in isolated places. If they have problems, help is not at hand

■ some people are more vulnerable than others to the harmful effects of solvents and may suffer lasting damage.

However, the substances themselves only rarely cause long-term damage to the liver, kidneys, lungs, bone marrow or nervous system is known, but it is not common and is generally reversible.

From *Solvents: A Parent's Guide*, HMSO, 1993

2

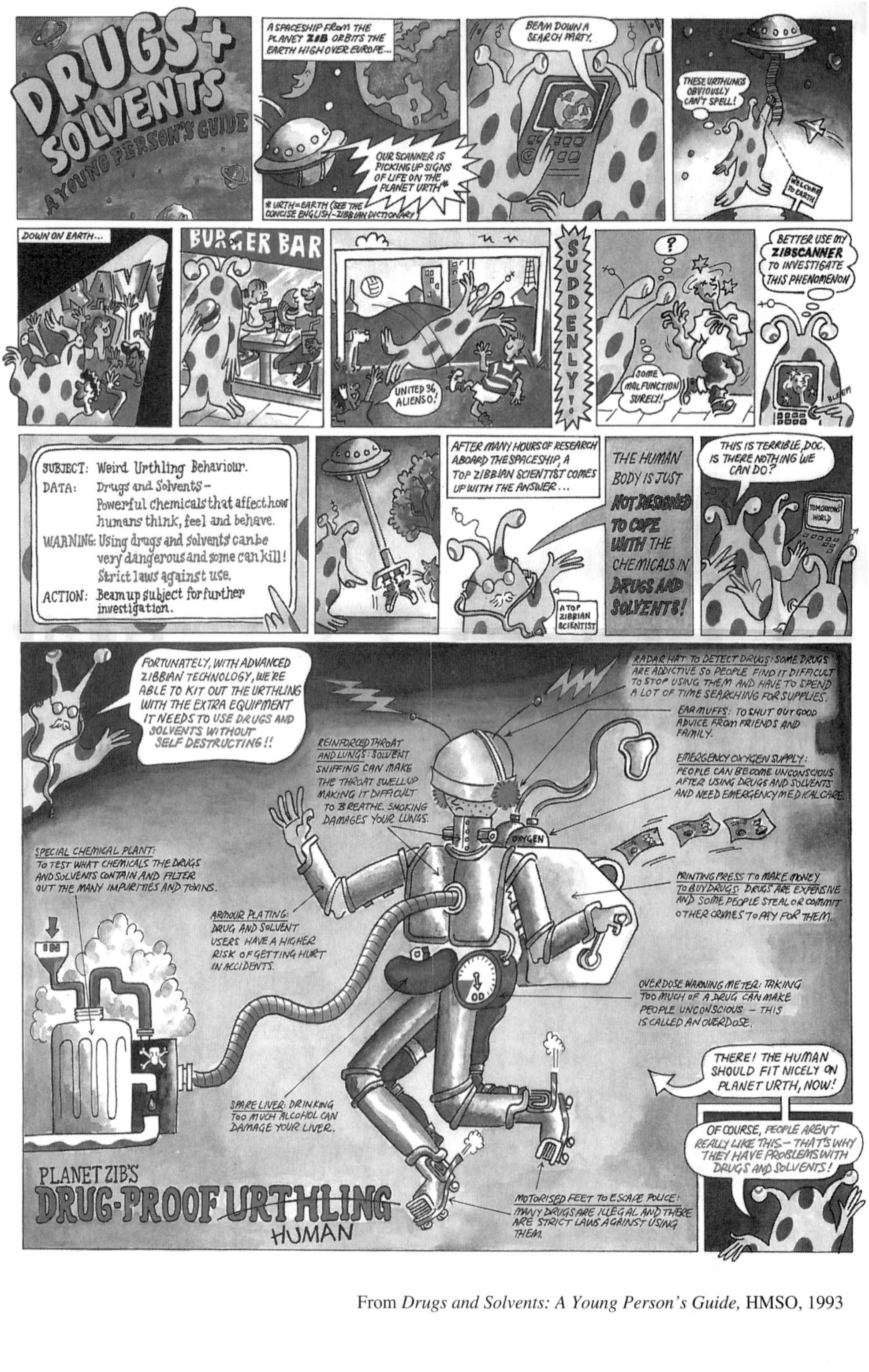

From *Drugs and Solvents: A Young Person's Guide,* HMSO, 1993

DICTIONARY

exertion   physical effort
formulation mixture
reversible   possible to treat

CLOSER READING

Compare the two leaflets under the following headings:

1 *Content*
- What areas have the writers focused on?
- Have they presented the information as a story or as a list of points?
- Have examples been used to illustrate the points?

2 *Layout*
- How has the information been presented? Look at the use of cartoons, pictures, lettering, bullet points etc.

3 *Language*
- What tone has the writer used? Is it serious or humorous?
- How formal or informal is the use of language?
- What level of vocabulary is used? How easy is it to understand?

4 Do you think each leaflet has been designed effectively for its audience? Would you change either? In what ways?

5 These leaflets were produced in the early 1990s, but different governments have different approaches to tackling the drug problem.

What advice would you give to a government employee who had the job of designing a drugs leaflet aimed at teenagers today?

3 & 4 Text books

The two extracts that follow are taken from history text books. The first, about the 'Space Race', was written in 1995 and is aimed at pupils aged 11 to 14. The second, about schools between 1700 and 1870, was written in 1987 and is aimed at pupils aged 14 to 16.

(You will find further information about some of the words in these extracts on page 28.)

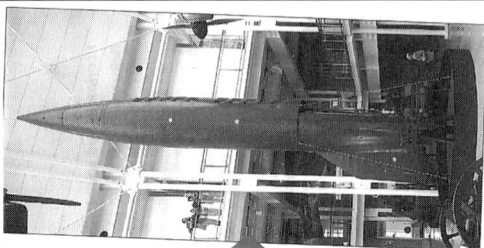

Source D The race into space

July 1969 — Armstrong and Aldrin land on the moon.

January 1967 — Three US astronauts killed in an accident testing the new Apollo spaceship.

February 1966 — Russian unmanned spaceship Luna 1X makes first ever soft landing on the moon.

December 1965 — American spaceships Gemini 6 and 7 link up in space.

March 1965 — Russian cosmonaut Leonov becomes the first man to walk outside a spaceship in space.

June 1963 — Valentina Tereshkova becomes the first woman in space.

February 1962 — John Glenn becomes the first American to orbit the Earth.

April 1961 — Yuri Gagarin becomes the first man in space.

October 1959 — Russian satellite Lunik 11 takes the first photographs of the dark side of the moon.

October 1957 — Russian satellite Sputnik becomes the first man-made object in space.

Source E Buzz Aldrin on the moon

At first the Soviet Union appeared to be well in the lead, especially in April 1961 when they astounded the world by sending the first man into space. Overnight, Yuri Gagarin became a world famous name. Two years and two months later the Soviet Union scored another success when Valentina Tereshkova became the first woman in space. In fact, the Americans were probably already in the lead.

The American spacecraft were far more advanced than their Soviet counterparts, which is why they were taking longer to develop. However, it was in the interests of NASA, the National Aeronautics and Space Administration, to give the impression that they thought the Russians were ahead. Then the US government would spend still more money on the space programme. In the end it cost them 25 billion dollars. Watched by an astonished world, live on their TV screens, Neil Armstrong and Buzz Aldrin left Apollo 11 and landed on the surface of the moon on 20 July 1969. The USA had won the Space Race.

After the race

Space travel did not end with Apollo 11. There were more Apollo missions to the moon and the Russians landed an unmanned lunar rover, Lunakhod. The Soviet Union concentrated on developing their Mir space station while NASA produced the reusable Space Shuttle which could land back on earth, unlike all previous spacecraft. The emphasis was now on scientific and military research. The public were no longer fascinated by space now that the race was over. Space exploration was no longer in the news.

Remember…

- The Space Race was part of the Cold War rivalry between the Superpowers – America and the Soviet Union.

Investigations

1 Why did the USA and the USSR want the German rocket scientists?

2 Read Source **B**.
   a) According to President Kennedy, why did America want to land a man on the moon?
   b) What other reasons do you think that there might have been which Kennedy does not mention?

3

The Space Race

Why did the USA and the USSR take part in the Space Race?

'We have the technology'

By September 1944 German scientists had developed the V2 rocket (Source **A**) and 1000 of these were to fall on the south-east of England before the Second World War was over. With the beginning of the Cold War both the USA and the USSR set out to produce rockets which could carry nuclear warheads. It was not just the German technology which they were both using, but also the German scientists. Werner von Braun, who had designed the V2, went to work in America along with many of his team.

The race to the moon

Ordinary Americans were convinced that the USA was the number one country in the world. They had won the war and they enjoyed a standard of living that was far higher than anywhere else. This certainty was shattered on 4 October 1957, when the Soviet Union launched the first ever satellite, Sputnik, into space. The Cold War was still at its height. It was now a matter of honour for the USA to overtake the Russians. The Space Race had begun. In 1961 President Kennedy officially announced the finishing post (Source **B**). It would be a race to the moon.

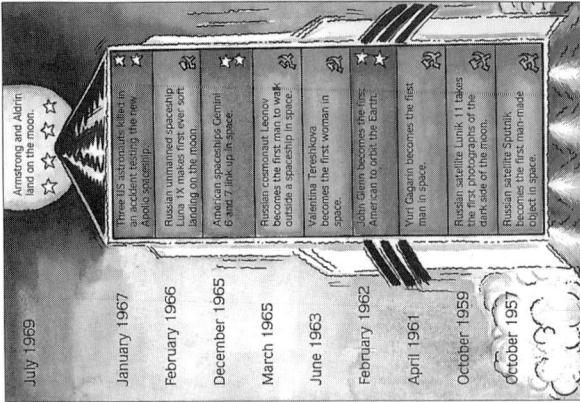

Source A A German V2 rocket in the Imperial War Museum, London. This could deliver an explosive warhead onto an English city and was too fast to be caught by a plane.

I believe that this nation should commit itself to achieving a goal, before this decade is out, of landing a man on the moon and returning him safely to earth. No single space project will be more exciting, or more impressive to mankind.

Quoted in *Parnell History of the Twentieth Century*, BPC

Source B US President Kennedy, May 1961

Source C On 12 April 1961 the Russian Yuri Gagarin orbited the earth once in his spacecraft, Vostok 1

From N. DeMarco and R. Radway, *The Twentieth Century World*, Stanley Thornes, 1995

SECONDARY EDUCATION FOR THE RULING CLASSES

The endowed grammar schools

The endowed grammar schools largely owed their beginnings to old bequests made in the Middle Ages which specified what subjects should be taught in the schools. These subjects were largely irrelevant to the needs of pupils during the Industrial Revolution. The value of the original endowments had fallen and many schools had begun to charge fees, thus no longer accepting those who could not pay – the free scholars – for whom the grammar schools had originally been intended.

In 1805, a legal decision effectively prevented grammar schools from changing their curriculum – they had to teach 'grammar', if that was laid down in their endowment – and it was not until 1840 that the Grammar Schools Act allowed them to change. By that time the demand for better education from the middle classes had stimulated a revival in schools. Many endowed grammar schools expanded and improved and some went on to become public schools.

The public schools

Some grammar schools had already developed into public schools by the middle of the eighteenth century. They had become boarding schools for the sons of rich people from all over the country. But the standard of education was poor, and at the start of the nineteenth century they were as set in their ways as the endowed grammar schools, with which they shared many common features. The vicious use of the birch and the general air of lawlessness and needless cruelty in these schools even led pupils to riot (such as the Great Rebellion of boys at Rugby School, in 1797).

Most public schools taught classics to the exclusion of every other subject. Lord John Russell (Prime Minister 1846–52) said that when he was at Westminster School, the teaching had consisted entirely of Latin. On half holidays, he and other boys had had to go to an outside teacher to be taught arithmetic and writing.

In the early nineteenth century, schools such as Westminster held their lessons in one huge school room. The boys sat on benches (or forms) with a desk in front of them. (This is why each group of boys, under an usher or assistant master, was known by the form it occupied – First Form, Second Form, and so on.)

By 1870, many new public schools had been founded and others had expanded. There were a number of reasons for this:

(a) The newly rich middle classes wanted their sons to be educated as young gentlemen; and they had the money to pay for it.

Charterhouse (founded 1611) – one of the great English public schools, The Illustrated London News, 1 March 1862

(b) The railways made it feasible for boarding schools to cater for pupils from all over the country.

(c) There were still relatively few good day schools which could provide a similar education.

(d) Communal life in a boarding school was praised for its own sake, irrespective of the quality of the school.

(e) Enterprising headmasters, like Dr Butler of Shrewsbury (who started the prefect system) and Dr Thring of Uppingham (who introduced music and organised games), radically altered the type and quality of the education offered by their schools.

Dr Thomas Arnold of Rugby School was probably the most famous and the most influential of these Victorian headmasters. He made Christianity and the Chapel the focus of school life and placed great emphasis on character-building through sport and the development of the prefect system. But he still emphasised the classics rather than the sciences and placed his trust in the birch rather than the carrot.

1 How did the Industrial and Transport Revolutions affect the development of the public schools?
2 What influence has the nineteenth-century public school system had on the state system of education today?

From P. Sauvain, *British Economic and Social History*, Stanley Thornes, 1987

D I C T I O N A R Y
the Cold War the continuous hostility between the USA and the Soviet Union after the Second World War

bequests gifts of money or property

feasible possible

irrespective regardless

Enterprising innovative and inventive

CLOSER READING

1 Look at the *layout* of the two extracts. List all the ways used by each writer to present the information. Explain how each of these devices aims to help the reader understand the information being given.

2 How has the *content* of each piece been presented? One is told as a dramatic story in which the main characters' feelings are described, while the other compares aspects of its subject and sometimes moves backwards as well as forwards in time.

3 Look at the *use of language* in each extract.

   a Write down any words that you do not fully understand. What does this tell you about the language level required to read each piece?

   b Write down any words that describe emotions. Which text contains more?

4 Evaluate the two extracts.

   • Do you think that they are appropriate for the audiences they were designed for?

   • Do you think that the greater the number of presentational devices the better? Or can you have too many?

   • Could either text be improved? How?

5 Imagine that you had to present the information on schools to a younger audience (Year 7, for example). Redesign the extract, thinking about layout, language and the way in which you present the content.

5 | The language development of twins

This is an extract from *The Cambridge Encyclopaedia of Language* by David Crystal. It discusses the ways in which the language development of twins differs from that of children born singly.

(You will find further information about some of the words in this extract on page 30.)

5

TWINS

The language learning environment of twins is unique. During their early years, their linguistic experience differs greatly from that of single children. Singletons receive most of their language stimulation from adults or older children, whose utterances provide a more advanced learning 'target'. Twins, however, spend a great deal of time together, with each learning from a linguistic setting in which the other speaker is at the same developmental linguistic level. In such circumstances, it is hardly surprising to find many twins developing a private form of communication.

One study found a great deal of private language play in early-morning twin conversations. At 33 months, for example, there were dialogues in which each child responded to features of pronunciation it noticed in the other:

A: zæki su
B: (*laughing*) zæki su zæki su (*both laugh*) æ:
A: api:
B: olp olt olt
A: opi: opi:
B: api: api: (*laughing*) api api api
A: ai ju
B: (*laughing*) ai ju api (*repeated several times*)
A: kaki (*repeated several times*)
B: ai i: o:
A: ai i: o o:

(E. O. Keenan, 1974, p. 171.)

To the outsider, this kind of dialogue might resemble a 'secret language', but it is no more than a form of phonetic play.

One of the most interesting features of twin language is the way in which they 'share' the response to an adult utterance:

MOTHER: What can you see in the picture?
TWIN A: A cat.
TWIN B: And a dog.

Observers have been struck by the intuitive way in which one twin is able to respond very rapidly to what the other has just said, and how the first twin is able to anticipate when to stop. They very seldom talk at the same time. Even very short utterances can be split in two:

MOTHER: What do you want me to read?
TWIN A: Puss.
TWIN B: In boots.

This kind of skill can only come from the frequent opportunities the twins have had to interact, in the early years. They know each other's rhythms, and each is able to predict a great deal of what the other is likely to say.

Perhaps because of this close dependence, twins are usually somewhat late in developing their individual language skills. When their language is formally assessed, during the third and fourth years, it is often found to be about 6 months behind the norm for singletons. On the other hand, there are certain aspects of their development that may be ahead of other children – notably, their ability to keep a conversation going, and to interact with adults. By age 7 or 8, the delay seems to have disappeared.

Poto and Cabenga

GRACE: Cabenga, padem manibadu peeta.
VIRGINIA: Doan nee bada tengkmatt, Poto.

Reported extracts of this kind from a twin conversation achieved world-wide publicity in the late 1970s. They came from the Kennedy twins of San Diego, California, who at the age of 8 were still using their own private language. They called themselves by different names in this language: Grace became 'Poto' and Virginia became 'Cabenga' – names which were later used as the title of a film about their early years.

Their totally unintelligible speech for a while promoted the impression that the children were mentally retarded, but this proved not to be so. In due course, a detailed study of their language came to be made. This indicated that their speech was not as alien as its bizarre sound had led people to believe. it was basically a severely distorted form of English, with some features of German, several idiosyncratic grammatical characteristics, and a proportion of invented vocabulary. What made it so difficult to follow (and also to analyse!) was its extremely rapid speed of articulation and its staccato rhythm – features that later transferred to their English, when therapists began to work with them.

There are probably special reasons for the late retention of private speech in this case. The children, it seems, had very little opportunity to hear good models of English speech in their early years. They saw few other children in the area where they lived. Their parents were both working, and during the day they were cared for by their German grandmother who spoke no English. There was also an expectation that they might be retarded (because of a history of convulsions), which affected the style of the parents' interaction. Left to themselves, the twins would have had little alternative but to develop their own medium of communication.

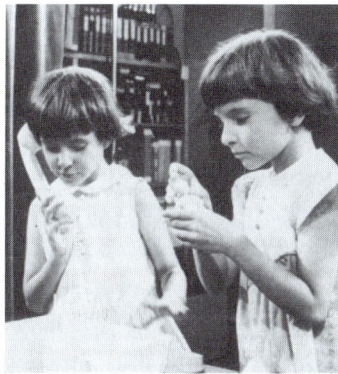

Secret languages

Twins have often been observed to talk to each other in a way that is unintelligible to adults or other children. The phenomenon has been variously labelled 'cryptophasia', 'idioglossia', or 'autonomous speech'. Estimates of incidence are uncertain, but some have suggested that as many as 40% of twin pairs develop some form of private speech, especially in the second year.

There seems to be no basis for the view that a completely different 'language' is involved. The patterns heard can largely be explained with reference to the children's efforts to cope with the kind of language used around them, and to the kind of processes that take place in normal language acquisition. The twin situation promotes the continued use of immature and idiosyncratic patterns of sound, grammar, and vocabulary, and a personal style of interaction often characterized by abnormal intonation and rhythm. These patterns become particularly noticeable when the children continue to use them past the normal period of 'baby talk'. In the most dramatic cases, private speech has lasted until age 5 or more, when it often attracts a great deal of publicity.

From D. Crystal, *The Cambridge Encyclopaedia of Language,* Cambridge University Press, 1987

C LOSER READING

1 Give reasons why, in general, twins learn language differently from singletons.

2 What are the distinctive features of the way twins use language?

3 What are the benefits and drawbacks for twins of the ways in which they learn and use language?

4 Look at the case study of the Kennedy twins (the section headed 'Poto and Cabenga').

  a Why has the writer included this?

  b Why did the twins develop and use a 'secret language' for so long?

  Use the information in the section 'Secret languages' in the third column of the extract to support your comments.

FURTHER ACTIVITIES

1 Write an information leaflet on a subject which you are *familiar* with. You will need to consider the following things:

a Subject
  • Interest or hobby (for example, pets, sport, collecting)
  • Issue (for example, animal rights, alcohol)

b Audience
  • Younger than you, your own age or adults
  • Male or female
  • Expert or non-expert

c Content
  • What are the important facts?
  • How are they to be presented? As a story? As a series of points?

d Layout
  • What presentational devices should be used?

e Language
  • Should it be formal or informal?
  • What level of language should be used?
  • What tone should be used?

2 In pairs or small groups, produce two information leaflets, *for different audiences*, on a subject which you are *unfamiliar* with. This will involve detailed research, and it is a good idea to share this out between you. You could find information from a range of places:

  • the school and local library
  • newspapers and magazines
  • interviews
  • CD-ROMs
  • visits to museums, galleries and other information centres
  • writing to the appropriate organisations.

Arrange a time for all the research to be done, and share out your findings between you. The information you have found should provide you with examples, statistics and case studies which you can use to illustrate your own ideas and information.

When you find information it is important to *select* what is essential and then re-present it in a way that is effective. To do that you need to take account of the list in Further Activity 1. Divide your pair or group into two, each choosing a different audience for the leaflet, and using different language and layout to communicate the information effectively.

3 Working in pairs, choose a text book from any subject that is currently in use in your school. Choose a page which you think does not present information well. Discuss *why* it doesn't work, asking yourselves the following questions:

  • Does it make the subject seem boring or irrelevant?
  • Is it too difficult or confusing?
  • Is the layout helpful and attractive?
  • Is the language easy to understand?

When you have finished discussing what is wrong with it, you now have the hard bit to do – how could you make it attractive to someone of your own age? Rewrite and redesign the page, using language and presentational devices that you think will make it more accessible and will bring the subject to life.

When you have finished, swap your new version with other pairs in the class and ask them to discuss your version, using the same questions (above) that you asked about the original.

INFORMATION

Instructions

Legal Writing

Information Writing

Biography

Interviews

Essays

Travel Writing

Diaries

Philosophical Writing

Autobiography

Social Commentary

Reportage

Reviews

Promotional Writing

Polemic

PERSUASION

4
Biography

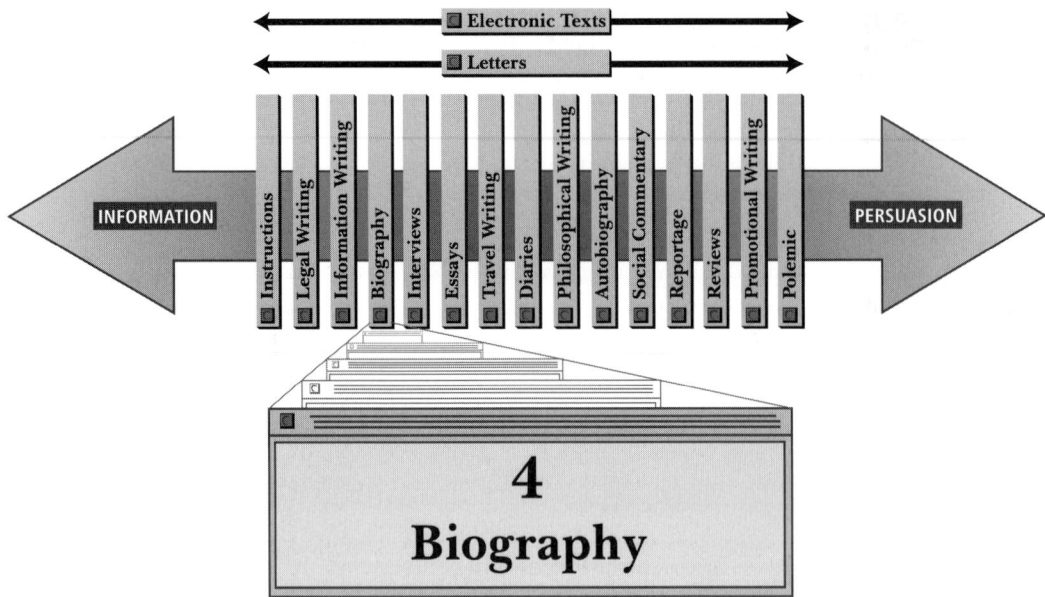

Biographies are the stories of people's lives, written by somebody else. Biographies are almost always written about famous people, or people who have done something that is thought to have been important by others living at the time or afterwards. Because of this, a biographer is usually most interested in showing how the person they are writing about came to be as they were, and how and why they achieved what they did. However much they sometimes try to be detached and objective, biographers usually have a point of view about the person they are writing about, whether they are praising them for what they have done, or attacking them for it.

What you will be asked to do, in looking at the passages that follow, is to identify the point of view of the author, and how this affects the way in which they present their material.

1 The murder of Julius Caesar

This is an extract from *The Life of Julius Caesar* by the Greek historian Plutarch, who wrote at the beginning of the 1st century AD. Plutarch was interested in seeing patterns in the way in which great men affected the development of events in the two great nations of the classical world, Greece and Rome. In 1579, another historian, Sir Thomas North, published a translation of Plutarch's *Parallel Lives of the Greeks and Romans* from Greek into English. It was this translation that William Shakespeare read, and used as the basis for his information, and even sometimes for his dialogue, in such plays as *Julius Caesar* and *Antony and Cleopatra*. The extract below is from North's famous translation.

Julius Caesar was a Roman general who was so successful that he became the most powerful man in the state. Although Rome was at that time a republic, Caesar's position made him king-like, and there were those in Rome who suggested that he should, in fact, become king. Others opposed this suggestion, which they thought would destroy their country's freedom. A group of those who were against Caesar got together and plotted to kill him. In the extract below, we read of the way in which Caesar is murdered and what happened afterwards to the men who murdered him.

(Some words are highlighted in the text. You will find further information about these words at the end of the passage.)

Then Casca behind him **strake** him in the neck with his sword. **Howbeit** the wound was not great or mortal, because, it seemed, the fear of such a devilish attempt did amaze him and take his strength from him, that he killed him not at the first blow. But, Caesar, turning straight unto him, caught hold of his sword and held it hard, and they both cried out, Caesar in Latin:

'O vile traitor Casca, what doest thou?'

And Casca in Greek to his brother:

'Brother, help me.'

10 At the beginning of this stir, they that were present, not knowing of the conspiracy, were so amazed with the horrible sight they saw, they had no power to fly, neither to help him, not so much as once to make an outcry. They on the other side that had conspired his death **compassed** him in on every side with their swords drawn in their hands, that Caesar turned him nowhere but he was stricken at by some, and still had naked swords in his face, and was hacked and mangled among them, as a wild beast taken of hunters. For it was agreed among them that every man should give him a wound, because all their parts should be in this murder. And then **Brutus** himself gave him one wound about his **privities**.

20 Men report also that Caesar did still defend himself against the rest, running every way with his body. But when he saw Brutus with his sword drawn in his

hand, then he pulled his gown over his head and made no more resistance, and was driven, either casually or purposely by the counsell of the conspirators, against the base whereupon **Pompey**'s statue stood, which ran all of a gore-blood, till he was slain. Thus it seemed that the image took just revenge of Pompey's enemy, being thrown down on the ground at his feet and yielding up his ghost there for the number of wounds he had upon him. For it is reported that he had three-and-twenty wounds upon his body; and divers of the conspirators did hurt themselves, striking one body with so many blows …

30   Caesar died at six-and-fifty years of age; and Pompey also lived not passing four more years than he. So he reaped no other fruit of all his reign and dominion, which he had so vehemently desired all his life and pursued with such extreme danger, but a vain name only and a superficial glory that procured him the envy and hatred of his country. But his great prosperity and good fortune, that favoured him all his lifetime, did continue afterwards in the revenge of his death, pursuing the murderers both by sea and land, till they had not left a man to be executed, of all of them that were actors or counsellors in the conspiracy of his death. Furthermore, of all the chances that happen unto men upon the earth, that which came to Cassius above all
40   others is most to be wondered at. For he, being overcome in battle at the **journey of Philippes**, slew himself with the same sword with which he strake Caesar.

Adapted from the 1595 edition of Plutarch's *Lives*, trans. Sir Thomas North

DICTIONARY

strake struck

Howbeit however

compassed surrounded

Brutus Caesar's heir, and the man he most trusted

privities private parts

Pompey a rival general whom Caesar had defeated

journey of Philippes battle of Philippi

C LOSER READING

1 Re-read the first paragraph and the dialogue that follows (lines 1–8). Note down how Caesar reacts to the attack on him.

2 Look again at lines 9–11. Say in your own words how those not involved in the conspiracy react to the attack.

3 Look at the rest of the second paragraph and the whole of the third (lines 12–29). Note down how Caesar deals with the attack and what makes him change his behaviour. Where does he die and why does this seem significant?

4 Re-read lines 30–34. What is Plutarch's summary of Caesar's achievements?

5 Re-read from line 34 to the end of the passage. What happens to all the conspirators after they have murdered Caesar? What is particularly notable about the way in which Cassius dies?

6 Most of the passage appears to be a straightforward account of Caesar's murder and of what happened afterwards.

- Pick out and write down any words or sentences in which Plutarch appears to be putting forward his own view of these events.
- In two or three sentences of your own, say what Plutarch's opinion of Caesar and of the conspirators appears to be.

2 The writings and friends of Dr Johnson

Samuel Johnson was a writer who lived from 1709 to 1784. He was one of the great literary men of his age, writing, on his own, a *Dictionary of the English Language*, and bringing out an edition of Shakespeare's plays. He was also known as a great conversationalist. The best known biography of Dr Johnson's life is the *Life of Johnson*, written after his death by his friend and admirer James Boswell.

The passages below give accounts of two aspects of Johnson's life, his writings and his relationships with friends.

(Some words are highlighted in the text. You will find further information about these words at the end of the passages.)

A

This year his old pupil and friend, David Garrick, having become joint **patentee** and manager of Drury-lane theatre, Johnson honoured his opening of it with a Prologue, which for just and manly dramatick criticism, on the whole range of the English stage, as well as for poetical excellence, is unrivalled … The most striking and brilliant passages of it have been so often repeated, and are so well recollected by all the lovers of the drama and of poetry, that it would be **superfluous** to point them out. In the Gentleman's Magazine for December this year, he inserted an 'Ode on Winter', which is, I think, an admirable specimen of his genius for **lyrick** poetry.

10 But the year 1747 is distinguished as the **epoch**, when Johnson's **arduous** and important work, his DICTIONARY OF THE ENGLISH LANGUAGE, was announced to the world, by the publication of its Plan or Prospectus.

How long this immense undertaking had been the object of his contemplation, I do not know. I once asked him by what means he had attained to that astonishing knowledge of our language, by which he was enabled to realise a design of such extent, and accumulated difficulty. He told me, that 'it was not the effect of particular study; but that it had grown up in his mind **insensibly**.' I have been informed by Mr James Dodsley, that several years before this period, when Johnson was one day sitting in his
20 brother Robert's shop, he heard his brother suggest to him, that a Dictionary of the English Language would be a work that would be well received by the

publick; that Johnson seemed at first to catch at the proposition, but, after a pause, said, in his abrupt decisive manner, 'I believe I shall not undertake it.' That he, however, had bestowed much thought upon the subject, before he published his 'Plan', is evident from the enlarged, clear, and accurate views which it exhibits.

B

Soon afterwards, he supped at the Crown and Anchor tavern, in the Strand, with a company whom I collected to meet him ... He was this evening in remarkable vigour of mind, and eager to exert himself in conversation, which he did with great readiness and fluency ...

When I called upon Dr Johnson next morning, I found him highly satisfied with his **colloquial** prowess the preceding evening. 'Well, (said he,) we had good talk.' BOSWELL. 'Yes, Sir; you tossed and gored several persons.'

The late Alexander, Earl of Eglintoune, who loved wit more than wine, and men of genius more than **sycophants**, had a great admiration of Johnson;
10 but from the remarkable elegance of his own manners, was, perhaps, too delicately sensible of the roughness which sometimes appeared in Johnson's behaviour. One evening about this time, when his Lordship did me the honour to sup at my lodgings with Dr Robertson and several other men of literary distinction, he regretted that Johnson had not been educated with more refinement, and lived more in polished society. 'No, no, my Lord, (said Signor Baretti,) do with him what you would, he would always have been a bear.' 'True, (answered the Earl, with a smile,) but he would have been a *dancing* bear.'

To **obviate** all the reflections which have gone round the world to Johnson's
20 prejudice, by applying to him the epithet of a bear, let me impress upon my readers a just and happy saying of my friend Goldsmith, who knew him well: 'Johnson, to be sure, has a roughness in his manner; but no man alive has a more tender heart. *He has nothing of the bear but his skin.*'

From J. Boswell, *Life of Johnson*, Clarendon Press, 1934

DICTIONARY

patentee registered licence-holder
superfluous unnecessary
lyrick private, as opposed to public or dramatic, poetry
epoch time
arduous difficult
insensibly without being noticeable
colloquial conversational
sycophants flatterers
obviate argue against, counter

C LOSER READING

1 Re-read through the first paragraph of Passage A (lines 1–9). What poem did Johnson publish in 1747?

2 Look again at the second paragraph of Passage A (lines 10–12). What other work did Johnson say he was going to write?

3 Re-read the last paragraph of Passage A (lines 13–26). Say in your own words how the idea of the Dictionary first came to Johnson, and how he prepared himself for writing it.

4 Look again through the whole of Passage A.
  - Underline all the adjectives (describing words, such as 'admirable') in the passage.
  - Make a list of them, and look up any meanings you are unsure of in the dictionary.
  - Using this list as evidence, write a few sentences in your own words summarising what seems to you to be Boswell's attitude to Johnson's writing. Use quotations from your list to back up your view.

5 Re-read the first two paragraphs of Passage B (lines 1–7). What did Boswell arrange, and how did Johnson behave? Say in your own words:
  - what you think Boswell meant by the metaphor 'you tossed and gored several persons';
  - what the metaphor is drawn from.

6 Look again at the third paragraph of Passage B (lines 8–18). What did the Earl of Eglintoune regret about Johnson's behaviour, and how would he have liked to change it?

7 Re-read the last paragraph of Passage B (lines 19–23). Say in your own words what Goldsmith said about Johnson, and what he meant by it.

8 Look through Passage B as a whole, and write two or three sentences summarising the view of Johnson you get from this passage. What kind of man does he appear to be, and what were the strengths and weaknesses commented on here?

3 **The actress and the president**

Marilyn Monroe (born Norma Jean Baker) lived from 1926 until 1962, and was perhaps the most well-known film-star of her generation. She was particularly famous for playing slightly scatty, very sexy blondes. She was twice married, and had several affairs, including a long-standing relationship with John (Jack) Kennedy.

The passage on pages 38–39, taken from *The Marilyn Scandal* by Sandra Shevey, describes the beginning of the end of her affair with John Kennedy, who was at that time President of the United States.

(Some words are highlighted in the text. You will find further information about these words at the end of the passage.)

The popular picture of Jacqueline Kennedy as an aloof, elegant lady is deceptive. On more than one occasion she is known to have put an end to Jack's affairs. Monroe was preceded in his affections by a similar type of girl. (Curiously, for all his sex appeal, Jack Kennedy was attracted to offbeat women. His fascination for Marilyn had probably as much to do with her appealing quality of **tentativeness** as it did with her body measurements.) Ralph Martin also refers to another affair with 'the girl with the snapping eyes', which began before Kennedy met Jackie and carried over into his marriage. Apparently the affair finished when Jackie found out about it and 10   determined to bring it to a halt.

It is possible that the same fate befell Marilyn once word of their affair drifted back to Washington. 'Jackie,' a friend told me, 'was mercurial. She would remain silent about Jack's **philandering**, and then all of a sudden, she would lay down the law.' In this instance, she made her position perfectly clear by announcing that she would not attend the Madison Square Garden $1,000-per-head birthday fundraiser due to be held on 19 May. If Monroe goes, I do not, was the implication. True to form, Jackie went fox hunting in Virginia, leaving her husband to cope with an affair which by then was doomed to extinction.

20   Perhaps wifely objections would have carried less weight had Kennedy not been diverted by a new romantic interest: 'A very attractive, medium-blonde, half-serious girl with a mysterious hidden quality' is how historian Martin describes Mary Meyer, an ideal Kennedy type who came into Kennedy's life at the opportune moment, causing someone to speculate that perhaps she was '**a Monroe decoy**'. Their relationship began shortly after Monroe's death and continued until Kennedy's assassination a year later. Ironically, Miss Meyer was also the victim of an assassin's bullet the following year.

Any flagging interest on Kennedy's part at this **juncture** was largely unknown to Monroe, who was busily making preparations to entertain him at the 30   birthday gala which was being planned by Democratic Party Chairman Arthur Krim, President of United Artists, the company which released *Misfits*. Jean Louis, the designer for *Misfits* and for **Something's Got to Give**, who had also been a Columbia staff designer in the forties when he fitted Marilyn for the costumes she wore in *Ladies of the Chorus*, was recruited by Marilyn to come up with something special for the occasion. 'I always thought she was cute,' he admits, 'but I never thought of her as being this cute.' The costume Jean Louis created was almost transparent (probably **peau-de-soie**), fashioned with lots of net and covered with rhinestones. (The stones were hand-sewn, smaller ones replacing the original larger ones which 40   were found to be too heavy.) Jean Louis remembers fitting Marilyn in her Brentwood house which had three bedrooms (in addition to a solar or sun room in the patio area, one of which Marilyn had transformed into a fitting room encased in glass. (She was shy and felt uncomfortable being fitted at the studio.) Although Monroe was, in James Bacon's word, 'built like a statue', she wanted her round, voluptuous breasts to appear pear-shaped and therefore asked designers to stitch beads in the appropriate areas. Jean Louis recalls that he was not told what the dress was for, but discovered the truth one afternoon when a call came through from Hyannisport.

50 Marilyn planned to leave for New York a couple of days early in order to rehearse the 'Happy Birthday' song she had been asked to sing. When the new Fox production chief got wind of her plans, however, word came down that she risked her job, since *Something's Got to Give* was already behind schedule having been delayed because Marilyn had picked up a 'flu bug in Mexico, which lingered into production, causing additional delays. Marilyn was also pregnant and beset by fears of miscarrying. Having lost one baby while filming *Some Like It Hot*, she was being particularly careful not to jeopardize her chances this time around. That the child was Kennedy's is almost certainly true, although the rumour was discounted even by Monroe's closest friends …

60 Monroe's appearance at the birthday gala was, in short, vulgar. Everything about is was wrong, and yet, in spite of that, her performance was enormously appealing. Firstly, the effect of having been ill and then being buoyed on vitamins was visible in the way Monroe seemed to strain in her delivery of the 'Happy Birthday' song. Then, her outfit was wrong: the wig was awful (it didn't seem to fit right) and the dress was too revealing (her body had, after all, matured). The worst part about it, however, was the change compared with the light, airy, effortless **ebulliency** of Monroe performing 'Diamonds Are a Girl's Best Friend'. (At that stage of her life her hair hadn't been frazzled from bleaching, and her figure still looked good in

70 scanty clothes.)

The performance, which lasted all of ten minutes, drained Monroe and it took her two and a half hours to recover before appearing at John Kennedy's Carlyle reception. Anyone who believes that this lady with the quirky nervous system could have done a Broadway show every night should have observed the effect of the brief Madison Square Garden appearance.

Arriving at the party in the very same gown she had worn on stage (referred to by the actress herself as 'skin and beads') all that appeared to be holding her up was willpower …

Adlai Stevenson said of Monroe that night: 'I do not think I have ever seen

80 anyone so beautiful in my life.'

From S. Shevey, *The Marilyn Scandal*, Sidgwick & Jackson, 1987

DICTIONARY

tentativeness shy hesitation

philandering flirting and having affairs

a Monroe decoy a companion who pretended to be with John Kennedy so as to draw attention away from his relationship with Marilyn Monroe

juncture time

Misfits the last complete film Marilyn Monroe made

Something's Got to Give the film Marilyn Monroe was making when she died

peau-de-soie a clinging silky material which makes the wearer appear almost naked

ebulliency bubbliness

(C)LOSER READING

1 Re-read the first three paragraphs of the passage (lines 1–27).
   - In your own words describe the relationship between Jacqueline and John Kennedy.
   - What reasons does the author suggest for John Kennedy ending his affair with Marilyn Monroe?

2 Look again at the fourth paragraph of the passage (lines 28–48).
   - What is your impression of the dress Marilyn Monroe had made for her appearance at the birthday gala?
   - Why does she have the fitting done at home?

3 Re-read the fifth paragraph of the passage (lines 49–59).
   - Why is the production company not pleased with her intention to go to New York?
   - What else do we learn about Marilyn in this paragraph?

4 Look through the passage from lines 60 to the end. Say in your own words your impression of Marilyn's appearance at Madison Square Garden, and at the party afterwards.

5 Draw up two columns, and head them Positive and Negative.
   - In the first column, note down all the positive comments and pieces of information given about Marilyn in the passage as a whole.
   - In the second column, note down all the negative comments and pieces of information given.
   - Look through your two lists, and write a short summary of how Marilyn appears to be at this stage in her life.

4 | Schindler's Ark

Schindler's Ark, by Thomas Keneally, is the story of a German porcelain manufacturer who saved thousands of Jewish people by employing them in his factory at a time when, under the Nazi régime, they would have otherwise ended up dying of starvation or in the gas chambers. Keneally's interest in Oskar Schindler is in why such an apparently unheroic man should have risked his life in this way. The book has now been made into a film under the title *Schindler's List*. The passage below is taken from the opening of the book.

(Some words are highlighted in the text. You will find further information about these words at the end of the passage.)

In Poland's deepest autumn, a tall young man in an expensive overcoat, double-breasted dinner jacket beneath it and – in the lapel of the dinner jacket – a large ornamental gold-on-black enamel **swastika**, emerged from a fashionable apartment block in Strazewskiego Street on the edge of the ancient city of Cracow, and saw his chauffeur waiting with fuming breath by the open door of an enormous and, even in this blackened world, **lustrous** Adler limousine.

'Watch the pavement, Herr Schindler,' said the chauffeur. 'It's icy like a widow's heart.'

10 In observing this small winter scene, we are on safe ground. The tall young man would to the end of his days wear double-breasted suits, would, being something of an engineer, always be gratified by large dazzling vehicles, would, though a German and at this point in history a German of some influence, always be the sort of man with whom a Polish chauffeur could safely crack a warm, comradely joke.

But it will not be possible to see the whole story under such easy character headings. For this is the story of the **pragmatic** triumph of good over evil, a triumph in eminently measurable, statistical, unsubtle terms. When you work from the other end of the beast, when you chronicle the predictable and

20 measurable success evil generally achieves, it is easy to be wise, wry, piercing, to avoid **bathos**. It is easy to show the inevitability by which evil acquires all of what you could call the real estate of the story, even though good might finish up with a few **imponderables** like dignity and self-knowledge. Fatal human malice is the staple of narrators, original sin is the mother-fluid of historians. But it is a risky enterprise to have to write of virtue.

In fact virtue is such a dangerous word that we have to rush to explain; Herr Oskar Schindler, chancing his glimmering shoes on the icy pavement in this old and elegant quarter of Cracow, was not a virtuous young man in the customary sense. In this city he kept house with his German mistress and

30 maintained a long affair with his Polish secretary.

Likewise he was a drinker. Some of the time he drank for the pure glow of it, at other times with associates, bureaucrats, **SS men** for more **palpable** results. Like few others, he was capable of staying canny while drinking, of keeping his head. That again, though, under the narrow interpretation of morality has never been an excuse for **carousing**. And although Herr Schindler's merit is well documented, it is a feature of his ambiguity that he worked within or, at least, on the strength of, a corrupt and savage scheme; one which filled Europe with camps of varying but consistent inhumanity and created a submerged, unspoken-of nation of prisoners. The best thing,

40 therefore, may be to begin with a tentative instance of Herr Schindler's strange virtue and of the places and associates to which it brought him …

It is certain that by this stage of his history, in spite of his liking for good food and wine, Herr Schindler approached tonight's dinner at Commandant Goeth's more with loathing than with anticipation. There had in fact never been a time when to sit and drink with Amon had not been a repellent business. Yet the revulsion Herr Schindler felt was of a **piquant** kind, an ancient exultant sense of abomination such as, in a medieval painting, the just show for the damned. An emotion, that is, which stung Oskar rather than unmanned him …

50 At the double doors giving on to the dining room, the Rosner brothers were playing, Henry on violin, Leo on accordion. On Hauptsturmführer Goeth's command they had taken off the tattered clothing of the camp paint shop where they worked in the daytime and adopted the evening suits they kept in their barracks for such events. Oskar Schindler knew that although the commandant admired their music the Rosners never played at ease in the villa. They had seen too much of Amon. They knew he was erratic and given to **ex tempore** executions. They played studiously and hoped that their music would not give offence.

At Goeth's table that night there would be seven men …

60 The guests were summoned to the table. Onion soup was carried in and served by the maid. While the guests supped and chatted, the Rosner brothers continued to play, moving in closer to the diners, but not so close as to **impede** the movements of the maid or of Ivan and Petr, Goeth's two Ukrainian orderlies. Herr Schindler, sitting between the tall girl whom Scherner had **appropriated** and a sweet-faced, small-boned Pole who spoke German, saw that both girls watched this maid. She wore the traditional domestic uniform, black dress and white apron. She bore no **Jewish star** on her arm, no stripe of yellow paint on her back, yet she was Jewish just the same. What drew the attention of the other women was the condition of her

70 face. There was bruising along the line of the jaw, and you would have thought Goeth had too much shame to display a servant in that condition in front of guests from Cracow. Both the women and Herr Schindler could see, as well as the injury to her face, a more alarming purple, not always covered by her collar, at the junction where her thin neck joined her shoulder.

Not only did Amon Goeth neglect to leave the girl unexplained in the background, but he turned his chair towards her, **gesticulating** with one hand, displaying her to the assembled company. Herr Schindler had not been at this house for six weeks now, but his informants told him the relationship between Goeth and the girl had developed this way. When with

80 friends he used her as a conversational device. He only hid her away when senior officers from beyond the Cracow region were visiting.

'Ladies and gentlemen,' he called, mimicking the tones of a fake-drunken **master of cabaret**, 'may I introduce Lena? After five months she is now doing well in cuisine and deportment.'

'I can see from her face,' said the tall girl, Scherner's, 'that she's had a collision with the kitchen furniture.'

'And the bitch can have another,' said Goeth with a genial liquid gurgle. 'Yes. Another. Couldn't you, Lena?'

'He's hard on women,' the SS chief boasted, winking at his tall consort.

90 Scherner's intention might not have been unkind, since he did not refer to Jewish women but to women in general. It was when Goeth was reminded of Lena's Jewishness that she took more punishment, either publicly, in front of dinner guests, or later, when the commandant's friends had gone home. Scherner, being Goeth's superior, could have ordered the commandant to stop beating the girl. But that would have been bad form, would have soured

the friendly parties at Amon's villa. Scherner came here not as a superior, but as a friend, an associate, a carouser, a savourer of women. Amon was a strange fellow, but no one could turn on parties the way he could …

[Dinner over, Schindler prepares to say goodnight and go home.]

100 He saw that Goeth, in his shirt sleeves, was disappearing out of the dining-room door, making for the stairwell supported by one of the girls who had flanked him at dinner. Oskar excused himself and caught up with the commandant. He reached out and laid a hand on Goeth's shoulder. The eyes the commandant turned on him struggled to focus. 'Oh,' said Goeth in a liquid way. 'Going, Oskar?'

'I have to be home,' said Oskar. At home was Ingrid, his German mistress.

'You're a bloody stallion,' said Goeth.

'Not in your class,' said Schindler.

'No, you're right. I'm a frigging Olympian. We're going, where're we
110 going …?' He turned the his head to the girl but answered the question himself. 'We're going to the kitchen to see that Lena's clearing away properly.'

'No,' said the girl, laughing. 'We aren't doing that.'

She steered him up the stairs. It was decent of her, the sisterhood in operation, to protect the thin, wounded girl in the kitchen.

Herr Oskar Schindler watched the uneven animal, the hulking officer, the slight, supporting girl, struggling crookedly up the staircase. Goeth looked like a man who would have to sleep until at least lunchtime, but Oskar knew the commandant's amazing constitution and the clock that ran in him. By
120 3 a.m. Goeth might even decide to rise and write a letter to his father in Vienna. By seven, after only an hour's sleep, he'd be on the balcony, infantry rifle in hand, ready to shoot any dilatory prisoners.

When the girl and Goeth reached the first landing, Schindler sidled down the hallway towards the back of the house …

In the kitchen of the villa, the maid, Helen Hirsch (Goeth called her Lena out of laziness she would always say) looked up to see one of the dinner guests in the doorway. She put down the dish of meat scraps she'd been holding and stood to attention with jerky suddenness. 'Herr …' She looked at his dinner jacket and sought the word for him. 'Herr Direktor, I was just
130 putting aside the leftovers for the Herr Commandant's dogs.'

'Please, please,' said Herr Schindler. 'You don't have to report to me, Fräulein Hirsch.'

He put his arm around her. He could surely feel the clenching of her body as he touched her cheek with his lips.

He murmured, 'It's not that sort of kiss. I'm kissing you out of pity, if you want to know.'

She couldn't avoid starting to weep. Herr Direktor Schindler bussed her hard

in the middle of the forehead, in the manner of Polish farewells at railway stations, a resounding Eastern European smack of the lips. She saw that he

140   had begun to weep too. 'That kiss is something I bring you from …' He waved his hand, indicating some honest tribe of men out in the dark, sleeping in tiered bunks or hiding in forests, people for whom by absorbing punishment from Hauptsturmführer Goeth she was in part a buffer.

Herr Schindler released her and reached into the side pocket of his jacket, bringing out a large confectionery bar. In its substance too it seemed pre-war.

'Keep that somewhere,' he advised her.

'I get extra food here,' she told him, as if it were a matter of pride that he wouldn't presume she was starving. Food, in fact, was the least of her worries.

150   She knew she would not survive in Amon's house, but it would not be for lack of food.

'If you don't want to eat it, trade it,' Herr Schindler told her. 'Or why not build yourself up?' He stood back and surveyed her. 'Itzhak Stern told me about you.'

'Herr Schindler,' murmured the girl. She put her head down and wept neatly, economically, for a few seconds. 'Herr Schindler, he likes to beat me in front of those women. On my first day here, he beat me because I threw out the bones from dinner. He came down to the basement at midnight and asked me where they were. For his dogs, you understand. That was the first

170   beating … I said to him … I don't know why I said it, I'd never say it now … Why are you beating me? He said, The reason I'm beating you now is you asking me why I'm beating you.'

She shook her head and shrugged, as if **reproving herself** for talking so much. She didn't want to say any more, she couldn't convey the history of her punishments, her repeated experience of the Hauptsturmführer's knuckles.

Herr Schindler bent his head to her and became even more confidential. 'Your circumstances are appalling, Helen,' he told her.

'It doesn't matter,' she said. 'I've accepted it.'

180   'Accepted it?'

'One day he'll shoot me.'

Schindler shook his head and she thought it was too **glib** an encouragement to her to hope. Suddenly, the good cloth and the **cosseted** flesh of Herr Schindler were a provocation. 'For God's sake, Herr Schindler, I see things. We were up on the roof on Monday, chipping off the ice, me and young Lisiek. And we saw the Herr Commandant come out of the front door and down the steps by the patio, right below us. And, there on the steps, he drew his gun and shot a woman who was passing. A woman carrying a bundle. Through the throat. Just a woman on her way somewhere. You know. She

190   didn't seem fatter or thinner or slower or faster than anyone else. I couldn't guess what she'd done. The more you see of the Herr Commandant, the

more you see that there's no set of rules you can keep to. You can't say to yourself, If I keep these rules, I'll be safe …'

Schindler took her hand and wrung it for emphasis. 'Listen, my dear Fräulein Helen Hirsch, for all that, it's still better than Majdanek or Auschwitz. If you can keep your health …'

She said, 'I thought it would be easy to keep my health in the commandant's kitchen. When I was sent here, from the camp kitchen, the other girls were jealous.'

200 A pitiful smile spread on her lips.

Schindler raised his voice now. He was like a man enunciating a principle of physics. 'He won't kill you, because he enjoys you too much, my dear Helen. He enjoys you so much he won't even let you wear the Star. He doesn't want anyone to know it's a Jew he's enjoying. He shot the woman from the steps because she meant nothing to him; she was one of a series, she neither pleased nor offended him. You understand that. But you … it's not decent, Helen. But it's life.'

Someone else had said that to her. Untersturmführer Leo John, a second lieutenant, the commandant's deputy. John had said, 'He won't kill you till 210 the end, Lena, because he gets too much of a kick out of you.' But coming from John it hadn't had the same effect. Herr Schindler had just condemned her to a painful survival.

He seemed to understand that she was stunned. He murmured encouragement. He'd see her again. He'd try to get her out. 'Out?' she asked. 'Out of the villa,' he explained, 'into my factory. Surely you have heard of my factory. I have an enamelware factory.'

'Oh yes,' she said like a slum child speaking of the **Riviera**. 'Schindler's Emalia. I've heard of it.'

'Keep your health,' he repeated. He seemed to know it would be the key. He 220 seemed to draw on a knowledge of future intentions – Himmler's, Frank's – when he said it.

'All right,' she conceded.

From T. Keneally, *Schindler's Ark*, Wheeler, 1994

DICTIONARY

swastika the Nazi party badge
lustrous shining
pragmatic practical, matter-of-fact
bathos ridiculous anti-climax
imponderables incalculable qualities
SS men Schutzstaffel, a very powerful military organisation
palpable measurable
carousing drinking, partying

> **piquant** interesting, exciting
>
> **ex tempore** sudden
>
> **impede** get in the way
>
> **appropriated** taken over
>
> **Jewish star** all Jews in Nazi Germany had to wear a yellow star to identify them
>
> **gesticulating** gesturing
>
> **master of cabaret** night-club announcer
>
> **reproving herself** telling herself off
>
> **glib** easy
>
> **cosseted** cared for
>
> **Riviera** an area of the southern French coast where the rich went on holiday

DICTIONARY

CLOSER READING

1 Look again at the opening three paragraphs of the passage (lines 1–15). In your own words, describe the kind of man Oskar Schindler appears to be.

2 Re-read the fourth paragraph of the passage (lines 16–25). What point is Keneally making here?

3 Look again at lines 26 to 41.
   • Make two columns and head them Positive and Negative. Under the first column, note down all the positive things we learn about Schindler in these paragraphs; in the second, note down all the negative things.
   • In your own words, write two or three sentences summing up your view of Schindler's character at this stage. Use quotations from the text to back up your points.

4 Re-read lines 42 to 58, and look through the preceding paragraphs for any mention of Amon Goeth. What kind of man is he, and what does Oskar Schindler feel about him?

5 Re-read lines 60 to 98.
   • Who is Lena, and what is Goeth's attitude to her?
   • How do the other guests react to Goeth's treatment of her?
   • Is there a difference between the way the men and the women react?
   • Which reaction does Oskar Schindler's position appear to be closer to?

6 Look again at lines 125 to 143. What does Schindler do, and how does Helen react?

7 Re-read the paragraphs describing Goeth's treatment of Helen and his shooting of the woman prisoner (lines 155–193). In your own words, write one or two sentences describing Helen's life with Goeth and her feelings about it.

8 Re-read from line 194 to the end of the passage. How does Schindler comfort Helen, and what advice does he offer her?

FURTHER ACTIVITIES

1
- Look again through Text no. 1, Plutarch's description of the assassination of Caesar.
- Working in pairs, compare your notes on the passage, and come to an agreement on your answers to Closer Reading question 5.
- Discuss what you think Plutarch's main interest in writing the passage was. Use one of the sentences below as the basis for your discussion, selecting words and sentences from the passage to back up your point of view.
    a *'Plutarch's main interest in the passage is to describe Julius Caesar's personality because …'*
    b *'Plutarch's main interest in the passage is to pinpoint the reasons for Caesar's assassination, so as to point up a moral about the behaviour of powerful men. This is demonstrated through the way in which Plutarch focuses on …'*
    c *'Plutarch's main interest in the passage is to demonstrate that killers never prosper. This is demonstrated through the way in which Plutarch focuses on …'*
- With another pair, compare your findings and agree on a common point of view. Prepare a presentation of this point of view to the class as a whole.
- As a class, discuss your findings.
- On your own, make notes on any points that strike you as particularly interesting, either because they back up your point of view, or because they argue against it.
- On your own, write a short summary (about 250 words) of what you think Plutarch's main purpose was in this passage, giving quotations from the text to back up your point of view.

2
- On your own, re-read both the passages in Text no. 2 (from the *Life of Johnson*). Look again at the notes you wrote in answer to Closer Reading question 4. You will need these in a minute.
- With a partner, decide which of you will work on Passage A, and which on Passage B. Each of you re-write the passage you have chosen to work on, taking out all the adjectives.
- Swap your re-written passages, and compare them both against the original. Discuss together what the differences are, particularly with reference to the passages' effect on the reader.
- On your own, write a short answer to the question below, using quotations from the text to back up your point of view.
    'Boswell's Life of Johnson gives us not so much a portrait of Johnson, as a picture of Boswell's own admiration for him.' Do you agree? Give reasons for your answer.

3
- On your own, write a list of five adverbs (if you are not quite clear what an adverb is, look up the definition in a dictionary before starting).

- With a partner, swap your lists and write a sentence using each of the adverbs you have been given.
- With your partner, look again through Text no. 3 (The Actress and the President), and note down all of the adverbs in the passage. Make a list of them and write down their definitions.
- With your partner, draw three columns, heading them Definite Fact, Probable Fact and Guesswork. Note down every statement that Sandra Shevey makes in one of the three columns. You may want to use the beginning of the chart below as a starting-point.

Definite Fact	Probable Fact	Guesswork
Jack Kennedy had affairs with other women before Marilyn	Jackie Kennedy may have had a hand in ending these affairs	Jackie ended the affair between Jack and Marilyn

- When you finished, number all the statements and total up how many of each you have in each column.
- On your own, use the findings in your chart to draw a pie-chart of the proportions of fact, probability and guesswork that there are in the passage.
- Again on your own, write a few sentences summarising your view of Sandra Shevey's method as a biographer, giving quotations from the text to back up your point of view.

4
- On your own, re-read Text no. 4 (Schindler's Ark) and look back through your answers to the Closer Reading questions.
- With a partner, go through the passage and note down whose point of view we are seeing the action from at each stage. Discuss whether it is always the same point of view, and, if it changes, where and why.
- On your own, write an answer to the question 'Just how objective is Thomas Keneally?' Use quotations from the text to back up your point of view.

5
- On your own, select a member of your family about whom to write a short biography.
- Make notes on your subject's life. Research any details you need to clarify. You may want to interview other people who know your subject, in order to get evidence from all sorts of different points of view.
- Choose **one** of the texts in this section, and write your subject's life, using that text as the model for your approach. Be careful to stick closely to the way in which the original text presents its subject when writing your biography.

Electronic Texts

Letters

INFORMATION

Instructions | Legal Writing | Information Writing | Biography | Interviews | Essays | Travel Writing | Diaries | Philosophical Writing | Autobiography | Social Commentary | Reportage | Reviews | Promotional Writing | Polemic

PERSUASION

5
Interviews

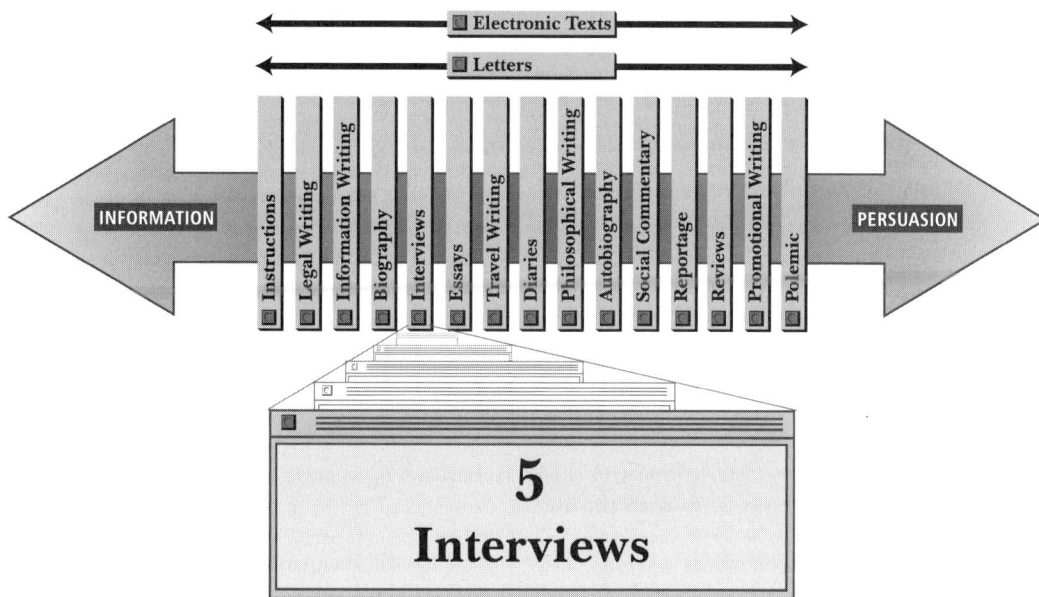

The type of information that an interviewer aims to get from an interviewee (the person being interviewed) depends on the purpose of the interview. Sometimes the purpose is to collect data – an example would be those interviews carried out by market researchers. Often interviewers aim to assess somebody's ability, for example in job interviews. Other interviews are designed to explore the personality of a celebrity (someone well known) – film stars, politicians and people currently in the news. These interviews have similarities with biographies (see pages 32–48) in that they give details about the interviewee's life and try to understand his or her personality. However, they are much shorter and focus mainly on what the interviewee is currently doing and planning to do.

An interview, if it is to be published, is also affected by the audience it is aimed at. If the audience wants simple entertainment they may want to read interviews to discover 'gossip' about famous people's private lives and relationships. A different audience may prefer a deeper insight into someone's personality and, if they are well known, how this relates to their behaviour in public life.

Another important factor in an interview is the relationship between the interviewer and interviewee. The two will have spent time face to face, will have formed opinions and may have developed a liking or disliking for each other. This may influence the interviewer when they finally write up the interview. There will have also been a lot of non-verbal communication – gestures, eye-contact, facial expressions and other body language – which might influence the way they feel about the interviewee.

Finally, the interviewer will select the information they feel to be important from what has been said, and they will give an interpretation of it. This means there is always the possibility of bias creeping in.

1   The job interview

Below are two extracts from interviews for a teaching job. (Q = question, A = answer)

A

Q: Please sit down. *(Points to an empty chair.)*

A: Er … thanks! *(Sits and relaxes.)*

Q: Now, Mr Johnson, I'd like to begin with a couple of questions about your relationship with pupils …

A: *(Interrupting.)* Good! That's what it's all about isn't it? Getting on together.

Q: An interesting view. Could you tell me about how you would try to get the best work out of pupils?

A: Well … I like children to see me as a kind of father figure, you know, someone they can trust and feel safe with. If kids are happy, they usually work better don't they?

Q: What would you do if a child was failing to hand in work and was disrupting your lessons?

A: Yes … I suppose that does happen from time to time. Perhaps they have problems at home? Or with their friends? I think you should chat with them and get them to open up – I'm sure that would improve things.

Q: Wouldn't you ever discipline a pupil?

A: Well, I don't like conflict, really. In the end, if someone doesn't work why should I force them to? I don't think it would get them anywhere. I teach this lad called David Ronson, he hates school – he hates teachers! *(Laughs.)* There's no point putting pressure on him, he would just explode! You know, the other day he threatened to throw another kid out of the window! That boy needs help, counselling or something. Education is low on his list of priorities.

B

Q: Please sit down. *(He pulls the chair over for her.)*

A: Thank you. *(She sits down with her back straight.)*

Q: I hope you're comfortable, Mrs Weatherall. I'd like to start by asking you about how you manage children in the classroom. How would you get the best out of pupils?

A: I feel it is very important to have the highest expectations of the children you teach. There is no point in making excuses for pupils because they might come from a difficult background or have problems. If you do that you're letting them down. No, the key is to push hard and challenge
10   them to fulfil their potential.

Q: What would your approach be to a child who fails to hand in homework or constantly misbehaves?

A: They need to know what the rules are and what the punishments are if they break the rules. They don't always know what is best for themselves – they will be grateful when they grow up and realise that we forced them back onto the straight and narrow.

Q: Would you think of asking the child about why they are misbehaving?

A: Yes, but only to point out that most answers that they give are probably just excuses. It is a hard world once they're looking for jobs – people
20   aren't sympathetic in the real world. One of the most important lessons they learn at school is to stand on their own two feet.

CLOSER READING

1 Rate each of the two interviewees from 1 to 10 (10 being the highest) for each of the following qualities:

  a sense of humour;
  b respect for children;
  c ability to discipline;
  d self-confidence.

Compare your answers with other people in the class, and discuss any differences you have.

2 What was the manner of each teacher during the interview? Look at what they do, what they say and how they say it.

3 How does the interviewer treat the interviewees differently? Look at what he does and how he adapts his questions. Explain these differences.

4 a What are the strengths and weaknesses of each interviewee?

  b Which teacher would you employ? Why? Compare your answers with others in the class.

  c What advice would you give each interviewee on how to improve their interview technique?

2 The evidence-gathering interview

This is the transcript of an interview which took place around 1815. The interview was carried out by Parliament as part of an investigation into the conditions in factories at the time. The woman being interviewed was called Elizabeth Bentley.

(Some words are highlighted in the text. You will find further information about these words at the end of the passage.)

EVIDENCE OF A FEMALE MILLHAND TO THE PARLIAMENTARY COMMISSIONERS

What age are you?
Twenty-three.

Where do you live?
At Leeds.

What time did you begin work at the factory?
When I was six years old.

At whose factory did you work?
Mr Burk's.

What kind of mill is it?
10   **Flax** mill.

What was your business in that mill?
I was a little doffer.

What were your hours of labour in that mill?
From 5 in the morning till 9 at night, when they were **thronged**.

For how long a time together have you worked that excessive length of time?
For about a year.

What were the usual hours of labour when you were not so thronged?
From six in the morning till 7 at night.

What time was allowed for meals?
20   Forty minutes at noon.

Had you any time to get your breakfast or drinking?
No, we had to get it as we could.

Do you consider doffing a laborious employment?
Yes.

Explain what you had to do.
When the frames are full, they have to stop the frames, and take the flyers off, and take the full bobbins off, and carry them to the roller, and then put empty ones on, and set the frame going again.

Does that keep you constantly on your feet?
30   Yes, there are so many frames and they run so quick.

Your labour is very excessive?
Yes, you have not time for anything.

*Suppose you **flagged** a little, or were late, what would they do?*
Strap us.

And they are in the habit of strapping those who are late in doffing?
Yes.

Constantly?
Yes.

Girls as well as boys?
40   Yes.

Have you ever been strapped?
Yes.

Severely?
Yes.

Is the strap used so as to hurt you excessively?
Yes it is … I have seen the **overlooker** go to the top end of the room, where
the little girls **hug the can to the backminders**; he has taken a strap, and a
whistle in his mouth, and sometimes he has got a chain and chained them,
and strapped them all down the room.

50   *What was his reason for that?*
He was very angry.

Did you live far from the mill?
Yes, two miles.

Had you a clock?
No, we had not.

Were you generally there in time?
Yes, my mother has been up at 4 o'clock in the morning, and at 2 o'clock in
the morning; the **colliers** used to go to their work at 3 or 4 o'clock, and when
she heard them stirring she has got up out of her warm bed, and gone out
60   and asked them the time; and I have sometimes been at Hunslet Car at
2 o'clock in the morning, when it was streaming down with rain, and we have
had to stay till the mill was opened.

You are considerably deformed in person as a consequence of this labour?
Yes I am.

And what time did it come on?
I was about 13 years old when it began coming, and it has got worse since; it
is five years since my mother died, and my mother was never able to get me a
good pair of **stays** to hold me up, and when my mother died I had to do for
myself, and got me a pair.

70   *Were you perfectly straight and healthy before you worked at a mill?*
Yes, I was as straight a little girl as ever went up and down town.

Were you straight till you were 13?
Yes, I was.

Did your deformity come upon you with much pain and weariness?
Yes, I cannot express the pain all the time it was coming.

Do you know of anybody that has been similarly injured in their health?
Yes, in their health, but not many deformed as I am.

It is very common to have weak ankles and crooked knees?
Yes, very common indeed.

80 *This is brought on by stopping the spindle?*
Yes.

Where are you now?
In the **poorhouse**.

State what you think as to the circumstances in which you have been placed during all this time of labour, and what you have considered about it as to the hardship and cruelty of it.

The witness was too much affected to answer the question.

From J. Carey (ed.), *The Faber Book of Reportage*, Faber & Faber, 1987

DICTIONARY

Flax fibre from plants, used to make cloth

thronged busy

flagged tired

overlooker person in charge

hug the can to the backminders part of the technical process in the mill

colliers miners

stays metal or bone inserts in clothes which act as supports

poorhouse a workhouse for the poor

CLOSER READING

1 This interview reads like a questionnaire; there is a series of set questions, most of which ask for brief answers. The interview would have been carried out with hundreds of millhands with the purpose of creating a picture of their lives. Most of the questions are **closed** – this means that they require a 'yes' or 'no' answer or a short factual response. This type of question provides data which can be counted up or measured, for example the number of 'yes' responses or lengths of time. A few of the questions are **open** – they ask for more detailed, personalised answers. These can be very varied and cannot be turned into statistics.

Write down **two** of the open questions in the passage and **two** of the closed ones.

2 Which questions ask for facts and which ask for opinions? Write down **three** that ask for opinions.

3 Write down any questions that **express** an opinion.

4 Even though this is a formal interview it creates a moving picture of this woman's life in the mill. Using the information you have gained from the interview, describe a normal day at the mill, writing as if you were a millhand.

3 The celebrity interview

This interview, with the cricketer Ian Botham and his son, is taken from *Hello!* magazine, a magazine which focuses on the lives of the rich and famous.

(Some words are highlighted in the text. You will find further information about these words at the end of the passage.)

'We're not like father and son,' explains Ian. 'He's 19 and I'm only 41, so we're more like brothers. It's like Viv Richards [Liam's godfather] and I, we're mates. Liam is a great mate. We have no secrets: if I'm in trouble and need £50, he'll give me £50. If he needs it, I'll give it to him. So, as mates, there is enormous **rivalry**. Whatever we do together, be it fish or play soccer, rugby, golf or tiddlywinks, or mess around with the cats and dogs on the lawn, there's a healthy element of competition.'

Ian wrote in his autobiography: 'It is the hope of every father who plays professional sports that he will one day be able to watch his son performing
10 at the same or higher level.' But, in cricket, it was always impossible for anyone to reach a higher level than the greatest wicket-taker in the history of English test cricket, scorer of 1,000 runs and 100 wickets in just 21 tests.

Ian Botham OBE – 'Beefy' – is a national hero: a TV personality who raised over £3 million for leukaemia research on long-distance walks. This is the man Liam has to confront back home in Yorkshire: a good dad who can be as hard as nails.

'We're both hard on the field, but Dad is also hard as a person,' discloses the son who once appeared on *Beadle's About* as part of a practical joke played on him by his father. 'I think I've got more of my mother's softer qualities. Dad's
20 had a lot of flack and that's made him hard. We differ in so far as I cope with aggravation a little better than he does.'

'Yeah,' ponders the man who re-enacted **Hannibal's crossing of the Alps**. 'He's a slightly watered-down version of what I was like at his age.' …

Ian admits he was away for most of his son's childhood. He was present at his birth in 1977 – 'mind-blowing, an experience I'll never forget' – only because a foot injury kept him out of a test against Australia.

'I didn't see much of Dad when I was a kid,' says Liam. 'It's only in the last three or four years I've really got to know him. We have a good relationship now. It would have been nice to get to know Dad earlier but there was no way
30 that was going to happen.'

'Unfortunately, in professional cricket you make sacrifices,' says Ian. 'One I've had to make is not having a family life. There have been chunks of Liam's life I haven't seen, but it was the way the dice landed. I wouldn't have swapped my life. When I was at home I was probably too strict. I didn't want to fall into the trap of coming back after being away for 11 and a half months and just spoil the kids rotten for three weeks and then go away again.

'That would have made it impossible for Kath, and for me, because every time I walked through the door the kids would have expected something. That's not what life is about. So I didn't come bearing gifts. It was my living,
40   not a holiday. It was hard on all of us.'

Liam says: 'My first memories of Dad are recognising him on TV and seeing him in papers and feeling proud. He was away a lot, so it was nice to "catch up" with him that way. All he wanted to do when he got home was relax and have nothing to do with cricket, so I never played that game with him in the garden. It would have been nice, but it didn't happen, so there was no point in being upset about it.'

'I used to be on the road for 49 to 50 weeks of the year,' says Ian. 'I was shattered when I got home. I'd just sleep the whole time.'

From I. Woodward, 'Ian Botham and Son Liam', Hello!, 1997

DICTIONARY

rivalry competition
Hannibal's crossing of the Alps Hannibal was a successful army commander who crossed the Alps on foot in 217 BC to defeat the Roman army.

CLOSER READING

1 In what ways are Ian and Liam Botham 'like brothers' rather than father and son?

2 How do we know that the interviewer thinks highly of Ian Botham? Find three examples.

3 The second half of the passage is about the Botham's family life.

   a Why did Ian Botham miss out on family life?

   b What did Liam Botham think about this as he grew up?

   c Is it possible to tell what the interviewer's opinion is of Ian Botham's absence as a father?

4 The interviewer's questions aren't included in this article – they aren't necessary for our understanding.

   Write down what you think the questions were.

4 | The in-depth interview

This interview appeared in *The Guardian*. Helen Mirren is a well-known actor who starred in the *Prime Suspect* series. She was being interviewed at the time *Some Mother's Son* was released, a film in which she starred.

(Some words are highlighted in the text. You will find further information about these words at the end of the passage.)

Sipping a second glass of white wine in a New York restaurant, Mirren looks softer and a little older than the character with whom she has become almost **synonymous** – Detective Chief Inspector Jane Tennison. Her strawberry blonde hair is cut longer and faint **crow's feet** creep away from the edges of her eyes. Her all-black outfit – a full-length leather coat over a long skirt – is stylish rather than fashionable.

By a neat, if not mightily significant, **irony**, *Some Mother's Son* arrives on our screens in the wake of Michael Collins, the Neil Jordan 'biopic' starring Liam Neeson which raised hackles among Irish Protestants and Fleet Street leader
10   writers. It was while living with Ulster-born Neeson in the early eighties that Mirren was first exposed at close quarters to the Irish conflict. She based her character in *Some Mother's Son* on a woman she met in the province at the time.

For the last 12 years, Mirren has shared a home in the Hollywood Hills with the American director Taylor Hackford (*An Officer And A Gentleman*) and her beloved catahoula hounds, though she insists she does not consider herself to be living in Los Angeles but merely 'spending part of my life there'. Even so, the idea that Hollywood now passes for Mirren's home seems oddly **incongruous**. She is one of those British institutions, like tea or the National
20   Health Service, whose merits have gone largely unrecognised across the Atlantic.

She has been one of the brightest lights of the English stage since joining the Royal Shakespeare Company at 18; and yet Mirren did not make her Broadway debut until two years ago. Her Oscar-nominated performance in *The Madness of King George* briefly made her a studio darling, but her films – a mixture of acclaimed **art-house** classics such as Peter Greenaway's *The Cook, The Thief, His Wife & Her Lover* and Hollywood turkeys like *The Mosquito Coast* – never **hit pay dirt** at the American box office.

Though she is still lusted after by a generation of British men who cherish
30   the memory of her snorkelling naked in her screen debut, *Age Of Consent*, it seems her slightly **hangdog** features have never quite fitted into Hollywood's **pasteurised aesthetic**.

Mirren suggests the reason is much simpler, however. 'It's because I'm not American. Americans have a very uncomfortable relationship with people who speak with an English accent. I think it comes from those Cecil B De Mille films where all the Romans were played by people with a British accent and all the good Jews from Jesus Christ onwards were played by Americans. They (Americans) have this terrible fear thinly disguised as admiration for Brits. The only kind of Brit you're allowed to be in America is a princess or a

40   duchess or a lord and then they really love you.' Or perhaps a tough-as-nails female homicide detective. *Prime Suspect* was both a critical and popular success in the US, exposing many Americans to Mirren's **understated** brilliance for the first time.

Mirren, who finished filming the final series of the Granada drama last summer, insists she doesn't miss Jane Tennison, though she came to admire her. 'I would have liked to have been more like her. It was great playing a character who embodied all the New Year's Eve resolutions that I make every year and significantly fail to achieve.'

Unlike Tennison, Mirren rarely fixes her **interlocutor** with her distinctive

50   greyish eyes ('the colour of dirty washing-up liquid' is how she usually describes them). Instead she finds a point in the middle distance, locking on to it as she **marshals** her thoughts into long, impressively complete sentences. She tackles her green salad with the same deliberation, **methodically** slicing the lettuce into strips then bundling it into neat bite-sized packages. Though she **exudes** a quiet assurance – talking through questions when she has not finished delivering the answer to an earlier one, for instance – she sprinkles her remarks with not entirely convincing **self-deprecation**. Running the gauntlet of photographers and TV cameras outside the Oscar ceremony might be fun 'if you were incredibly beautiful … and totally confident about

60   the way you look,' she allows, 'but if you're not it's a nightmare.' But isn't Mirren famous for being gorgeous? 'No. I'm famous for being cool about not being gorgeous.'

Enough people disagree with her assessment that when she appeared naked on the cover of the *Radio Times* in October, millions of men developed an unusually keen interest in that week's TV listings. Mirren says she agreed to pose nude for the edition celebrating 50 years of the BBC radio programme *Woman's Hour* because she was tickled by the idea. 'I did it because it was the *Radio Times*. The *Radio Times*!' The resulting cover, she thought, was 'jolly' rather than sexy. 'I didn't happen to be wearing anything but you would

70   never have guessed that from the picture.' Mirren was selected for the *Radio Times* cover because she turned 50 last year, an event which horrified those who still remember her wildly **sensual** performances with the RSC in the late 1960s.

Mirren herself insists she is unmoved by the landmark birthday. 'It wasn't a big deal for me. I think you have these crises of "Oh my God, who am I? What am I doing? Where am I going? Why haven't I done this and that and the other? I look hideous, it's all over for me," but they usually happen at 12.30 at night on a Tuesday evening when you're forty three and a half or thirty five and three quarters. To me they've never happened on any

80   particular birthday.'

Though it is a regular **gripe** of middle-aged Hollywood actresses that there are few decent film roles for women over 50, Mirren says she has noticed no fall-off in the demand for her services. She doesn't know whether being the

other side of 50 will slow her career, she says, 'but I tell you it's a lot better than being a 50-year-old ballet dancer or soccer player because we deal in the business of being a human being. That's my business, if you know what I mean. It's reflecting what it is to be a human being, all the time, **constantly regurgitating** different improvisations on the theme of being a human being.' Mirren considers starting another sentence then checks herself. That
90   would be talking about acting.

Ian Katz, 'The Mother of all Roles', *The Guardian*, 4 Jan 1977

DICTIONARY

synonymous interchangeable
crow's feet wrinkles at the corners of the eyes
irony coincidence
incongruous inappropriate
art-house a type of film made for a minority 'high-brow' audience
hit pay dirt made lots of money
hangdog downcast
pasteurised aesthetic a kind of art where everything has to be perfect
understated restrained, not 'over-the-top'
interlocutor questioner
marshals organises
methodically systematically, step-by-step
exudes gives off
self-deprecation putting oneself down
sensual physical, sexual
gripe complaint
constantly regurgitating repeatedly churning out

CLOSER READING

1 Look at the description of Mirren. What does the interviewer say about her **appearance** and her **manner**?

2 Summarise what Mirren's opinions are about the following:
   • her lack of film success in America
   • her looks
   • her age
   • why she acts.

3 Find examples in the passage which show the interviewer's **admiration** for Mirren, and examples where he is **critical**.

4 Compare this interview with the one from *Hello!* (pages 55–56). You could look at the following areas:
   • whether the focus is more on the interviewee's private life or their public life (acting or sport);
   • whether or not the interviewer is critical of the interviewee;
   • how much is direct quotation and how much of the article is the interviewer's own views;
   • how much the interviewee's appearance, body language and manner are referred to.

FURTHER ACTIVITIES

1 Working in groups of four, role play an interview situation. One person is the interviewer, two are interviewees and one is an observer.

a The observer's role is to watch how well the interviewees cope with the interview: what they say, how they say it and their body language. Also, they should see if the interviewer treats each interviewee in the same way or differently.

b The interviewer should prepare a list of questions (five should be enough) . These should all be open questions (see page 54 for a definition of open questions) which require the interviewee to give detailed and personal answers.

c The two interviewees should decide what kind of characters they are. They will need to decide whether they will:
  • be confident
  • behave in a formal or informal way
  • give short or detailed answers.

d You could choose any job; what is important is that the main focus of the interview is the personal qualities of the interviewee. Some possibilities are:
  • teaching
  • shop work
  • computer operation
  • marketing
  • charity work
  • law
  • medicine
  • design or architecture
  • office work.

After the interviews, the observer should report back on what they have seen, giving advice to the interviewees. It may be helpful to record the interviews so that they can be played back and each person can have a chance to comment. If the interviews are videotaped, it will be possible to record the body language used too.

2 Carry out a survey on a topic that interests you. You will need to design a series of questions (about ten) to gather information. Some of the questions should be closed and some open (see the definition of these terms on page 54).

You can carry out your survey by interviewing people face to face, or by photocopying your questions and handing them out as questionnaires to be completed. Remember to leave plenty of space for people to write responses to open questions!

Your closed questions could take any of the following forms:
- ones that require yes or no answers
- multiple choice
- a series of statements that could be put in rank order.

When you have collected your data you should write a report. Use the following structure:

a Begin with an introduction which explains why you chose your topic and what you were trying to find out.

b Include charts and graphs showing the results of your closed questions.

c Write summaries of the answers to your open questions.

d Finish with an analysis of what the answers show about people's opinions concerning your topic.

Some possible topics are:
- attitudes towards the monarchy
- animal rights
- teenage problems
- school uniform
- drug abuse
- equal opportunities
- the qualities of a good teacher
- crime and punishment.

3 Many interviews are carried out to find out more about what someone is like, what experiences they have had and what views they hold.

Working in pairs, take it in turns to carry out an in-depth interview with each other. Devise a series of open questions (about ten) that you can ask your partner which will reveal the type of person he or she is.

Your questions could be based on the following areas:
- important experiences
- family background
- hopes for the future
- feelings about the present
- relationships
- opinions about current issues in the news or society.

You should be prepared to ask extra questions, if necessary, to encourage the interviewee to explain things more clearly, or so that you can explore their life and views in more detail.

If possible, tape-record the interview so that you can listen properly without having to worry about taking notes. You will also be able to quote your interviewee directly.

Write up your interview as though it were to be published in a magazine (you can choose which). Remember the following things:

- Select the most interesting sections of the interview.
- Don't include all the 'er's and 'um's! If your interviewee did hesitate a lot you could comment on that.
- If possible, try to avoid using the questions in your article – this way it will appear less artificial and will 'flow'.
- Include your own observations about your interviewee's body language and tone of voice.
- Decide which parts you are going to quote directly and which parts you are going to summarise.
- Try to come to an overall conclusion about your interviewee.

Electronic Texts

Letters

INFORMATION — Instructions · Legal Writing · Information Writing · Biography · Interviews · Essays · Travel Writing · Diaries · Philosophical Writing · Autobiography · Social Commentary · Reportage · Reviews · Promotional Writing · Polemic — PERSUASION

6
Essays

It is one of the curious facts about school life that you are frequently asked to indulge in activities that you will rarely, if ever, have to undertake again – and one of these is the writing of essays.

Just what is an essay? According to the Oxford English Dictionary it is 'A composition of moderate length on any particular subject, or branch of a subject; originally implying want of finish, "an irregular undigested piece", but now said of a composition more or less elaborate in style, though limited in range.' In other words, it is a short piece of writing on pretty well any subject, but presenting more of the characteristics of an observation, an idea, than of a finished piece of reasoning.

Nowadays, in the world beyond school, essays are almost only ever encountered in newspapers and magazines, but in earlier centuries they were a respectable branch of writing, in which a gentleman could express his thoughts on the world around him.

In the passages that follow, you will be asked to look at what ideas are being put forward, and how the ideas link to the style in which they are being expressed.

1 Him Indoors

This is a piece of writing by Phil Hogan taken from the *Observer* newspaper, in which the author, a contemporary journalist, is giving a taste of his life and experiences.

(Some words are highlighted in the text. You will find further information about these words at the end of the passage.)

'You'll have plenty of time when we get back from dropping the kids off at school,' she says through a mouthful of toothpaste foam. 'It's only a *curtain pole*.'

I'm no expert, but I appreciate enough of the complexities of home improvement to know that *nothing* is only a curtain pole. Especially at 8.22 am, when the kids are still in their pyjamas, I'm still in the bath, the Cornflakes are still in the packet and the polish I'm meant to slap on three pairs of shoes, none of them mine, is still in the tin.

'I won't have time,' I say. 'I've got to iron a shirt.'

10 'Why can't you be a bit more organised?' she begins, but is luckily interrupted by the blood-curdling screech of our ill-positioned fire alarm, which goes off when the toast is done or when someone walks past our house eating extra-strong mints.

She rushes off in a panic, leaving me to meditate on the kind of imbecile who is so disorganised that he doesn't have time to fit a curtain pole before going to work …

By the time I have cut myself shaving, reclaimed an old T-shirt from the rag drawer, emptied the kids' hot-water bottles down the toilet and cursed the inventor of the double bunk, who obviously never made a bed in his life, I go
20 downstairs to find two of the children dressed, cleanly shod and wrestling about on the carpet while the third, likewise **accoutred**, takes a rotten tomato, because we have no rotten lettuce left, out to the rabbit. 'Right, what needs doing?' I demand, a freshly baptised master of the situation.

'Nothing,' she says with a well-organised smile, shutting a lunch box with an irritatingly efficient click, and gathering up bags, homework and coats with an unnecessarily **rhetorical** flourish. 'We just need to get them out to the car.'

They pile with enthusiasm into the back of our *fantastic* new P-reg metallic green Fiat Ulysse people carrier, which was bought under a brilliant finance scheme that has a built-in safeguard to prevent you ever actually owning it.
30 In return, the dealership signs a form promising not to tell your neighbours that you're not as well off as they think you are.

The kids fight over who gets the seat by the electric window, while I switch on the indicators instead of the windscreen wipers, fiddle with the immobilising thing and the headlights that turn into machine guns and try to remember where the car hides the radio when you lock it up for the night. All the seats swivel round and turn into tables so you can stop on the motorway for a game of poker if you want.

Half an hour later, we're back from school and I'm up the ladder and in a sweat. I have to leave the house in 25 minutes. The ironing board with my
40   unironed shirt is standing in the corner like a **reprimand** on four legs. My wife has warmed up some croissants and put them on a tray with some coffee. To get my prizes, all I have to do is take one piece of wood down and put another up in its place, fit three brackets in a straight line, saw the pole, fit the finials, which is an expensive new word for 'ends', and then stand back whistling and wiping imaginary dirt from my hands.

My wood is prepared. I know it will fit because my genius carpenter of a neighbour was kind enough to cut it for me, or at least sensible enough not to lend me his electric saw when I turned up on his doorstep with my tail wagging like a dog with an 8ft-long stick to throw.

50   Now, I'm on my own. There's a tussle with the screws but I win it in straight sets. I prise the old narrow plank off and ease in my wider one and fix the centre screw. *Yes*. But 15 of my minutes have gone. I try another screw. Funny, the holes are in the wrong place … I unscrew it again and try it upside down. The holes are in the wrong place, only now in an upside-down way.

I am the picture of **equanimity**. I put my junior school tool kit away. I will try again at the weekend. Even as I brand a hot, soily wrinkle into my white shirt with an iron that has been sharing the cupboard with a box of potatoes, I hear myself saying, it's only a *curtain* pole.

P. Hogan, 'Him Indoors', *Observer Life*, 16 March 1977

DICTIONARY	
accoutred	dressed, kitted out
rhetorical	showy
reprimand	rebuke, telling-off
equanimity	calm and balance

CLOSER READING

1 Re-read the first five paragraphs of the passage (lines 1–16). Summarise in your own words what Phil Hogan has been asked to do and what he feels about it.

2 Look again at the sixth paragraph (lines 17–23). Note down what has changed since the opening of the passage.

3 Re-read the seventh paragraph (lines 24–26). What do you learn about Phil Hogan's feelings in this paragraph? Pick out any words and phrases that give you a clue to his feelings and note them down.

4 Look again at the next two paragraphs (lines 27–37). Note down what these paragraphs are about. In one or two sentences, say what you think these two paragraphs add to the essay as a whole, and why. Pick out words and phrases from the text to back up your point of view.

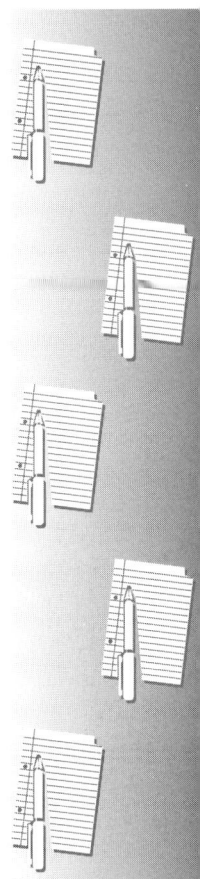

5 Re-read the next three paragraphs (lines 38–54). Summarise what happens in this part of the text.

6 Look again at the last paragraph of the passage (lines 55–58). In your own words, say what Phil Hogan's attitude is at the end of the essay, and how it has altered from that displayed in the opening paragraphs. Pick out words and phrases from the text to back up your point of view.

2 My First Visit to the Photographer

This essay is by Frans Bengtsson, a Swedish writer active in the middle of the 20th century. He was interested in history and in the natural world. In this essay, he tells of his feelings as a small child on being told that he is going to have his photograph taken.

(Some words are highlighted in the text. You will find further information about these words at the end of the passage.)

The photograph is probably still somewhere to be found. I came upon it some years ago, and remember it well as being in no way remarkable; a boy of about four or five, I should think, dressed up in his best clothes, is seen standing on the floor, his arm in a somewhat strained manner around the neck of a younger sister. She, in her turn, has been placed on a stool somewhat too high to suit the pose in question, and sits in **placid** contentment, playing with her fingers and obviously pleased with her pretty little frock. To the face of the boy, however, where no trace of either happiness or contentment can be seen, the photographer has not succeeded
10 in **cajoling** any smile, although to the **initiated** his expression, apart from a certain wildness about the eyes, is surprisingly composed. No sign of inward turbulence in the form of swollen eyelids or noticeable **wanness** is apparent; but this may well have been obliterated by the process of touching up which is one of the secrets of photographic artistry.

Be that as it may; I can only record that the actual taking of this particular photograph represents the most terrifying moment of my whole experience. I should never have remembered the occasion, of course, had it not been for this unique sensation of horror; but as it is I remember the details vividly.

We, my parents, my sister and I, were on a visit to my grandmother, who
20 lived at Kristianstad in a house which possessed a **window mirror**. This mirror was an unfailing source of delight and I used to sit in front of it whenever I had the chance, watching the continuous procession of life in the East High Street approach and pass by. Going out into the street and meeting other boys whom I did not know was both unpleasant and humiliating, but to sit by the window mirror was sheer bliss. When one fine day it was announced, that my sister and I were to be dressed up and taken

to the photographer's, the scheme of the universe was rudely interrupted. From the very start this proposition sounded an alarming one, and became even more so when I found out that our parents were not going to be
30   photographed, but only we children. In my experience unpleasant things such as the taking of **castor oil** or going to bed early were invariably reserved for children – never for their parents. I had no clear idea of what was meant by being photographed, except that in some way one became a picture on a piece of paper, and that a great deal seemed to indicate that this came about under hideous circumstances. Old men who had ceased to be of any use were often photographed and hung up on the wall; we had some of the sort at home ourselves. I felt that the situation was serious, particularly as here at grandmother's I was like a plant uprooted from its mould and had neither **scullerymaid** nor **stableboy** to turn to in an emergency. Under normal
40   conditions the truth of matters could nearly always be found out from them, as opposed to which the explanations given by one's parents were often unsatisfactory, and sometimes completely untrue, in particular when they attempted to comfort one in the face of some danger, warn one against something amusing, or forbid one something good to eat. The **aura** of respect which surrounded my father made it quite impossible for me to speak to him on important subjects, but for want of a better informant I asked my mother, while she was brushing and dressing me, whether it hurt very much to be photographed.

'Hurt, what nonsense,' she said in her cheerful manner, 'there is nothing that
50   *can* hurt. The photographer has a big sort of **contrivance** that he takes photos with. You stand in front of it, and he stands behind it with his head underneath a cloth, and hey presto! it's all over.'

Thus spoke my mother in her innocence; and at the sound of her words, the **latent** and deadly fear within me spread to undreamed of proportions. I began to scream with all my might, clinging to her and imploring to be let off. I promised that I would always be good and obedient if only I were spared this ordeal. I knew that I had often been naughty, but did I really deserve such a punishment? Surely a good whipping was sufficient. Whether I said, or sobbed, all this I do not know; in any case I remember thinking it.
60   My mother was astounded, could not understand what I meant, and kept on repeating that it was all over in a moment, and did not hurt; I only howled the louder, until my father poked his head in at the door, and ordered me in tones of thunder to be quiet.

Nowadays I realise more clearly that parents do not always have an easy time of it with their children. It might be thought that my mother had said nothing to make me hysterical, apart from which I ought to have been able to enquire more closely of her as to what was frightening me; but at the time, although I was not afraid of her, this seemed quite impossible. Why? one wonders. In all probability because one of the strongest instincts is the fear of
70   making oneself ridiculous. Laugh at me, by all means, when I say something funny, or which I myself think is funny; but for Heaven's sake never laugh when I say something silly in earnest, because this is completely unendurable. Children – or at least, some children – feel this; and it is fortunate that the acute sensitiveness to one own comical stupidities

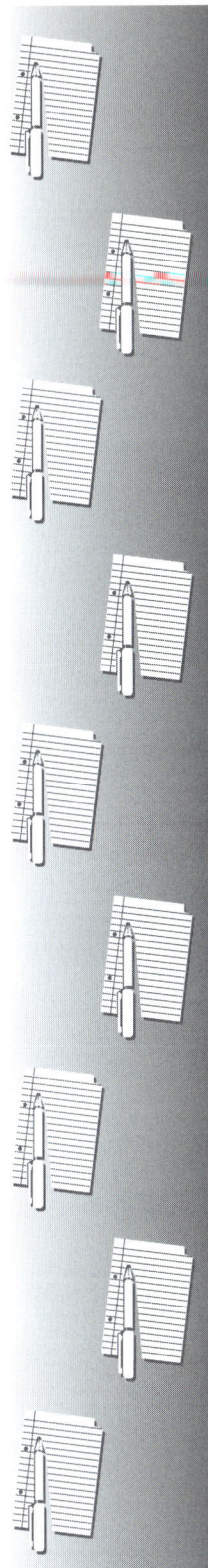

gradually becomes dulled as one grows up, thereby restraining many an otherwise obvious case of suicide.

Not only, therefore, did I refrain from asking any more questions, but I made no attempt to explain the reason for my howling, and this in itself suggests the existence of some shadow of doubt in my own mind with regard

80   to the theory about being photographed; a doubt, however, in no way comparable to the degree of terror I felt. For as a result of my mother's fearful piece of information, the said theory became clear, logical, and from an abstract point of view entirely acceptable. Her words engraved themselves on my consciousness: 'He has a big sort of contrivance that he takes photos with ...'. I happened to know what was meant by the word contrivance (this was before a subsequent acquaintanceship with the telephone and numerous other modern 'contrivances') for in an attic at home, standing against one of the walls, was a large and elderly **mangle**, a curious object, the like of which I have never seen since, with several pairs of rollers one above the other. This

90   mangle, which probably dated from the 18th century, refused on occasion to function satisfactorily, and I had recently heard my father refer to it with emphasis as 'a useless contrivance, only fit for firewood'. It was easy to understand, after thinking the matter over, that being photographed must entail, amongst other things, being pressed through some sort of a mangle. 'He stands behind it with his head underneath a cloth ...'. The reason for this precaution became obvious – in order, of course, to avoid being spattered with blood.

The thought of my late grandfather, hanging in a state of photography on the wall at home, gave necessary confirmation to my theory that it must be a

100   question of mangling. I remembered him before he was photographed as an exceptionally large, red, stout gentleman, once an artillery sergeant major in the town, who had spent an enviable life driving about and firing off a cannon. Since then, however, he had been photographed, and was now imprisoned behind glass, in a frame, completely flattened out. One could still see plainly that it was grandfather, although apparently all the blood had been squeezed out of him, shrivelling him up in some way that I could not altogether fathom. It was said that he 'had a stroke', and one could well understand that drastic treatment of some sort had been necessary before drawing him through the mangle, so large and stout as he had been.

110   In this **martyrdom** of the imagination, it may seem shocking that I should have believed my parents capable of wishing to see me mangled and pasted onto cardboard. Admittedly, and as was usual at that time, I lived in modified terror of my father, but he was by no means a monster, merely somewhat heavy-handed when occasion demanded. In actual point of fact, the dreadful train of my thoughts probably originated from a well-developed **ethical** consciousness. I realised that I was a naughty and troublesome child, and that a punishment of this sort was reasonable enough in itself. It is possible – although my chronology may be at fault – that the crushing of my sister's finger with a stone during the course of a battle of wills between the two of us

120   may have preceded the photography; while she, at the first opportunity, had taken her revenge by hitting me in the neck with a broken brass doorhandle, which laid me out bleeding and unconscious on the floor. These happenings,

according to my conception of things at the time, may have been the reason why we were both considered eligible to be photographed, though in my sister's case matters were easier, she being too young and too stupid to realise what was in store.

Of the actual walk to the photographer's, in the company of both our parents, I remember nothing. Possibly I may have entertained hopes to the last that the whole thing was a threat, and that we should turn back at the
130 door. The photographer lived two flights up; one went in through a doorwayand then up some stairs on the left. On either side of the entrance were glass cases full of photographs, in particular one of an individual with a long moustache, standing beside a whiteclad female, who looked as though his teeth had been pressed forward through his mouth during the ordeal of photography, and at the sight of whom everything collapsed for me. I resisted desperately all the way up the stairs, probably to the accompaniment of loud yells; how I was transported up, whether by the scruff of my neck or otherwise I do not know, my memory being a blank until I actually stood before the dreaded 'contrivance'. The photographer was a thin, pale man
140 who seemed to have a great deal of arranging to do, and who tried various methods of cheering me up, the point of which I could not understand at all; this sort of frantic and useless effort, made by all photographers, has always been, to me, one of the many mysteries of existence. He put his head under the cloth, and I knew that the moment had come. The head, however, popped most unexpectedly out again. 'Keep quite still, please,' he said, and I take it for granted that even my heart obeyed him and suspended action. He lifted a little lid from the contrivance, and after a moment put it on again. 'There now,' he said, 'that's all.'

I felt myself sink with shame. I was so thoroughly ashamed that, after
150 returning to grandmother's not even the beloved mirror window was able, that day, to give me any pleasure; and although my mother often tried to find out the reason for my strange behaviour on this unique occasion, she was not allowed to know anything about it until at least twenty years later.

This is the story of my first visit to the photographer, and one of my clearest early recollections. In its way it may be quite an instructive story, not unsuitable for the unhappy parents of children who create hideous and inexplicable scenes of violent obstinacy, simply because they are the victims of an uncontrollable imagination, or have become involved with some vision of terror which it is impossible to explain to the grown-ups.

F. Bengtsson, 'My First Visit to the Photographer', in *A Walk to Ant Hill and Other Essays*, ed. M. Roberts and E. Schubert, Chatto & Windus, 1950

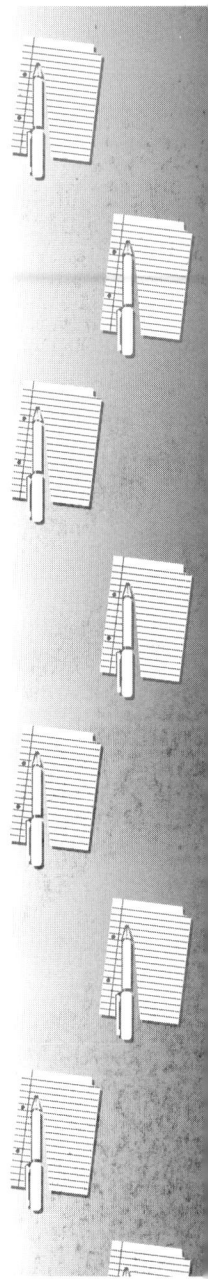

DICTIONARY

placid calm
cajoling wheedling, persuading
initiated those in the know
wanness pallor, paleness
window mirror a mirror mounted in such a way as to reflect events going on in the street outside
castor oil a pale yellow oil with a slightly bitter taste, used as a medicine
scullerymaid a servant working in the kitchen

stableboy a servant working in the stables

aura atmosphere

contrivance mechanical object

latent hidden

mangle a machine for pressing the water out of clothes after washing, made up of several rollers through which the clothes were squeezed

martyrdom suffering

ethical moral

(C)LOSER READING

1 Re-read the first two paragraphs (lines 1–18). Note down the main piece of information which Bengtsson introduces to the reader, and the point at which the reader is given this information.

2 Look again at the next three paragraphs (lines 19–63). Note down two of Bengtsson's initial reasons for being uneasy about being photographed.

3 Re-read the sixth paragraph (lines 64–76). What reasons does Bengtsson give for children being unwilling to confide their fears to their parents?

4 Look again at the next two paragraphs (lines 77–109). What does Bengtsson expect to happen to him at the photographer's? List three reasons for his belief.

5 Re-read the following paragraph (lines 110–126). What reasons does Bengtsson give for believing his parents capable of treating him in the way that he is expecting?

6 Look again at the next two paragraphs (lines 127–153). In your own words, describe what actually happens, and what Bengtsson feels about it.

7 In the final paragraph (lines 154–159), Bengtsson talks of the incident as having been 'instructive'. Write a short paragraph saying what 'moral' he draws from the story, and whether you agree with him. Give examples to back up your point of view.

3 | The modern schoolmaster

This is an extract from 'The Old and New Schoolmaster' by Charles Lamb, in which the author muses on the nature of schoolteaching and schoolteachers. Lamb was a writer of light and humorous pieces at the beginning of the 19th century. Having gone to school with the Romantic poet Coleridge, he remained life-long friends with him and, through him, with other poets such as William Wordsworth. His sister, Caroline, was an ill and unhappy woman, who killed their mother in a fit of insanity, and was in and out of mental hospitals for the rest of her life. Lamb consistently cared for and looked after her for as long as he lived.

(Some words are highlighted in the text. You will find further information about these words at the end of the passage.)

The modern schoolmaster is expected to know a little of everything, because his pupil is required not be entirely ignorant of anything. He must be **superficially**, if I may say so, **omniscient**. He is to know something of pneumatics; of chemistry; of whatever is curious or proper to excite the attention of the youthful mind; an insight into mechanics is desirable, with a touch of statistics; the quality of soils, etc., botany, the constitution of his country, *cum multis aliis*. You may get a notion of some part of his expected duties by consulting the famous **Tractate on Education**, addressed to Mr Hartlib.

10 All these things – these, or the desire of them – he is expected to instil, not by set lessons from professors, which he may charge in the bill, but at school intervals, as he walks the streets, or saunters through green fields (those natural instructors), with his pupils. The least part of what is expected from him is to be done in school hours. He must **insinuate** knowledge at the *mollia tempora fandi*. He must seize every occasion – the season of the year – the time of the day – a passing cloud – a rainbow – a waggon of hay – a regiment of soldiers going by – to inculcate something useful. He can receive no pleasure from a casual glimpse of Nature, but must catch at it as an object of instruction. He must interpret beauty into the picturesque. He cannot
20 relish a beggar-man, or a gipsy, for thinking of the suitable improvement. Nothing comes to him, not spoiled by the sophisticating medium of moral uses. The Universe – that Great Book, as it has been called – is to him, indeed, to all intents and purposes, a book out of which he is doomed to read tedious homilies to distasting schoolboys …

Boys are **capital fellows** in their own way, among their mates; but they are unwholesome companions for grown people. The restraint is felt no less on the one side, than on the other. Even a child, that 'plaything for an hour,' tires *always*. The noises of children, playing their own fancies – as I now hearken to them, by fits, sporting on the green before my window, while I am
30 engaged in these grave speculations at my neat suburban retreat at Shacklewell – by distance made more sweet – inexpressibly take from the labour of my task. It is like writing to music. They seem to modulate my **periods**. They ought at least to do so – for in the voice of that tender age there is a kind of poetry, far unlike the harsh prose-accents of man's conversation. I should but spoil their sport, and diminish my own sympathy for them, by mingling in their pastime.

I would not be **domesticated** all my days with a person of very superior capacity to my own – not, if I know myself at all, from any considerations of jealousy or self-comparison, for the occasional communion with such
40 minds has constituted the fortune and felicity of my life – but the habit of too constant **intercourse** with spirits above you, instead of raising you, keeps you down. Too frequent doses of original thinking from others restrain what lesser portion of that faculty you may possess of your own. You get entangled in another man's mind, even as you lose yourself in another man's grounds. You are walking with a tall **varlet**, whose strides out-pace yours to **lassitude**. The constant operation of such potent agency would reduce me, I am convinced, to imbecility. You may derive thoughts from others; your way of thinking, the mould in which your thoughts are cast, must be your own. Intellect may be **imparted**, but not each man's intellectual frame.

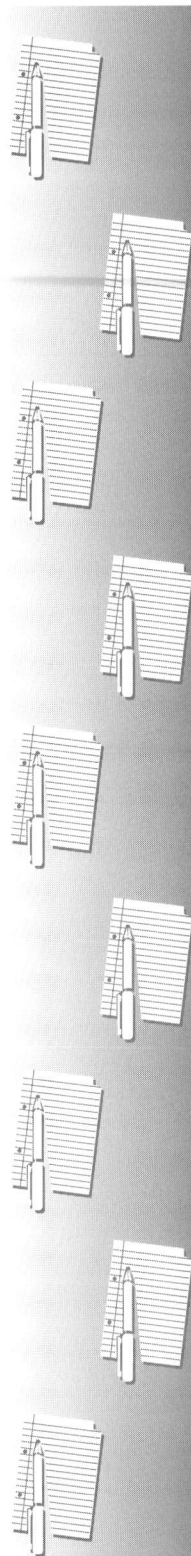

From C. Lamb, 'The Old and New Schoolmaster', *The Essays of Elia*, 1823 edition

72

DICTIONARY

superficially on the surface

omniscient all-knowing

cum multis aliis with much else

Tractate on Education study of education

insinuate slip in

mollia tempora fandi the most suitable time to speak

capital fellows nice people

periods sentences

domesticated living with

intercourse conversation

varlet rogue

lassitude exhaustion

imparted taught

CLOSER READING

1 Re-read the first two paragraphs (lines 1–24). In your own words, summarise what the 'modern schoolmaster' has to do, and when he has to do it.

2 Look again at the third paragraph (lines 25–36). What is Lamb's attitude to children, and why does he not want to spend time with them?

3 Re-read the final paragraph (lines 37–49). List the reasons Lamb gives for not wanting to spend too long with people who are more intelligent than he is.

4 Look again at the last sentence of the passage (lines 47–49). Re-write the sentence in your own words, and then write two or three sentences of your own, saying whether or not you agree with what Lamb is saying here. Give reasons for your point of view.

4 | How We Laugh and Cry Over the Same Things

Michel Eyquem de Montaigne was a 16th-century French writer. The times he lived through were often troubled and turbulent, particularly with violent clashes between French Catholic and Protestant forces, while Montaigne himself had his own physical difficulties to contend with, being plagued with gall-stones. Throughout his life, Montaigne thought and wrote about the experiences of human beings, how they behave, and how they ought to behave. His view was one of thoughtful tolerance, with a great belief in reason as a force for good.

In the passage below, from 'How We Laugh and Cry Over the Same Things', Montaigne explores the way in which we feel and express our emotions. He suggests that things are by no means as simple as they may at first appear.

(Some words are highlighted in the text. You will find further information about these words at the end of the passage.)

When we read in history books about the way in which Antigonus was angry with his son for bringing him the head of King Pyrrhus, his enemy, who had just been killed fighting him in battle, and that, when he saw the head, he burst into bitter tears; or when we are told of the way in which the Duke of Lorraine mourned the death of Charles of Bourgogne, whom he had just defeated, and how he wore mourning for Charles' death at his funeral; or when we learn that, at the battle of Auroy which the Count of Montfort won against Charles of Blois, the victor mourned deeply when he came across the dead body of his opponent, we should not be too quick to cry, with
10   Petrarch, that:

> … so with every human soul,
> Lest our true feelings we discover,
> Each in its opposite we cover.

The histories relate that when Caesar was presented with the head of Pompey, he turned his face away, as if from an ugly and unpleasant sight. They had known each other for a long time, during their involvement in affairs of the state, and their lives had run parallel for many years, and so it should not be assumed that Caesar's disgust was entirely assumed, as some writers have suggested …

20   For the fact of the matter is that, although most of our actions may well be play-acting and lies, and that it may well sometimes be true that,

> the legatee's tears are a mask for his smile,

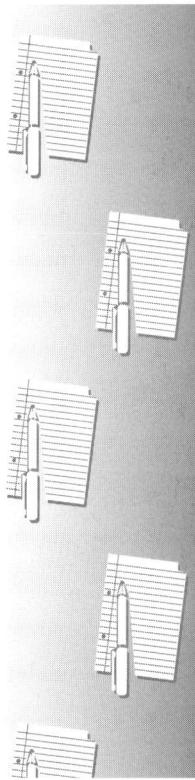

in general, as these examples have shown, our souls are often moved by different and opposite feelings **simultaneously**. For just as it is said that our bodies contain a variety of contrary **humours**, of which one is most usually dominant, so too with our souls: they are buffeted hither and thither by different emotions, each master of the field at different times. But the mastery is never so complete that other weaker emotions cannot make a counter-attack and take charge for a moment. It is because of this that we can

30   see children, who are spontaneous and natural, laughing and crying at the same time over the same thing; but none of us can claim, when setting out on a journey, however much it has been longed for, that we leave friends and family behind without a tremor; and that, even if the tears do not actually escape, we do not mount our horses with a sad, dejected expression … So it is not surprising that a man should mourn the death of someone whom they still have no wish to see alive again.

When I swear at my **valet**, there is no holding back, I give it everything I have, but, the moment passed, if he needs anything from me, I am happy to help him in any way I can: I can switch from one mood to another in an

40   instant. When I call him a layabout and an ass, I don't mean him to be labelled like that for ever, nor am I contradicting myself if I sometimes call him a good fellow. No emotion possesses us wholly and entirely …

If someone sees how on occasions I appear cold towards my wife, while at other times I am warm and loving, and assumes that either one or other attitude is false and assumed, then that person is an idiot. Nero, bidding farewell to his mother, whom he had ordered to be drowned, nevertheless felt all the emotion due to this maternal leave-taking, and was stricken with pity and horror …

We may pursue vengeance for an injury with single-minded intent, and feel

50   deep satisfaction when we achieve our end, but we can weep nonetheless; it is not our victory that we are weeping for; as far as that is concerned, our feelings have not changed at all, but our souls see things now in a different light and show up another aspect of the affair: for everything can be seen from all sorts of different points of view. Kinship, old friendships catch at our imagination and fill our feelings for an hour; but their passage is so fleeting that we scarcely feel it and it is soon gone.

> There is nothing swifter than the human spirit
> In thinking, or in moving from thought to action.
> The soul is therefore mobile, more so than any other

60   object we can perceive in Nature. (Lucretius)

Thus, if we seek to be consistent and unvarying at all times, we are making a mistake. When **Timoleon** wept for the assassination he had committed after so much careful and mature reflection, he was not weeping for the freedom he had restored to his homeland, he was not mourning the dead tyrant, but he was weeping for his brother. Once one part of his duty had been carried out, there was room for another to find expression.

From M. Montaigne, 'How We Laugh and Cry Over the Same Things', author's trans.

DICTIONARY

simultaneously at the same time

humours in medieval times, it was believed that a person's physical and emotional character was determined by four fluids, or humours, which existed in different people in different proportions, and shaped their attitudes in different ways

valet personal servant

Timoleon a Corinthian who, in about 365 BC, in order to protect democracy, killed his brother Timophanes, who was seeking to become a dictator

CLOSER READING

1 Re-read the first two paragraphs (lines 1–19). In these paragraphs we read of four people who were responsible for the deaths of others. Draw up three columns, and list in them:
 • who was killed
 • who was responsible for their death
 • how the person responsible felt.

2 Look again at the third paragraph (lines 20–36). In your own words, summarise the point that Montaigne is making here.

3 Re-read the fourth and fifth paragraphs (lines 37–48). Montaigne gives two examples from his own life to back up his argument. Say what these examples are, and, using your own experience, write two or three sentences saying whether you agree with him or not.

4 Look again at the last two paragraphs (lines 49–66). Summarise in your own words the point that Montaigne is making here.

FURTHER ACTIVITIES

1
 • In groups of four, divide the passages in this section between you, so that each person is concentrating on **one** passage.
 • Re-read the passage you are working on, and note down in a few sentences what the passage is about and what the 'moral' of the passage seems to be. For instance, you might say that the Phil Hogan passage (Text no. 1) is about putting up a curtain rail, and that the moral is that nothing is as straightforward as it might appear at first sight.
 • In your group, compare your findings, and note down any similarities and differences between the passages, and the way in which they link morals and stories together.

- In pairs, select **two** of the passages which seem to you to be particularly effective, and discuss in detail how they get their ideas across.
- In your pair, write a leaflet aimed at Year 9 students, entitled 'A Guide to Good Essay Writing'. Make your leaflet clear and attractive. You may want to include illustrations.

2

- Working in a pair, select **one** of the passages from the section which particularly interests you. Discuss between you exactly what the passage is about and how the author backs up his point of view. Make notes of your discussion.
- On your own, use your notes to write an essay in answer to the passage you have chosen, arguing an opposing point of view. Stick as closely as you can to the style and method of the passage you have chosen to argue against.

3

- In small groups, look through the essay titles below. Discuss each one, and make brief notes for possible essays on that subject.
  a A Day in the Life of a Tea Bag
  b A Walk on the Wild Side
  c Peace
  d 'The Price of Freedom is Eternal Vigilance'. Discuss.
- As a class, pool your ideas. Make notes on any examples and approaches that seem to you particularly effective.
- In pairs, choose **one** topic, and together write the opening paragraph for an essay on that subject.
- On your own, write an essay on one of the titles listed below. You may use the one you have worked on with a partner, and take the opening paragraph you have already written as a starting point, or you may start completely afresh. Whatever you decide, remember to make your essay lively and personal, using examples drawn from your own experience to back up the point that you are making.

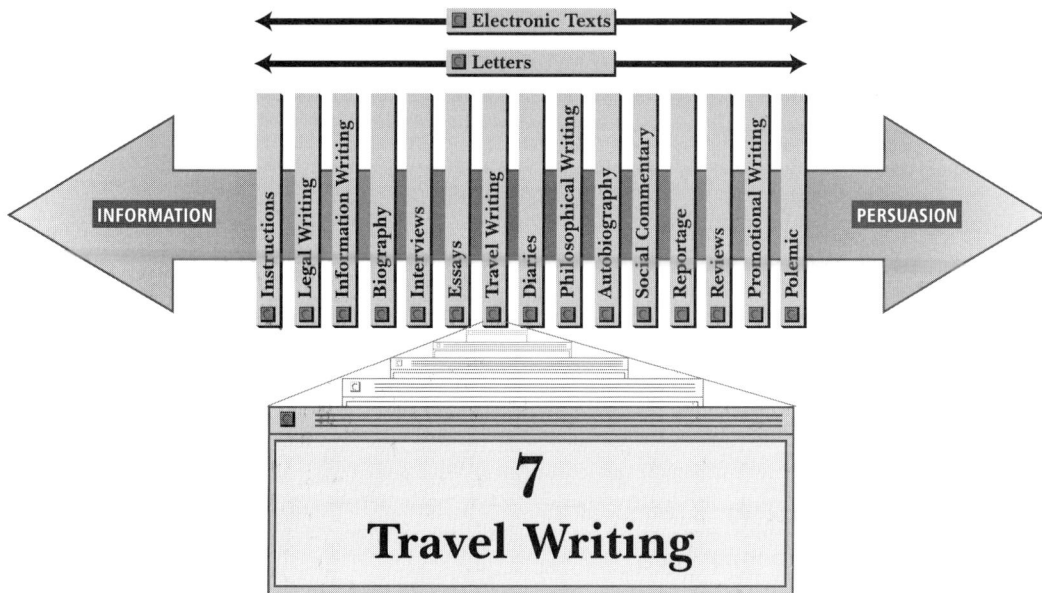

Electronic Texts

Letters

INFORMATION — Instructions — Legal Writing — Information Writing — Biography — Interviews — Essays — Travel Writing — Diaries — Philosophical Writing — Autobiography — Social Commentary — Reportage — Reviews — Promotional Writing — Polemic — PERSUASION

7
Travel Writing

Travel writing is a record of someone's experiences away from home. This can range from a description of a society in a different part of the world to comments on a town in the writer's native country which they had not previously visited.

The simplest and most common form of travel writing is the postcard that people send when on holiday. This usually describes, briefly, what the person has done and whether they like where they are staying. Two types of travel writing closely associated with this are holiday brochures and travel guides. Holiday brochures are covered in a different chapter (Promotional Writing) as they are trying to sell a place as well as describing it. Travel guides vary – some are clearly trying to promote a destination while others try to give a more balanced view. There is an example of a travel guide in this chapter.

Other people write about travels which were not so much holidays as attempts to describe different parts of the world. Sometimes writers wish to explore their own responses to different societies and cultures. By seeing how other people live they can reflect on their own lifestyles – this may make them more critical or more appreciative of their own society.

As with any type of writing where opinions are expressed, writers' individual values and preferences will influence what they say. It is common for two people to visit a city or country and come away with two opposing views because of their personal taste and the experiences they had on their visit.

1 | A travel guide

This is an extract from a guide book, *The Rough Guide to Kenya*, by Richard Trillo. It gives advice on what to do and where to go when visiting Kenya's national parks.

(Some words are highlighted in the text. You will find further information about these words at the end of the passage.)

THE PARKS

In these animal-rich national parks, the first realization of where you are – among real, uncaptured wildlife – is truly **arresting**. Which parks to visit can seem at first a pin-in-the-map decision: any of them can provide a store of amazing sight and sound impressions.

AMBOSELI and TSAVO are the two most accessible, with ever-busy game lodges, well-worn trails, large numbers of tourists in the high seasons, and large, if brutally diminished, herds of elephant. Amboseli is perhaps least recommended of the popular parks, despite its position at the foot of Kilimanjaro: it is just too small and too well trodden, and it's still recovering
10   from heavy flooding in 1993. Tsavo, in contrast, is huge enough to escape company completely, except at MZIMA SPRINGS, for which it's worth being part of the crowd if necessary.

MAASAI MARA has the most fabled reputation, with horizons of wildlife on every side. Somewhat isolated in the west, it requires a specific, usually there-and-back, visit, but it's well worth the effort (and perhaps the cost), especially during the yearly WILDEBEEST MIGRATION that takes place sometime between July and November. The Mara is also *the* place to see lions – lots of them – and one of the best places to see naturally constituted elephant herds.

SAMBURU and MERU, on the north side of Mount Kenya, have different
20   varieties of animals, such as northern species or races of giraffe, zebra, antelope and ostrich. Samburu – dry, thorny and split by the Ewaso Nyiro river – is increasingly popular and noted for its CROCODILES and LEOPARDS, albeit baited ones. Meru, however, is perhaps the most beautiful Kenyan park – isolated, **verdant** and surprisingly unvisited.

Animal watching

Game viewing soon loses its more self-conscious aspects. Our wildlife colour section will help you identify the larger mammals you're likely to encounter. RANGERS can usually be hired for the day and, if you have room, someone with intimate local knowledge and a trained eye is a good companion. Knowing
30   some **Swahili** animal names is a help (see p.527). Most of the lodges and tented or luxury *banda* camps have their own **4WD** vehicles and run regular 'game drives'. These can be very worthwhile because the drivers usually know

the animals and the area. Expect to pay between $30 and $40 per person for scheduled departures and around $120 to $150 for exclusive use of the vehicle for two to three hours.

The usual pattern is two (or sometimes three) game drives a day: at dawn, mid-morning and late afternoon (though if you keep this up for more than a day or two you'll be exhausted – best to skip one). In the middle of the day, the parks are usually left to the animals; you'll be told it's because they are all hiding. A more likely reason is that the midday hours are a lousy time to take pictures. The animals are around, if sleepy, and if you can put up with the heat while most people are safely in the lodges, it can be a tranquil and satisfying time.

To see as much as possible, stop frequently to scan with BINOCULARS, watch what the herds of antelope and other grazers are doing (a predator will usually be watched intently by them all), and talk to anyone you meet on your way. The best time of day is sunrise, when **nocturnal animals** are often still out and about and you might see that weird dictionary leader, the aardvark.

From R. Trillo, *The Rough Guide to Kenya*, 5th revised edn, Rough Guides/Penguin, 1996

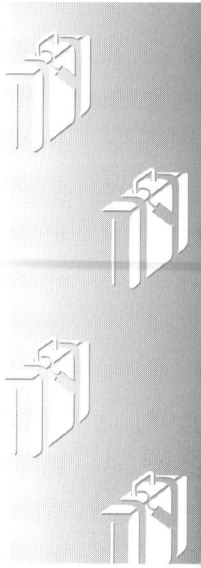

DICTIONARY

arresting breath-taking
verdant green
Swahili the official language of Kenya
4WD four-wheel-drive
nocturnal animals animals that live at night

CLOSER READING

1 The writer mentions five different parks. Write down the name of each park and then write next to it what he says is **good** about it and what are the **drawbacks** (if any).

When you have done this, try to sum up what the writer thinks makes a park worth visiting. Do you agree with him?

2 The writer puts a number of words in SMALL CAPITALS so that they stand out. Explain, for each word, why you think he has done this.

3 a List **eight** pieces of advice you are given about animal watching.

   b This advice tells you about what the writer thinks you should do to get the most out of watching animals. It also tells you about his view of what makes a good holiday. Which of the statements below best fits his view?
   • It is best to relax and take things easy.
   • Keep yourself to yourself.
   • Mix in with the Kenyans and learn as much as you can.
   • Don't trust anyone.
   • See as much as you can.

When you have chosen your statement, give some reasons to justify your choice.

2 Amazon Adventure

The following passage is taken from an account of an expedition to South America led by the travel writer, Redmond O'Hanlon. He was accompanied by his friend, Simon. The other people are local people he had hired to help them on a journey down a tropical river.

(Some words are highlighted in the text. You will find further information about these words at the end of the passage.)

Simon and I were having our difficulties. It was possible that some of them **stemmed from** his reluctance to eat anything that we caught and cooked – piranha soup, say, or the occasional guan, a chicken-like bird, that Culimacaré had been lucky enough to shoot. Simon hated it whenever we gutted an animal, and had taken to eating only the spam and rice that we had brought along as reserve stores and now nearly exhausted. But most of our difficulties probably resulted from having to be together – always. That morning, listening to Simon's projected **itinerary**, I had one thought: homicide. But first we had to find the Maturaca.

10   I shone my torch across our tarpaulin and carefully noted the positions of two scorpions. There would be a scorpion, I calculated, under every eleventh leaf. They had been caught by the rising water, and, like all the other refugees of the jungle floor, had to camp with us on islands that were never more than ten yards by twenty. I collected my wet clothes from the parachute-cord line strung up over our heads and shook them free of the insects crawling all over them. There was nothing particularly alarming in this morning's collection: no huge *veintecuatros*, so called because their bite hurts for twenty-four hours; no *catanare*, tiny ants that sting like wasps. I changed quickly out of my dry clothes, and made a brief tick check by
20   torch-light.

Dawn filtered down. Frogs and cicadas began to call. The mosquitoes scrambled. Chimo, Culimacaré and Pablo cut fresh poles and we set off, punting our heavy canoes with difficulty. The channels were never very wide – fifteen feet at the most – but our ten-foot poles rarely touched bottom, and we had to push against the soft bank. Most of the time we couldn't punt at all, and had to pull the boats forward, standing on submerged branches up to our waists or necks, easing the hull over fallen trees, hacking a way through the branches. That morning, in two hours, we travelled two hundred yards.

30   Once in the water, pushing the boats along, we were never very comfortable. First, there were the ants, not the dangerous ones, but thousands and thousands of your ordinary, everyday biting ant, which went for your head and neck and had a knack for fastening on, just beyond reach, to the centre of your back.

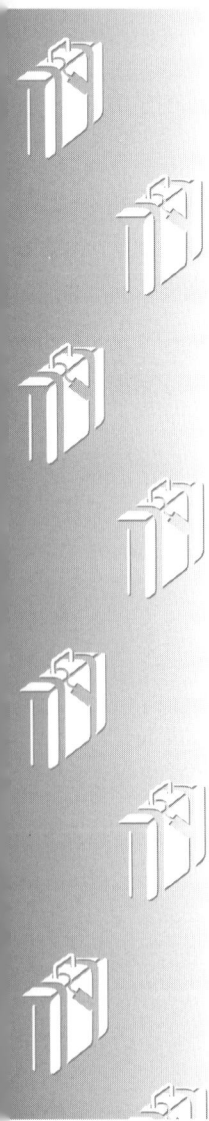

Then there was the wasp and the hornet, which hung their nests from a twig or fixed them to the back of a leaf suspended over the water. As we cleared a passage with our machetes it was impossible to spot their yellow-brown cones. The cry *'Avispa!'* **galvanised our limbs** in the most extraordinary way: wherever you were, you dived for the water and, once there, you held your

40 hat tight over your face to protect your eyes. On the back, a wasp-sting was tolerable; on the neck, very painful; and a hornet sting, anywhere, was very, very painful. By now Simon had developed, on principle, a dislike of water of any kind. With the cry *'Avispa!'*, he was always the last to **relinquish** the boat, and always an easy target: Simon got stung on the *head* by everything.

From R. O'Hanlon, 'Amazon Adventure', in *Granta*, Winter 1986

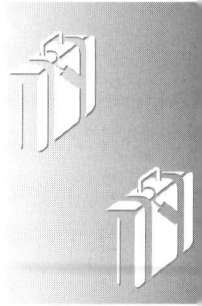

DICTIONARY

stemmed from arose out of

itinerary route

galvanised our limbs brought us suddenly to life

relinquish leave

CLOSER READING

1 Comments about Simon open and close the extract. He is quite a comic character as he seems totally unsuited to this type of travel. Find **two** reasons, one in the opening paragraph and one in the closing one, as to why he is a failure on this expedition.

2 Another reason why the passage is funny is because O'Hanlon describes very unpleasant conditions in a very matter-of-fact way. For example:

> *I shone my torch across our tarpaulin and carefully noted the positions of two scorpions. There would be a scorpion, I calculated, under every eleventh leaf.*

Rather than being horrified by being surrounded by scorpions, he uses calm, scientific language like 'carefully noted' and 'calculated'. Find other examples in the passage where O'Hanlon describes unpleasant experiences in a calm, understated way.

3 In this passage the writer describes his experiences in graphic detail. This means that the descriptions are full of strong and vivid pictures, which create an impression in the reader's mind of what it actually felt like. This is because writers who are describing places and people that their readers will be unfamiliar with need to help the reader experience them through the senses: sight, sound, smell, touch and taste.

This extract focuses in particular on sight and touch. Find examples of extraordinary sights and sensations in the passage.

3 Travels With a Donkey

This is an extract from a book by Robert Louis Stevenson, which describes his travels in France in the late 19th century. As the title of the book suggests, a donkey was his main form of transport. The extract describes a particularly unpleasant part of his journey.

(Some words are highlighted in the text. You will find further information about these words at the end of the passage.)

All the way up the long hill from Langogne it rained and hailed alternately; the wind kept freshening steadily, although slowly; plentiful hurrying clouds – some dragging veils of straight rain-shower, others massed and luminous as though promising snow – careered out of the north and followed me along my way. I was soon out of **the cultivated basin** of the Allier, and away from the ploughing oxen, and such-like sights of the country. Moor, heathery marsh, **tracts** of rock and pines, woods of birch all jewelled with the autumn yellow, here and there a few naked cottages and bleak fields, – these were the characters of the country. Hill and valley followed valley and hill; the little
10 green and stony cattle-tracks wandered in and out of one another, split into three or four, died away in marshy hollows, and began again **sporadically** on hillsides or at the borders of a wood.

There was no direct road to Cheylard, and it was no easy affair to make a passage in this uneven country and through this **intermittent** labyrinth of tracks. It must have been about four when I struck Sagnerousse, and went on my way rejoicing in a sure point of departure. Two hours afterwards, the dusk rapidly falling, in a lull of the wind, I **issued from** a fir-wood where I had long been wandering, and found, not the looked-for village, but another **marish** bottom among rough-and-tumble hills. For some time past I had
20 heard the ringing of cattle-bells ahead; and now, as I came out of the skirts of the wood, I saw near upon a dozen cows and perhaps as many more black figures, which I **conjectured** to be children, although the mist had almost unrecognisably exaggerated their forms. These were all silently following each other round and round in a circle, now taking hands, now breaking up with chains and **reverences**. A dance of children appeals to very innocent and lively thoughts; but, at nightfall on the marshes, the thing was eerie and fantastic to behold. Even I, who am well enough read in Herbert Spencer, felt a sort of silence fall for an instant on my mind. The next, I was pricking Modestine forward, and guiding her like an unruly ship through the open.
30 In a path, she went **doggedly** ahead of her own accord, as before a fair wind; but once on the turf or among heather, and the brute became demented. The tendency of lost travellers to go round in a circle was developed in her to the degree of passion, and it took all the steering I had in me to keep even a decently straight course through a single field.

While I was thus desperately tacking through the bog, children and cattle

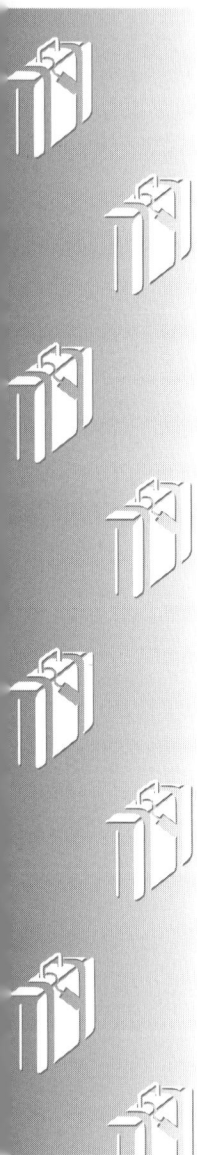

began to disperse, until only a pair of girls remained behind. From these I sought direction on my path. The peasantry in general were **but little disposed to counsel a wayfarer**. One old devil simply retired into his house, and barricaded the door on my approach; and I might beat and shout myself

40 hoarse, he turned a deaf ear. Another, having given me a direction which, as I found afterwards, I had misunderstood, complacently watched me going wrong without adding a sign. He did not care a stalk of parsley if I wandered all night upon the hills! As for these two girls, they were a pair of impudent sly sluts, with not a thought but mischief. One put out her tongue at me, the other bade me follow the cows; and they both giggled and jogged each other's elbows. The Beast of Gévaudan ate about a hundred children of this district; I began to think of him with sympathy.

From R. L. Stevenson, *Travels with a Donkey*, Chatto & Windus, 1900

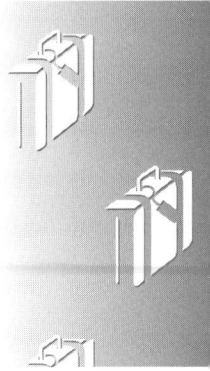

DICTIONARY

the cultivated basin the catchment area of the river which was used for agriculture

tracts areas

sporadically in an unplanned way

intermittent incomplete, stopping and starting

issued from came out of

marish marshy, swampy

conjectured guessed

reverences bows

doggedly determinedly

but little disposed to counsel a wayfarer unwilling to give advice to a traveller

CLOSER READING

1 This extract emphasises how vulnerable the lone traveller can be. Out of their normal surroundings people may be faced with unexpected and unwanted events which they may not be able to deal with.

Find evidence from the extract which shows Stevenson's vulnerability. You could make your notes under the following headings:

- the weather
- the landscape
- the inhospitable local people
- the behaviour of the donkey.

2 Using your notes from Question 1, explain what kind of person Stevenson appears to be and how he must have felt at this stage in his travels.

3 The second paragraph (lines 13–34) adds to our feeling that Stevenson felt alone in a strange world. How does he create a sense of unreality? You could focus in particular on the description of the children dancing in a circle.

4 Amurath to Amurath

Amurath to Amurath, published in 1911, was written by Gertrude Bell and describes her travels through Turkey. The first extract is taken from the Preface, in which she explains why she wrote about her travels. The second extract, taken from a later section in the book, describes the beginning of a journey into the desert.

(Some words are highlighted in the text. You will find further information about these words at the end of the passages.)

A

When I was pursuing along the banks of the Euphrates the leisurely course of oriental travel, I would sometimes wonder, sitting at night before my tent door, whether it would be possible to **cast into shape the experiences that assailed me**. And in that spacious hour, when the silence of the embracing wilderness was enhanced rather than broken by the murmur of the river, and by the sounds, scarcely less primeval, that wavered round the camp fire of my nomad hosts, the task broadened out into a shape which was in keeping with the surroundings. Not only would I set myself to trace the story that was **scored** upon the face of the earth by mouldering wall or half-choked dyke, by

10 the thousand **vestiges** of former culture which were scattered about my path, but I would attempt to record the daily life and speech of those who had inherited the empty ground whereon empires had risen and expired. Even there, where **the mind ranged out unhindered** over the whole wide desert, and thought flowed as smoothly as the flowing stream – even there I would realise the difficulty of such an undertaking …

B

I had determined to journey back behind this great dividing line, to search through regions now desolate for evidences of a past that has left little historic record, calling upon the **shades** to take form again upon the very ground whereon, substantial, they had played their part. So on a brilliant morning Fattuh and I saw the caravan start out in the direction of Baghdad, not without inner heart-searchings as to where and how we should meet it again, and having loaded three donkeys with all that was left to us of worldly goods, we turned our faces towards the wilderness … Now no one rides into the desert, however uncertain the adventure, without a keen sense of

10 exhilaration. The bright morning sun, the wide clean levels, the knowledge that the problems of existence are reduced on a sudden to their simplest expression, your own wit and endurance being the sole determining factors – all these things brace and quicken the spirit. The spell of the waste seized us as we passed beyond the sulphur marshes; Hussein Onbashi held his head higher, and we gave each other the **salaam** anew, as if we had stepped out into another world that called for a fresh greeting.

'At Hit,' said he, and his words went far to explain the lightness of his heart, 'I have left three wives in the house.'

'Mashallah!' said Fattuh, 'you must be deaf with the gir-gir-gir of them.'

20 'Eh billah!' assented Hussein, 'I shut my ears. Three wives, two sons and six daughters, of whom but two married. Twenty children I have had, and seven wives; three of these died and one left me and returned to her own people. But I shall take another bride this year, please God.'

'We Christians,' observed Fattuh, 'find one enough.'

'You may be right,' answered Hussein politely; 'yet I would take a new wife every year if I had the means.'

'We will find you a bride in Kebeisah,' said I.

Hussein **weighed this suggestion**.

'The maidens of Kebeisah are fair but wilful. There is one among them, her
30 name is Shemsah – wallah, a picture! a picture she is! – she has had seven husbands.'

'And the maidens of Hit?' I asked. 'How are they?'

'Not so fair, but they are the better wives. That is why I choose to remain in Hit,' explained Hussein. 'The bimbashi would have sent me to Baghdad, but I said, 'No, let me stay here; the maidens of Hit do not expect much.' Your Excellency may laugh, but a poor man must think of these things.'

We rode on through the **aromatic scrub** until the black masses of the Kebeisah palm-groves **resolved** into tall trunks and feathery **fronds**. The sun stood high as we passed under the village gate and down the dusty street that
40 led to the Mudir's compound. We tied our mares to some mangers in his courtyard and were ourselves ushered into his reception-room, there to drink coffee and set forth our purpose. The leading citizens of Kebeisah dropped in one by one, and the talk was of the desert and of the dwellers therein. The men of Kebeisah are not Arab, Bedouin; they hold their mud-walled village and their 50,000 palm-trees against the tribes, but they know the laws of the desert as well as the nomads themselves …

From G. Bell, *Amurath to Amurath,* Heinemann, 1911

DICTIONARY	**cast into shape the experiences that assailed me** make sense of the things that happened to me
	scored marked
	vestiges traces
	the mind ranged out unhindered one could think freely
	shades spirits of the past
	salaam a Turkish greeting
	weighed this suggestion considered this
	aromatic scrub sweet-smelling vegetation
	resolved changed
	fronds palm leaves

C)LOSER READING

1 Look at extract A. What was Bell's main reason for writing about her travels? Choose from the following:
   - She wanted to impress her readers with her knowledge of Turkey.
   - She wanted to clarify her own thoughts and feelings through writing.
   - She wanted to show that women could rise to the challenge of travelling in far away places.
   - She wanted to explore the links between Turkey's past and the lives of those who lived there now.
   - She wanted to explain why Turkey had become a difficult and unpredictable place to live in.

2 Now look at extract B. Find evidence to show that Bell had mixed feelings about venturing out into the desert.

3 Bell includes many details which show that this was a different culture to her own. Write about how it was different, commenting on the following things:
   - the use of Turkish expressions;
   - the conversation of her fellow travellers;
   - the lives of those who live in the desert.

FURTHER ACTIVITIES

1 Think of a holiday you have had recently. It could have been abroad or in this country. Write about your experiences, focusing on describing the place itself and the sort of things you can do there.

Before writing, take account of the following things:

- What was distinctive about the place you visited? Was it different from where you live? Or was it very similar and like many other places? How did people behave towards you? Were there any habits or customs that you needed to be aware of?

- In order to make your account come to life you need to describe the sights, sounds and smells that you remember from your visit.

- What advice would you give to someone thinking of visiting this place? Is it worth it? Are there things to look out for? Are there dangers? How should you prepare for the visit?

2 This task should be carried out in pairs or groups. Imagine that you have been asked to write a guide to the place where you live for people who are thinking of visiting. You could, if you prefer, choose a town or city near to you that you know well.

Your guide could include information on the following areas:

- places to stay
- places to visit
- things to avoid
- important people
- facilities for people of different ages, for example young children, teenagers, adults
- shopping
- eating out and night-life
- leisure activities.

You may need to do a lot of research to find the information you need, and this should be divided between you. Local libraries have some of this information, as do tourist information centres.

When you have gathered your information together, divide the sections between you. Make sure that you set out your advice clearly, using maps and illustrations where helpful. The introduction to 'Information Writing' on page 21 gives detailed guidance on how to communicate information effectively.

Remember, you are not trying to sell this place: you are giving honest advice to someone who might visit. You can be as critical as you like!

3 Much travel writing involves the writer discussing a country or place which is totally new to them, a place in which they feel a complete outsider because it is different from what they are used to.

> One writer, Jonathan Swift, wrote a spoof travel book called *Gulliver's Travels* in 1726. In it he described how Gulliver set out on various journeys overseas. During his travels he came into contact with many strange (invented) types of people. Below is an extract in which Gulliver describes an incident that happened in a country where everything, including the people, was twelve times larger than normal.
>
> (Some words are highlighted in the text. You will find further information about these words at the end of the passage.)

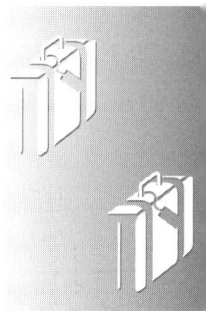

I slept about two hours, and dreamed I was at home with my wife and children, which aggravated my sorrows when I awaked and found myself alone in a vast room, between two and three hundred foot wide, and above two hundred high, lying in a bed twenty yards wide. My mistress was gone about her household affairs, and had locked me in. The bed was eight yards from the floor. **Some natural necessities** required me to get down; **I durst not presume to call**, and if I had, it would have been in vain with such a voice as mine at so great a distance from the room where I lay, to the kitchen where the family **kept**. While I was under these circumstances, two rats crept up the curtains, and ran smelling backwards and forwards on the bed. One of them

10

came up almost to my face, whereupon I rose in a fright, and drew out my **hanger** to defend myself. These horrible animals had the boldness to attack me on both sides, and one of them held his fore-feet at my collar, but I had the good fortune to rip up his belly before he could do me any mischief. He fell down at my feet, and the other, seeing the fate of his comrade, made his escape, but not without one good wound on the back, which I gave him as he fled, and made the blood run trickling from him. After this **exploit** I walked gently to and fro on the bed, to recover my breath and loss of spirits. These creatures were of the size of a large **mastiff**, but infinitely more nimble and

20   fierce, so that if I had taken off my belt before I went to sleep, I must have **infallibly** been torn to pieces and devoured. I measured the tail of the dead rat, and found it to be two yards long, wanting an inch; but it went against my stomach to drag the carcass off the bed, where it lay still bleeding; I observed it had yet some life, but with a strong slash cross the neck, I thoroughly dispatched it.

From J. Swift, *Gulliver's Travels,* ed. P. Dixon and J. Chalker, Penguin, 1967

DICTIONARY

Some natural necessities 'the call of nature', that is, the need to go to the toilet

I durst not presume to call I didn't dare to call out

kept currently were

hanger a type of sword

exploit adventure

mastiff a large dog

infallibly without fail

Imagine that you travel to an island, which no one from your country has ever visited before, and you come across a strange people. Describe your experiences for people back home. You might discuss some of the areas listed in Activity 2. In addition you could describe:

- any strange customs the people have;
- the buildings they live in;
- the creatures that live on the island;
- any other aspect which you think your audience may find interesting.

Electronic Texts

Letters

INFORMATION

Instructions
Legal Writing
Information Writing
Biography
Interviews
Essays
Travel Writing
Diaries
Philosophical Writing
Autobiography
Social Commentary
Reportage
Reviews
Promotional Writing
Polemic

PERSUASION

8
Diaries

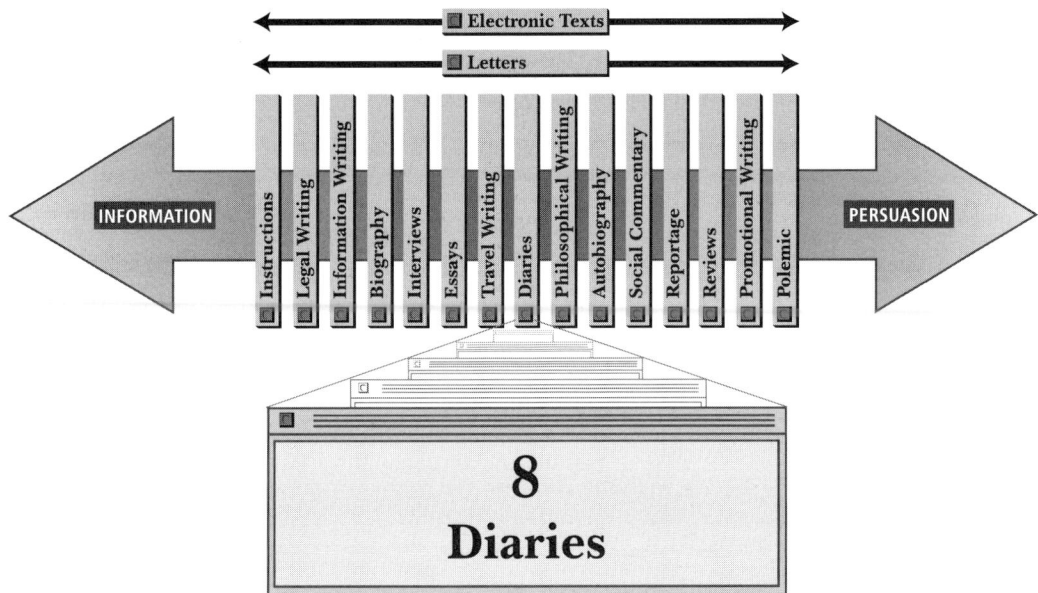

Diaries are day-to-day accounts of someone's own experiences. They are like autobiographies in that they are a record of someone's life. One difference, however, is that they are more immediate accounts of events, as the memories are fresh and the writer has had little time to reflect on what has happened. Therefore events are not interpreted in the light of the whole life but rather in terms of the writer's feelings and understanding at that time.

There are different kinds of diaries. Some diaries are basically factual records of events – although inevitably the writer will select and focus on what they believe to be important. Other diaries are used to interpret what has happened, expressing feelings and opinions.

Another important consideration for a diarist is that of audience. Most diaries are private and are concerned with the writer's personal world. With these diaries the audience is the writer himself or herself – it is a way of clarifying and reflecting on one's feelings. Some diaries, however, are written with the intention that they are published. These diaries might comment on the public world, discussing such areas as politics, current affairs, social issues and important events. If a diary is to be published the writer will need to consider the same issue facing the autobiographer – how do I wish to present myself to the public?

1 | Contrasting accounts

The two texts below are imaginary diary entries written by two characters from *Romeo and Juliet* by William Shakespeare. They were written after a ball held by Lord Capulet, the head of the Capulet family who despised another family called Montague. Romeo, a Montague, had gate-crashed the ball with a group of friends because he had hoped to meet Rosaline, the girl he thought he was in love with. However, he met Juliet who he fell in love with at first sight. During the ball, Tybalt, a member of the Capulet family, had spotted Romeo and was furious that Romeo had dared to enter the Capulet home.

(Some words are highlighted in the text. You will find further information about these words at the end of the passages.)

A | ROMEO'S ACCOUNT

I hardly know how to begin! I thought that I was destined to die a lonely and unfulfilled man. Rosaline, who I wrote about so passionately yesterday, has now been **banished** from my mind. My love for her was but a shadow compared to that which I feel now towards Juliet. And what is more, she will return my love! How can anyone devote their time to senseless **brawling** when love brings much greater rewards! There was another squabble in the town earlier today, but these things seem meaningless to me.

At the ball tonight she stood out as a jewel amongst grey stones. When I saw her the rest of the world disappeared, and through word and deed we
10 expressed the depth of our feelings.

The one sour note was Tybalt – that stupid, foul-tempered and arrogant man rages over the most **petty** things. It was fortunate that old Capulet prevented him from **brandishing** his sword and creating the usual **carnage**. (I understand Tybalt was one of those involved in that futile skirmish earlier today.)

As I write this a word returns to my mind and fills me with **apprehension** – Capulet. Juliet is a Capulet. In that word lies danger. But what does danger mean to me now? And what is in a name?

B | TYBALT'S DIARY

I barely have the patience to write! Montague! I loathe the word! I won't be satisfied until all Montagues are either dead or banished from this town for eternity. Today I threw myself into a heroic fight with some of the Montagues and their servants. It is important that I take every opportunity to **assert** the superiority of the Capulets.

This evening, though, has driven me to distraction! At Capulet's banquet I realised that damned Montague, Romeo, had sneaked in behind a disguise. Not only is he a Montague but he is a **snivelling** fool who is always moping about – not a real man at all. As if this wasn't bad enough, he was trying to profess his 'love' to Juliet – Capulet's only daughter! She is a foolish little girl who should have spat in his face rather than kissed it.

10

When I offered to remove the wretch at once, Capulet, the old fool, actually prevented me from taking action and humiliated me in front of the other guests. He does not realise that our family honour comes above all things; we must protect our name at all costs.

DICTIONARY

banished removed

brawling fighting

petty unimportant

brandishing waving threateningly

carnage bloodshed

apprehension worry about the future

assert show

snivelling whining

CLOSER READING

1 Re-read Romeo's diary.

   a Write down words to describe Romeo's feelings. What does he value most in life?

   b What does Romeo think of the following characters:
   • Tybalt
   • Juliet
   • Capulet
   • himself?

2 Re-read Tybalt's diary.

   a Write down words that describe Tybalt's feelings. What does he feel are the most important things in life?

   b What is Tybalt's opinion of the following characters:
   • Romeo
   • Juliet
   • Capulet
   • himself?

3 How do you account for the differences in these two diary entries which are about similar events?

2 The Diary of Anne Frank

Anne Frank, a young Jewish teenager, wrote her diary during the Second
World War. She lived in Holland, which was eventually occupied by the Nazis.
The Nazis persecuted the Jews, and Anne's family felt it was necessary to hide
in the sealed-off back rooms of an Amsterdam office building. They were safe
for two years, but were eventually betrayed and Anne died in the
concentration camp at Belsen. She did not write her diary expecting it would
be published; it was found by accident.

The first extract is taken from early in the diary and explains why she began it.
The second extract is taken from a much later section and shows her
attempting to understand her own character.

(Some words are highlighted in the text. You will find further information
about these words at the end of the passages.)

A SATURDAY, 20TH JUNE, 1942

I haven't written for a few days, because I wanted first of all to think about
my diary. It's an odd idea for someone like me to keep a diary; not only
because I have never done so before, but because it seems to me that neither
I – nor for that matter anyone else – will be interested in the **unbosomings** of
a thirteen-year-old schoolgirl. Still, what does that matter? I want to write,
but more than that, I want to bring out all kinds of things that lie buried
deep in my heart.

There is a saying that 'paper is more patient than man'; it came back to me
on one of my slightly **melancholy** days, while I sat chin in hand, feeling too
10 bored and limp even to make up my mind whether to go out or to stay at
home. Yes, there is no doubt that paper is patient and as I don't intend to
show this cardboard-covered notebook, bearing the proud name of 'diary', to
anyone, unless I find a real friend, boy or girl, probably nobody cares. And
now I come to root of the matter, the reason for my starting a diary: it is that
I have no such real friend.

Let me put it more clearly, since no one will believe that a girl of thirteen
feels herself quite alone in the world, nor is it so. I have darling parents and
a sister of sixteen. I know about thirty people whom one might call friends –
I have strings of boy friends, anxious to catch a glimpse of me and who,
20 failing that, peep at me through mirrors in class. I have relations, aunts and
uncles, who are darlings too, a good home, no – I don't seem to lack
anything. But it's the same with all my friends, just fun and games, nothing
more. I can never bring myself to talk of anything outside **the common
round**. We don't seem to be able to get any closer, that is the root of the
trouble. Perhaps I lack confidence, but anyway, there it is, a stubborn fact
and I don't seem to be able to do anything about it.

Hence, this diary. In order to **enhance** in my mind's eye the picture of the
friend for whom I have waited so long, I don't want to set down a series of

bald facts in a diary like most people do, but I want this diary itself to be my
30 friend, and I shall call my friend Kitty. No one will grasp what I am talking
about if I begin my letters to Kitty just out of the blue, so, **albeit** unwillingly, I
will start by sketching in brief the story of my life.

B TUESDAY, 1ST AUGUST, 1944

Dear Kitty,

'Little bundle of contradictions.' That's how I ended my last letter and that's
how I'm going to begin this one. 'A little bundle of contradictions,' can you
tell me exactly what it is? What does contradiction mean? Like so many
words, it can mean two things, contradiction from without and contradiction
from within.

The first is the ordinary 'not giving in easily, always knowing best, getting in
the last word,' **enfin**, all the unpleasant qualities for which I'm renowned.
The second nobody knows about, that's my own secret.

10 I've already told you before that I have, as it were, a dual personality. One
half embodies my **exuberant** cheerfulness, making fun of everything, my
high-spiritedness, and above all, the way I take everything lightly. This
includes not taking offence at a flirtation, a kiss, an embrace, a dirty joke.
This side is usually lying in wait and pushes away the other, which is much
better, deeper and purer. You must realise that no one knows Anne's better
side and that's why most people find me so **insufferable**.

Certainly, I'm **a giddy clown** for one afternoon, but then everyone's had
enough of me for another month. Really, it's just the same as a love film is for
deep-thinking people, simply a **diversion**, amusing just for once, something
20 which is soon forgotten, not bad, but certainly not good. I loathe having to tell
you this, but why shouldn't I, if I know it's true anyway? My lighter **superficial**
side will always be too quick for the deeper side of me and that's why it will
always win. You can't imagine how often I've already tried to push this Anne
away, to cripple her, to hide her, because after all, she's only half of what's
called Anne: but it doesn't work and I know too why it doesn't work.

I'm awfully scared that everyone who knows me as I always am will discover
that I have another side, a finer and better side. I'm afraid they'll laugh at
me, think I'm ridiculous and sentimental, not take me seriously. I'm used to
not being taken seriously but it's only the 'light-hearted' Anne that's used to
30 it and can bear it; the 'deeper' Anne is too frail for it. Sometimes, if I really
compel the good Anne to take the stage for a quarter of an hour, she simply
shrivels up as soon as she has to speak, and lets Anne number one take over,
and before I realise it, she has disappeared.

Therefore, the nice Anne is never present in company, has not appeared one
single time so far, but almost always **predominates** when we're alone. I know
exactly how I'd like to be, how I am too ... inside. But, alas, I'm only like that
for myself. And perhaps that's why, no, I'm sure it's the reason why I say I've
got a happy nature within and why other people think I've got a happy
nature without. I am guided by the pure Anne within, but outside I'm
40 nothing but a **frolicsome** little goat who's broken loose.

From *The Diary of Anne Frank*, trans. B. M. Mooyart-Doubleday, Pan, 1954

DICTIONARY

unbosomings confessions

melancholy sad

the common round ordinary things

enhance clarify

albeit even though

enfin finally

exuberant lively

insufferable unbearable

a giddy clown a joker

diversion light entertainment

superficial unimportant, trivial

predominates takes over

frolicsome playful

CLOSER READING

The first two questions focus on extract A.

1 a What are Anne's reasons for writing her diary?

b Why does she believe that other people wouldn't be interested in reading her diary?

2 What does a diary provide that her friends and family don't?

The next two questions relate to extract B.

3 She describes herself as 'a bundle of contradictions'. What are the two sides of her character? Find evidence to back up your views.

4 Which side of her character does she reveal to her diary? How does this tie in with your response to Question 1?

3 | War diary

Sarah Macnaughtan wrote her diary with the intention that it should be published. She had already written some novels. It recounts her experiences in Belgium, helping wounded soldiers near the front line during the First World War. She worked from a bombed-out railway station at Furnes. During this time she gained a reputation for being a hard worker, even though secretly she suffered from ill-health.

(Some words are highlighted in the text. You will find further information about these words at the end of the passage.)

21 November 1914   I am up to my eyes in soup! l have started my soup-kitchen at the station, and it gives me a lot to do. Bad luck to it, my cold and cough are pretty bad!

It is odd to wake in the morning in a frozen room, with every pane of glass green and thick with frost, and one does not dare to think of Mary and morning tea! When I can summon enough **moral courage** to put a foot out of bed I jump into my clothes at once; half dressed I go to a little tap of cold water to wash, and then, and for ever, I forgive entirely those sections of society who do not **tub**. We brush our own boots here, and put on all the clothes we possess, and then descend to a breakfast of Quaker oat porridge with bread and margarine. I wouldn't have it different, really, till our men are out of the trenches; but I am hoping most fervently that I shan't break down, as I am so 'full with soup'.

Our kitchen at the railway-station is a little bit of a passage, which measures eight feet by eight feet. In it are two small stoves. One is a little round iron thing which burns, and the other is a sort of little 'kitchener' which doesn't! With this equipment, and various huge **'marmites'**, we make coffee and soup for hundreds of men every day. The first convoy gets into the station about 9.30 a.m., all the men frozen, the black troops nearly dead with cold. As soon as the train arrives I carry out one of my boiling 'marmites' to the middle of the stone entrance and ladle out the soup, while a Belgian Sister takes round coffee and bread …

After the first convoy of wounded has been served, other wounded men come in from time to time, then about 4 o'clock there is another trainload. At ten p.m. the largest convoy arrives. The men seem too stiff to move, and many are carried in on soldiers' backs. The stretchers are laid on the floor, those who can **'s'asseoir'** sit on benches, and every man produces a 'quart' or tin cup. One and all they come out of the darkness and never look about them, but rouse themselves to get fed, and stretch out poor grimy hands for bread and steaming drinks. There is very little light – only one oil-lamp, which hangs from the roof, and burns dimly. Under this we place the 'marmites', and all that I can see is one brown or black or wounded hand stretched out into the dim ring of light under the lamp, with a little tin mug held out for soup. Wet and ragged, and covered with sticky mud, the wounded lie in the **salle** of the station, and, except under the lamp, it is all quite dark. There are dim forms and frosty breaths, and a door which bangs continually, and then the train loads up, the wounded depart, and a heavy smell and an empty pot are all that remain. We clean up the kitchen, and go home about 1 a.m. I do the night work alone …

1 December   Mrs Knocker and Miss Chisholm and Lady Dorothy went out to Pervyse a few days ago to make soup, etc., for Belgians in the trenches. They live in the cellar of a house which has been blown inside out by guns, and take out buckets of soup to men on outpost duty. Not a glimpse of fire is allowed on the outposts. Fortunately the weather has been milder lately, but soaking wet. Our three ladies walk about the trenches at night, and I come home at 1 a.m. from the station. The men of our party meanwhile do some housework. They sit over the fire a good deal, clear away the tea-things, and when we come home at night we find they have put hot-water bottles in our

bed and trimmed some lamps. I feel like Alice in Wonderland or some other
50 upside-down world. We live in much discomfort, which is a little unnecessary;
but no one seems to want to undertake housekeeping.

I make soup all day, and there is not much else to write about. All along the
Yser the Allies and the Germans confront each other, but things have been
quieter lately. The piteous list of casualties is not so long as it has been. A
wounded German was brought in today. Both his legs were broken and his
feet frost-bitten. He had been for four days in water with nothing to eat, and
his legs unset. He is doing well.

On Sunday I drove out to Pervyse with a kind friend, Mr Tapp. At the end of
the long avenue by which one approaches the village, Pervyse church stands,
60 like a **sentinel** with both eyes shot out. Nothing is left but a blind stare.
Hardly any of the church remains, and the churchyard is as if some devil had
stalked through it, tearing up crosses and kicking down graves. Even the
dead are not left undisturbed in this awful war. The village (like many other
villages) is a mass of gaping ruins – roofs blown off, streets full of holes, not a
window left unshattered, and the guns still booming.

From H. Blodgett (ed.), *The English Woman's Diary*, Fourth Estate, 1992

DICTIONARY

moral courage strength of character
tub bath
'marmites' cooking pots
's'asseoir' sit up
salle main room
sentinel guard

CLOSER READING

1 The opening three paragraphs (lines 1–22) describe her lifestyle at this time.
   a What is her life at home like? Why does she accept this kind of lifestyle?
   b What is her life at work like? Describe the conditions she has to work in.

2 Look at how she describes the soldiers in the fourth paragraph (lines 23–39). Find all the phrases that describe them, and explain what this tells you about them and Macnaughtan's feelings towards them. You could set your ideas out in a table like the one below.

Descriptive phrase	What this tells you about:	
	the soldiers	Macnaughtan's feelings

3 The entry for 1 December provides more details about her lifestyle and work.
   a What is the relationship between the women and the men who work at the soup kitchen?
   b What is your reaction to the way they treat the German soldier?

4 How does the description of the church, the graveyard and the village at Pervyse add to our understanding of Macnaughtan's impressions of the war?

4 | The Fire of London

Samuel Pepys lived between 1633 and 1703, keeping a diary between 1660 and 1669 (he gave up because he felt his eyesight was failing). It is unlikely that he ever thought it would be published. Its appeal today lies in the detailed description of one man's development in a particular moment in history. He lived during an exciting time in history and met some of the most important people of the day. The passage below describes his reactions to the Fire of London in 1666.

(Some words are highlighted in the text. You will find further information about these words at the end of the passage.)

September 2nd (Lord's Day). Some of our mayds sitting up late last night to get things ready against our feast to-day, Jane called us up about three in the morning to tell us of a great fire they saw in the City. So I rose and slipped on my night-gowne and went to her window, and thought it to be on the back-side of Marke-lane at the farthest; but, being unused to such fires as followed, I thought it far enough off; and so went to bed again and to sleep. About seven rose again to dress myself, and there looked out at the window and saw the fire not so much as it was, and further off. So to my closett to set things to rights after yesterday's cleaning. By and by Jane comes and tells me
10   that she hears that above 300 houses have been burned down to-night by the fire we saw, and that it is now burning down all Fish-street, by London Bridge. So I made myself ready presently and walked to the Tower, and there got up upon one of the high places, Sir J. Robinson's little son going up with me; and there I did see the houses at that end of the bridge all on fire, and an infinite great fire on this and the other side the end of the bridge. So with my heart full of trouble, I down to the water-side, and there got a boat and through bridge, and there saw a **lamentable** fire. Poor Michell's house, as far as the Old Swan, already burned that way, and the fire running further. Everybody **endeavouring** to remove their goods, and
20   flinging into the river or bringing them into lighters that lay off; poor people staying in their houses as long as till the very fire touched them, and then running into boats, or clambering from one pair of stairs by the water-side to another. And among other things the poor pigeons, I perceive, were **loth to** leave their houses, but hovered about the windows and balconys till they were, some of them burned, their wings, and fell down. Having staid, and in an hour's time seen the fire rage every way, and nobody, to my sight, endeavouring to quench it, but to remove their goods and leave all to the fire; and having seen it get as far as the Steele-yard, and the wind mighty high and driving it into the City, and every thing after so long a drought
30   proving combustible, even the very stones of churches, I to White Hall and there up to the King's closett in the Chappell, where people come about me and I did give them an account dismayed them all, and word was carried into the King. So I called for and did tell the King and Duke of Yorke what I saw,

and that unless his Majesty did command houses to be pulled down nothing could stop the fire. They seemed much troubled, and the King commanded me to go to my Lord Mayor from him and command him to spare no houses, but to pull down before the fire every way. The Duke of York bid me tell him that if he would have any more soldiers he shall. Here meeting with Captain Cocke, I in his coach which he lent me, and Creed with me to Paul's, and

40   there walked along Watling-street as well as I could, every creature coming away loaden with goods to save, and here and there sicke people carried away in beds. Extraordinary good goods carried in carts and on backs. At last met my Lord Mayor in Canning-street like a man spent, with a handkercher about his neck. To the King's message he cried, like a fainting woman, 'Lord! what can I do? **I am spent**: people will not obey me. I have been pulling down houses, but the fire overtakes us faster than we can do it.' That he needed no more soldiers; and that, for himself, he must go and refresh himself, having been up all night. So he left me, and I him, and walked home, seeing people all almost **distracted**; and no manner of means used to

50   quench the fire. The houses, too, so very thick thereabouts, and full of matter for burning, as pitch and tarr, in Thames-street; and warehouses of oyle, and wines, and brandy and other things. I saw Mr Isaake Houblon, the handsome man, prettily dressed and dirty, at his door at Dowgate receiving some of his brothers' things, whose houses were on fire: and, as he says have been removed twice already, and he doubts (as it soon proved) that they must be in a little time removed from his house also, which was a sad consideration.

From *Everybody's Pepys*, ed. O. F. Marshall, G. Bell & Sons, 1926

DICTIONARY

lamentable disastrous
endeavouring attempting
loth to very unwilling to
I am spent I am exhausted
distracted mad with worry

CLOSER READING

1 Look at the opening few sentences. How does Pepys create a sense of impending disaster that people were unprepared for?

2 In many ways this piece is like reportage (see pages 141–153). It gives a detailed eye-witness description of a major event.
  a How does Pepys give you a sense of the place in which the fire happened?
  b Which details emphasise the tragedy of the fire?

3 What kind of social world does Pepys live in; in other words, who does he mix with? Give examples.

4 Find evidence of Pepys's own reactions to the fire. Are these necessary, or would you prefer it if he just showed you what was happening?

FURTHER ACTIVITIES

1 This task is best done individually. Think back over the last week. Choose something that happened which stands out in your memory.

a Write down the facts of what happened.

b Now write down your feelings about what happened, and what you think it showed about the people involved.

c Now write a diary entry as if you were one of the other people involved. He or she may see things very differently to you. In particular, they will be describing their feelings about you! Also, they may have different views about the people involved and may not know all the facts of the situation that you know.

2 You will need to work in pairs for this task. Invent a situation where someone did something which he or she later regretted. (You could, if you wish, base it on something that happened to one of you in real life.) Write two diary entries, one each:

a an entry for a private diary in which you write the truth about what happened and what you felt;

b an entry for a public diary, one that will be published, in which you try explain how you behaved so that people will be sympathetic to you.

Before writing, you will need to agree about the following:

- the details of what actually happened;
- where it happened;
- the people who were involved;
- the behaviour of the people involved;
- the real reasons why the central character behaved as he or she did;
- the reasons that are going to be put forward in the 'published' diary entry.

Think of how **each** of the above may be presented differently to convey different accounts of the events.

3 Some people write diaries as a way of exploring their feelings and their identity – who they really are.

Choose an event in your life which made you think seriously about the kind of person you are. It could be a moment of crisis where you revealed your true character. It might be an occasion when you reacted to something in a way which even surprised yourself.

Write the diary entry for the day the event happened. Record what happened, how you felt and what you learnt about yourself.

4 Some diarists, like Sarah Macnaughtan and Samuel Pepys, use their diary to record their personal responses to public events.

In groups, gather together copies of recent newspapers – daily, tabloid, broadsheet, local etc. Cut out stories that interest you and take turns to discuss your views using the following headings:

- What were your emotions as you read the story?
- What do you think about the people in the story? What would their feelings have been?
- How would you feel if you had been involved in the story?
- Do the stories have an impact on your personal life?
- How does the story make you feel about your society?

When you have finished your discussion, each person should choose one or two of the stories and record his or her personal response, using the headings for the discussion if they help.

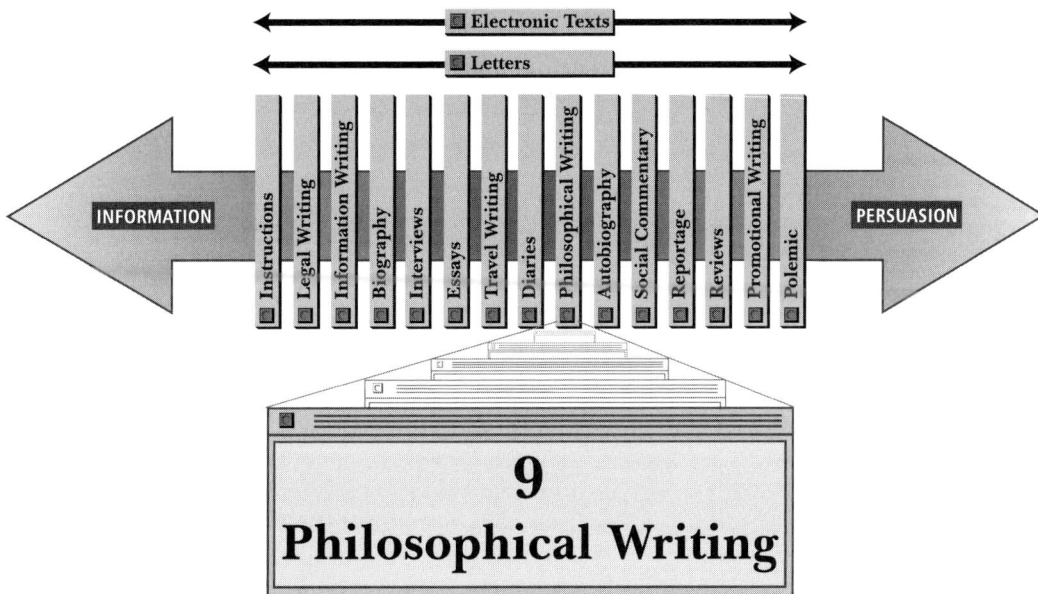

The diagram shows a spectrum between INFORMATION (left arrow) and PERSUASION (right arrow), with vertical bars labelled (left to right): Instructions, Legal Writing, Information Writing, Biography, Interviews, Essays, Travel Writing, Diaries, Philosophical Writing, Autobiography, Social Commentary, Reportage, Reviews, Promotional Writing, Polemic. Above the bars are two double-headed arrows labelled Electronic Texts and Letters.

9
Philosophical Writing

Philosophy means, literally, the 'love of wisdom', and is concerned with trying to understand, through enquiry and analysis, the nature of the life we are living, what we know, and how we know it.

Because philosophers are dealing with the way in which we know and understand things, they use language in a very careful, precise way, trying to make what they say as clear and logical as possible.

In the texts that follow, you will be asked to examine a range of philosophical writing, drawn from different times and different cultures, and to look at the ways in which the writers invite the reader's agreement with the theories they are putting forward.

1 | A Socratic dialogue

Plato is perhaps the most famous philosopher of Western culture. He lived in the city-state of Athens, between about 427 and 347 BC. He studied philosophy under Socrates, and most of his writings are concerned with what Socrates said and did. Socrates was a bold and original thinker, who taught philosophy by holding discussions with his students. Some of the things that he was supposed to have taught alarmed the people ruling Athens at the time, and Socrates was put into prison and condemned to death. He was sentenced to kill himself by swallowing poison.

In the passage below, an extract from the *Phaedo*, Plato describes how friends of Socrates went to visit him in his cell, upset that he was not fighting against his death sentence, and how Socrates convinced them that such behaviour would be highly illogical in a philosopher. The passage starts with Socrates speaking.

(Some words are highlighted in the text. You will find further information about these words at the end of the passage.)

'Let's discuss it among ourselves ...: do we suppose that death is a reality?'

'Certainly,' rejoined Simmias.

'And that it is nothing but the separation of the soul from the body? And that being dead is this: the body's having come to be apart, separated from the soul, alone by itself, and the soul's being apart, alone by itself, separated from the body? Death can't be anything else but that, can it?'

'No, it's just that.'

'Now look, my friend, and see if maybe you agree with me on these points; because through them I think we'll improve on our knowledge of what we're
10 examining. Do you think it befits a philosophical man to be keen about the so-called pleasures of, for example, food and drink?'

'Not in the least, Socrates,' said Simmias.

'And what about those of sex?'

'Not at all.'

'And what about the other services to the body? Do you think such a person regards them as of any value? For instance, the possession of smart clothes and shoes, and the other bodily adornments – do you think he values them highly, or does he **disdain** them, except in so far as he's absolutely compelled to share in them?'
20 'I think the philosopher disdains them.'

'Do you think in general, then, that such a person's concern is not for the body, but, so far as he can stand aside from it, is directed towards the soul?'

'I do.' ...

'And it is it just this that is named "death" – a release and parting of soul from body?'

'Indeed it is.'

'And it's especially those who practise philosophy **aright**, or rather they alone, who are always eager to release it, as we say, and the occupation of philosophers is just this, isn't it – a release and parting of soul from body?'

30   'It seems so.'

'Then wouldn't it be absurd, as I said at the start, for a man to prepare himself in his life to live as close as he can to being dead, and then to be resentful when that comes to him?'

'It would be absurd, of course.'

'Truly then, Simmias, those who practise philosophy aright are **cultivating dying**, and for them, least of all men, does being dead hold any terror. Look at it like this: if they've set themselves at odds with the body at every point, and desire to possess their soul alone by itself, wouldn't it be quite illogical if they were afraid and resentful when that came about?'

DICTIONARY

disdain despise
aright correctly
cultivating dying preparing the ground for death

CLOSER READING

1 The passage above is laid out as a conversation, but in fact it is Socrates who makes all the main points, isn't it? Simmias is there for Socrates to try his ideas out on, and to agree with what he puts forward. Concentrating only on what Socrates says, number each of Socrates' remarks 1–10, so that the sentence beginning 'Let's discuss it …' (line 1) is number 1, the paragraph beginning 'And that it is nothing …' (lines 3–6) is number 2, and so on.

2 Take each of the ten points in turn, and write a short summary, not more than one or two sentences, of each point that Socrates is making.

3 Write your summaries on separate pieces of paper, so that you can shuffle them about on the table in front of you.

4 Arrange your summaries into what seems to you to be the most logical order. This may be the same order as in the original passage, or it may not.

5 Write out the development of Socrates' argument as a flow-chart. It may start like the one below:

Philosophers are more concerned with the soul than with the body

↓

Body and soul are separated in death

↓

2 An exposition of the cause of lengthy hopes, and how they may be cured

This passage is from *The Remembrance of Death and the Afterlife*, by the 11th-century Muslim writer Al-Ghazali. He lived from 1058 until 1111 and spent most of his life in Baghdad, where he was honoured as a wise and devout man. He wrote many books in which he commented on the meaning of the teachings of Mohammed, the founder and prophet of Islam.

In the passage that follows, Al-Ghazali is talking about the importance of constantly keeping in mind that the most important thing in a person's life is not what he or she achieves in this world, but how he or she is prepared for the life after death, through their understanding of and obedience to God.

(Some words are highlighted in the text. You will find further information about these words at the end of the passage.)

Know that lengthy hopes have two causes, the first of which is ignorance, and the second of which is love of the world.

As regards the latter, [the problem is that] when man comes to love the world, and its desires, pleasures and attachments, then taking leave of it weighs heavily upon his heart, which will thus avoid thinking of death, which is the instrument of the separation; for everyone who conceives a dislike for something will fend it off. Man is **infatuated** with **vain** hopes, and ever fills his soul with hoping for that **which is conformable** to his preferences; and the only thing which conforms to them is that he should remain in the world.

10 Thus he never **ceases** to imagine this and count upon it within himself, along with the accessories of such permanence, including the wealth, family, accommodation, acquaintances, riding beasts and other means of life which he needs in this world. In this manner his heart becomes attached to this notion and cannot progress beyond it, being distracted thereby from the remembrance of death and not deeming it to be **nigh**.

When in certain circumstances the question of death and the need to prepare for it occur to him, he **procrastinates**, and makes promises to himself, saying, 'There are yet many days before you until you grow mature; then you can repent.' And when he grows to maturity he says, 'Not until you become an

20 old man.' But when he becomes an old man he says, 'Not until you finish building this house', or 'establishing this farm', or 'return from this voyage', or 'conclude the setting-up of this son, and provide for him and arrange a house for him', or 'not until you have subdued this enemy who takes such pleasure in your misfortunes'. Thus it is that he unceasingly procrastinates and delays, never plunging into one task without there being consequent upon its completion ten others, and in this gradual fashion procrastinates day after day, led by one task to another, or rather, to several others, until he

is snatched away by his fate at some moment he never expected, at which his sorrows grow long and protracted.

30   The most frequent cry of the dwellers in the **Inferno** is 'shall'. 'O woe,' they cry, 'because of "shall!"' For the unfortunate procrastinator is unaware that what induces him to postpone something today will still be with him tomorrow, and that it will, with the passage of time, grow in strength and firmness. He thinks it conceivable that the man who plunges into the world and pays it heed might have time to spare. What folly! No-one has time to spare from it save he who has cast it aside.

> No man has had his needs fulfilled therein;
> one desire ends only in another.

40   The root of all these hopes is the love of the world, and finding comfort therein, neglecting the saying [of the Prophet] (may God bless him and grant him peace): 'Love whomsoe'er you will, for you shall surely leave him.'

As for the matter of ignorance, this consists in a man's setting his confidence in his youth, and considering that death cannot be near while he remains young. This unfortunate wretch fails to consider that were the old men of his land to be tallied up they would amount to no more than a tenth of the men of the land. They are so few simply because death is more common in youth: for every old man that dies a thousand children and young men pass away. Alternatively, he may consider death to be unlikely by reason of his health, and discount the possibility of sudden death, being quite unaware that it is
50   far from unlikely, or that, should it truly be unlikely, then sudden illness is not; and every illness makes its appearance suddenly, and when it has come death is no longer improbable.

If this heedless man would but think, and come to realise that death has no fixed time as to youth, middle age or decrepitude, and that it does not know winter from summer, autumn from spring, or day from night, his awareness would be greater and he would busy himself with preparing for it. But ignorance of these matters, combined with the love of this world, invites him to prolong his hopes and neglect any consideration of the **proximity** of death. Always does he think that death is ahead of him, but does not reckon
60   upon its befalling him and that before long he will tumble into it. Constantly does he imagine that he will be following funeral cortèges, and never imagines that his own cortège will some day be followed, because witnessing the demise of others is something which is often repeated and has become familiar. But as far as his own death is concerned, he has no experience of it, and cannot imagine that he will experience it, for it has never transpired; and when it does it will never do so again: it will be the first and the final time.

The way forwards for him is to compare himself with others, and to appreciate that his own funeral cortège must itself be followed, and that he
70   himself must needs be **interred** in his grave, and that it may well be that the unfired brick with which his tomb will be covered has already been made, all unbeknown to him. Thus it is that his procrastination is sheer ignorance …

There exists no medicine which will induce one to contemplate death with one's heart comparable to that of looking to those of one's peers and companions who have passed away, and to the manner in which death came to them at a time they had never expected. At this time, a man who has made preparations has triumphed mightily, but as for him who was beguiled by lengthy hopes, he has failed most manifestly.

80   Let man in every hour look to his limbs and his extremities. Let his thoughts dwell upon how the worms must needs devour them, and upon the fashion in which his bones shall rot away. Let him wonder whether the worms are to begin with the pupil of his right eye or of his left; for there is no part of his body that shall not be food for the worm. He can do nothing for himself but to understand, and to act sincerely for the sake of God (Exalted is He!). And in like fashion, let him meditate upon that which we shall presently relate concerning the Punishment of the Grave, the Inquisition of Munkar and Nakir, and the Congregation and Quickening, together with the terrors of the Resurrection, and the sounding of the Call on the Day of the Greatest Exposition. For it is thoughts such as these which prompt anew the

90   remembrance of death in the heart, and summon one to make ready for it.

From Al-Ghazali, *The Remembrance of Death and the Afterlife*, trans. T. J. Winter, Islamic Texts Society, 1989

DICTIONARY

infatuated deeply in love with

vain foolish, worthless

which is conformable to which fits in with

ceases stops

nigh near

procrastinates puts off

Inferno hell

proximity closeness

interred buried

CLOSER READING

1 Number the paragraphs in the passage 1–9, and write a short sub-heading for each one, summarising what Al-Ghazali says in that paragraph.

2 Al-Ghazali gives three main reasons why people think too much of this life and not enough of the world to come. Write two or three sentences in your own words, saying what these three reasons are.

3 Say in your own words what Al-Ghazali recommends as the 'cure' for love of this world.

3 Of Ideas in general, and their Original

This extract is taken from *An Essay Concerning Human Understanding* by John Locke. Locke was a British philosopher who lived and wrote at the end of the 17th century. His main concerns were with seeking to work out a system of ideas which would enable all people to live together in equality and freedom. It was to a great extent his ideas which formed the basis of the American Constitution.

As well as political philosophy, though, Locke was also deeply interested in the nature of knowledge – how we know things, and where our ideas come from. It is this line of thinking which he is exploring in the passage below.

(Some words are highlighted in the text. You will find further information about these words at the end of the passage.)

1   Every Man being conscious to himself, That he thinks, and that which his Mind is employ'd about whilst thinking, being the *Ideas*, that are there, 'tis past doubt, that Men have in their Minds several *Ideas*, such as are those expressed by the words, *Whiteness, Hardness, Sweetness, Thinking, Motion, Man, Elephant, Army, Drunkenness*, and others: It is in the first place then to be enquired, How he comes by them? I know that it is a received Doctrine, That Men have native *Ideas*, and original Characters stamped upon their Minds, in their very first Being. This Opinion I have at large examined already; and, I suppose, what I have said in the **fore-going** Book, will be much more easily admitted, when I have shewn, whence the Understanding may get all the *Ideas* it has, and by what ways and **degrees** they may come into the Mind; for which I shall appeal to every one's own Observation and Experience.

2   Let us then suppose the Mind to be, as we say, white Paper, void of all Characters, without any *Ideas*; How comes it to be furnished? Whence comes it by that vast store, which the busy and boundless Fancy of Man has painted on it, with an almost endless variety? Whence has it all the materials of Reason and Knowledge? To this I answer, in one word, From *Experience*: In that, all our Knowledge is founded; and from that it ultimately derives it self. Our Observation employ'd either about *external*, **sensible** *Objects; or about the internal Operations of our Minds*, **perceived** *and reflected on by our selves, is that, which supplies our Understandings with all the materials of thinking*. These two are the Fountains of Knowledge, from whence all the *Ideas* we have, or can naturally have, do spring.

3   First, *Our Senses*, conversant about particular sensible Objects, do *convey into the Mind*, several distinct *Perceptions* of things, according to those various ways, wherein those Objects do affect them: And thus we come by those *Ideas*, we have of *Yellow, White, Heat, Cold, Soft, Hard, Bitter, Sweet*, and all those which we call sensible qualities, which when I say the senses convey into the mind, I mean, they from external Objects convey into the mind what produces there those

Perceptions. This great Source, of most of the *Ideas* we have, depending wholly upon our Senses, and derived by them to the Understanding, I call *SENSATION*.

4 Secondly, The other Fountain, from which Experience furnisheth the Understanding with *Ideas*, is the *Perception of the Operations of our own Minds* within us, as it is employ'd about the *Ideas* it has got; which Operations, when the Soul comes to reflect on, and consider, do furnish the Understanding with another set of *Ideas*, which could not be had from things without: and such are, *Perception, Thinking, Doubting, Believing, Reasoning, Knowing, Willing*, and all the different actings of our own Minds; which we being conscious of, and observing in our selves, do from these receive into our Understandings, as distinct *Ideas*, as we do from Bodies affecting our Senses. This Source of *Ideas*, every Man has wholly in himself: And though it be not Sense, as having nothing to do with external Objects; yet it is very like it, and might properly be call'd internal Sense. But as I call the other *Sensation*, so I call this *REFLECTION*, the *Ideas* it affords being such only, as the Mind gets by reflecting on its own Operations within it self. By *REFLECTION* then, in the following part of this Discourse, I would be understood to mean, that notice which the Mind takes of its own Operations, and the manner of them, by reason whereof, there come to be *Ideas* of these Operations in the Understanding. These two, I say, *viz.* External, Material things, as the Objects of *SENSATION*; and the Operations of our own Minds within, as the Objects of *REFLECTION*, are, to me, the only Originals, from whence all our *Ideas* take their beginnings. The term *Operations* here, I use in a large sense, as comprehending not **barely** the Actions of the Mind about its *Ideas*, but some sort of Passions arising sometimes from them, such as is the satisfaction or uneasiness arising from any thought.

5 The Understanding seems to me, not to have the least glimmering of any *Ideas*, which it doth not receive from one of these two. *External Objects furnish the Mind with the* Ideas *of sensible qualities*, which are all those different perceptions they produce in us: And the *Mind furnishes the Understanding with* Ideas *of its own Operations* ...

6 He that attentively considers the state of a *Child*, at his first coming into the World, will have little reason to think him stored with plenty of *Ideas*, that are to be the matter of his future Knowledge. 'Tis by degrees he comes to be furnished with them: And though the *Ideas* of obvious and familiar qualities, imprint themselves, before the Memory begins to keep a Register of Time and Order, yet 'tis often so late, before some unusual qualities come in the way, that there are few Men that cannot recollect the beginning of their **acquaintance** with them: And if it were worth while, no doubt a Child might be so ordered, as to have but a very few, even of the ordinary *Ideas*, till he were grown up to a Man. But all that are born into the World being surrounded with Bodies, that perpetually and diversly affect them, variety of *Ideas*, whether care be taken about it or no, are imprinted on the Minds of Children. *Light*, and *Colours*, are busie at hand every where, when the Eye is but open; *Sounds*, and some *tangible Qualities* fail not to solicite their proper Senses, and force an entrance to the Mind; but yet, I think, it will be granted easily, That if a Child were kept in a place, where he never saw any other but Black and White, till he were a Man, he would have no more *Ideas* of Scarlet or Green, than he that from his Childhood never tasted an Oyster, or a Pine-Apple, has of those particular Relishes.

From J. Locke, *An Essay Concering Human Understanding*, ed. P. H. Nidditch, Clarendon Press, 1975

ⓒ CLOSER READING

1 Locke has numbered the paragraphs of this passage 1–6. In your own words, write a sub-heading for each paragraph, summarising what Locke says in that paragraph.

2 Locke has set his thoughts out in what he felt to be a logical order, one proposition depending on the previous one.

- List all the propositions made in this extract.
- Set them out as a flow-chart. You may like to use the diagram below to help you begin.

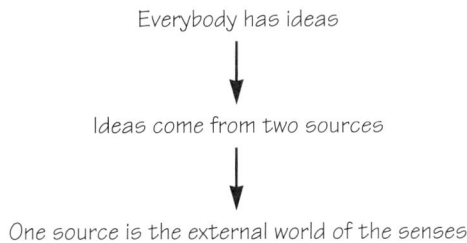

Everybody has ideas

↓

Ideas come from two sources

↓

One source is the external world of the senses

3 Go through the passage again carefully, and note down any points at which you would want to stop Locke and ask him a question.

- Make a list of these questions.
- Swap your list with a partner.
- Try to answer as many of your partner's questions as you can.

4 | The anthropic principle

This extract is from *A Brief History of Time* by Stephen Hawking. Currently Professor of Mathematics at Cambridge University, Hawking was born in Oxford in 1942, exactly 300 years after the death of Galileo. Despite the fact that he is disabled with Motor Neurone Disease, which has reduced his mobility to a minimum, he studied physics at the University of Oxford, and then went on to take a postgraduate degree at Cambridge.

In *A Brief History of Time*, Hawking set out as clearly as he could the current thinking about the physical universe and the concept of time. In the passage

> below, Hawking is looking at the different ways in which our understanding of the universe may be shaped by our own way of seeing and thinking.
>
> (Some words are highlighted in the text. You will find further information about these words at the end of the passage.)

If the universe is indeed **spatially** infinite, or if there are infinitely many universes, there would probably be some large regions somewhere that started out in a smooth and uniform manner. It is a bit like the well-known horde of monkeys hammering away on typewriters – most of what they write will be garbage, but very occasionally by pure chance they will type out one of Shakespeare's sonnets. Similarly, in the case of the universe, could it be that we are living in a region that just happens by chance to be smooth and uniform? At first sight this may seem very improbable, because such smooth regions would be heavily outnumbered by chaotic and irregular regions.

10 However, suppose that only in the smooth regions were galaxies and stars formed and were conditions right for the development of complicated self-replicating organisms like ourselves who were capable of asking the question: Why is the universe so smooth? This is an example of the application of what is known as the **anthropic principle**, which can be paraphrased as 'We see the universe the way it is because we exist.'

There are two versions of the anthropic principle, the weak and the strong. The weak anthropic principle states that in a universe that is large or infinite in space and/or time, the conditions necessary for the development of intelligent life will be met only in certain regions that are limited in space

20 and time. The intelligent beings in these regions should therefore not be surprised if they observe that their locality in the universe satisfies the conditions that are necessary for their existence. It is a bit like a rich person living in a wealthy neighbourhood not seeing any poverty.

One example of the use of the weak anthropic principle is to 'explain' why the **big bang** occurred about ten thousand million years ago – it takes about that long for intelligent beings to evolve. As explained above, an early generation of stars first had to form. These stars converted some of the original hydrogen and helium into elements like carbon and oxygen, out of which we are made. The stars then exploded as supernovas, and their debris

30 went to form other stars and planets, among them those of our own solar system, which is about five thousand million years old. The first one or two thousand million years of the earth's existence were too hot for the development of anything complicated. The remaining three thousand million years or so have been taken up by the slow process of biological evolution, which has led from the simplest organisms to beings who are capable of measuring time back to the big bang.

Few people would quarrel with the validity or utility of the weak anthropic principle. Some, however, go much further and propose a strong version of the principle. According to this theory, there are either many different

40 universes or many different regions of a single universe, each with its own initial configuration and, perhaps, with its own set of laws of science. In most of these universes the conditions would not be right for the development of

complicated organisms; only in the few universes that are like ours would intelligent beings develop and ask the question: 'Why is the universe the way we see it?' The answer is then simple: If it had been different, we would not be here!

50 The laws of science, as we know them at present, contain many fundamental numbers, like the size of the electric charge of the electron and the ratio masses of the proton and the electron. We cannot, at the moment, predict the values of these numbers from theory – we have to find them by observation. It may be that one day we shall discover a complete unified theory that predicts them all, but it is also possible that some or all of them vary from universe to universe or within a single universe. The remarkable fact is that the values of these numbers seem to have been very finely adjusted to make possible the development of life. For example if the electric charge of the electron had been only slightly different, stars either would have been unable to burn hydrogen and helium, or else they would not have exploded. Of course, there might be other forms of intelligent life, not dreamed of even by writers of science fiction, that did not require the light of
60 a star like the sun or the heavier chemical elements that are made in stars and are flung back into space when the stars explode. Nevertheless, it seems clear that there are relatively few ranges of values for the numbers that would allow the development of any form of intelligent life. Most sets of values would give rise to universes that, although they might be very beautiful, would contain no one able to wonder at that beauty. One can take this either as evidence of a divine purpose in Creation and the choice of the laws of science or as support for the strong anthropic principle.

From S. Hawking, *A Brief History of Time*, Bantam Press, 1988

DICTIONARY

spatially with regard to space
anthropic principle the principle that theories of the universe are limited by the need to allow for man's existence in it as an observer, so that we can only see what we, as human beings, can see, not what necessarily what is actually there
big bang the enormous explosion which is thought to have been at origin of our universe

CLOSER READING

1 Look again at the first paragraph of the extract and work out what is the main point that Hawking is making here. Write down in your own words, using two or three sentences, the main argument Hawking is putting forward here.
2 Re-read the next three paragraphs, from line 16 to line 46. Summarise in your own words the two different versions of the anthropic principle.
3 Look again at the final paragraph of the extract. What is Hawking saying about the values of numbers and their relationship to the development of life? Summarise his point in two or three sentences of your own.
4 Re-read the last two sentences of the extract, from line 63 to line 67. Summarise in your own words the point that Hawking is making here.

FURTHER ACTIVITIES

1 Working on your own, look again at Text no. 1, the passage from Plato. Imagine that Simmias is writing to a friend, Alexias, after Socrates has died. Alexias is deeply upset at Socrates' death, and Simmias is comforting him by telling him what Socrates felt about dying. Write the letter Simmias would have written. Simmias is writing to a friend, so the letter will be informal in style. Look at the Letters section of this book (pages 194–203) to remind yourself of the style and layout for this kind of letter.

2 Working with a partner, look again at Text no. 1. Imagine that you had both been present at this conversation.

- Go through the passage, and note down the points where you would have wanted to ask Socrates a question.
- Write down the questions you would have wanted to ask, or the points you would have wanted to make.
- Re-write the passage, putting in your questions, and the answers you think Socrates might have given.

3 • Working on your own, look back at Text no. 1. This is written as a conversation, which is the way in Socrates developed his teaching, talking to friends and developing his ideas through asking and answering questions. This kind of philosophical writing is called 'Socratic dialogue'. Look carefully at how the argument is developed through the conversation, and at the kind of things Simmias says.

- Choose one of the other texts from this section, and re-write it as a Socratic dialogue. You will need to be clear what the argument of the passage is, and how you will develop it in conversation form. You may want your conversation to have more than two people discussing the ideas. Make up names and characters for the different people speaking.

4 • Working in a small group, brainstorm on to paper a number of questions about life which puzzle you. For instance, how do we know people and things continue to exist when we can no longer see them? How do we know that we exist? Who or what is God? How do we know …? You can have as few or as many questions as you like.

- On your own, choose from the questions your group came up with the one that interests you most, and try to answer it. You can model your answer on the style of one of the writers in this section, or you can write in a style of your own. Remember, though, that your answer will need to be carefully argued, with reasons given to convince the reader that what you are saying must be true.

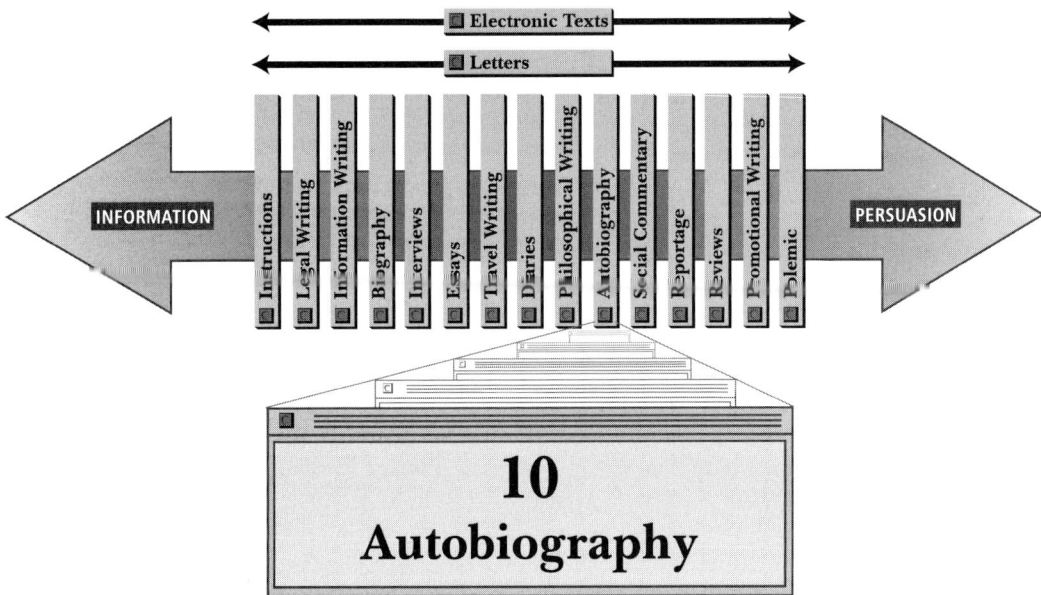

Electronic Texts
Letters

INFORMATION ← → PERSUASION

Instructions · Legal Writing · Information Writing · Biography · Interviews · Essays · Travel Writing · Diaries · Philosophical Writing · Autobiography · Social Commentary · Reportage · Reviews · Promotional Writing · Polemic

10
Autobiography

Autobiography is writing in which someone attempts to explore and understand their own life. Usually the writer recounts all the significant events of their life from birth, sometimes even discussing their parents' and grandparents' lives where these have an influence on their own. The writer tries to select the key events, relationships, influences and achievements in their life – it would be very dull if every event was recorded. It is in the selection and interpretation of these things that the writer tries to explain their life.

Autobiographies are similar to two other types of writing – biographies and diaries (see chapters 4 and 8). Like biographies, they are accounts of individuals' lives. However, they are different because when writing about your own life you have unique access to everything that happened to you and therefore may be able to give a fuller picture – there is no need for speculation. Also, when writing about your own life you are likely to want to explain why you did things, possibly presenting your actions in a more positive light than someone else might.

Like diaries, autobiographies are accounts of a person's own experiences. However, diaries are usually written on a daily basis and therefore only try to understand events on a day to day basis. An autobiography will attempt to interpret a whole lifetime and will therefore examine the way that that life has been shaped.

1   Teenage memoirs

Read the following extracts from Nicholas Fisk's autobiography *Pig Ignorant*. The first extract is taken from the opening of the book, the second from a later section where he deals with his relationships with women.

(Some words are highlighted in the text. You will find further information about these words at the end of the passages.)

A   Here he comes! Walking towards us! I see him distinctly, clear as day! – No, wait. That's not true. I don't see him distinctly at all. *What we are looking at is a walking, talking, breathing, solid ghost. Not the ghost of someone dead: I am still alive. His flesh is my flesh, his heartbeat is my heartbeat.*

Because he is me. But so long ago …

Muvver's darling

He's sixteen and a half. He is about six feet tall, fair-haired, ginger-jacketed, grey-trousered, pink-faced. He parts his hair right over on one side, which gives him a schoolboyish look. He bites his nails but will soon give up *that*
10   schoolboy habit. For Nick, school is over! He's free! He's his real self at last!

Where is he? On the pavement of a middle-class London suburb. There are big, solid, Victorian houses on either side of the road. The front doors have stained-glass picture panes, solid brass door-knockers, glossy coats of dark paint.

The house that is his home has three and a half storeys of big rooms; and a full-size cellar. The whole tree-lined street is full of houses just like his, occupied by single families or even by a pair of old ladies like the Misses Albery next door.

These houses still stand but now they are split up into flats and flatlets. The
20   once almost-empty street is today lined, bumper to bumper, with cars.

Correction: not all these houses still stand. One was knocked out like a tooth. We will come to that later, when Britain's Prime Minister, Neville Chamberlain, bleats his Declaration of War; when Herr Hitler shrieks his defiance; when, night after night, the air-raid sirens wail and hoot like gibbons; and the full-size cellars come into their own.

A car is stopping outside No. 44, where his friend Peter lives. A Sunbeam saloon with a fawn body, black wings and a golden polished-brass radiator. Lucky old Peter, having a Pa with a car. Not many people have cars. The streets belong to errand boys, cats and dogs, horse-drawn milk floats, lorries
30   delivering Corona soft drinks, postmen with **conical** hats peaked in front and behind, and 'Wallsie' the Walls Ice-Cream man pedalling his freezer-box **trike**.

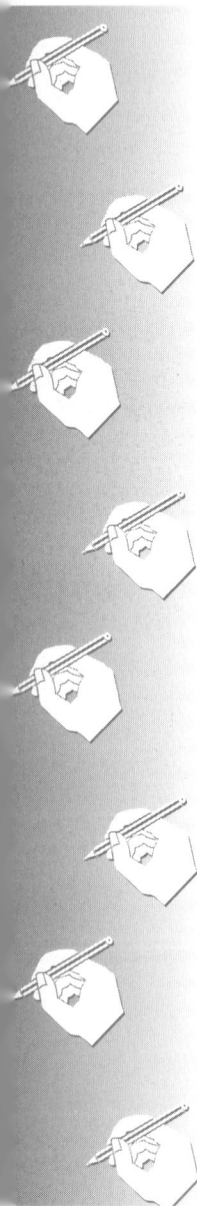

Wait! Suddenly Nick looks a little different. His shoulders are taut and hunched, his face is pinker, his footsteps seem to have a slight swaggering, 'don't-care' swing.

Why? There's that gang of whistling errand boys – four of them, doing circles on their heavy basket-carrying bikes. Nick's had trouble with errand boys. Errand boys gang up on you. You're riding your priceless, precious lightweight bike – Dunlop Sprite tyres, Simplex **derailleur**, three-speed gear,
40 dropped handlebars, rat-trap pedals; and all at once there they are, the whistling errand boys, several of them, with their bikes blocking the road and their mouths grinning and their dirty teeth showing.

"Ere, that's a noice boike! How much it corsst? Yer muvver buy it for yer?'

'Gotta lovely muvver, 'aven't chew? Fur coat an' all. No. 38, we seen 'er.'

'Gotta lovely sister, too. Gor …!'

The fat, worn tyres of their front wheels **butt** against the delicate, shiny front wheel of your lightweight. A dirty hand locks on to your clean handlebars. No escape.

'Yerr, real noice boike for a real noice boy. Muvver's boy!'

50 'Yerr, proper little muvver's darling! Real muvver's boy!'

But that happened years and years ago, when he was twelve or thirteen. Just a kid. He's not a kid any more. I mean, just look at him! That sports coat, those polished shoes with toe caps. And that pipe in his jacket pocket. A pipe, and an ounce of **Players Navy Mixture**! He gave up fags months ago. Christine said, 'I can't *stand* men smoking *ciggies*, they look sort of *nancy*. I mean, pipes, that's different. I like a man who smokes a pipe.' So he bought a pipe. Because of Christine. Christine Endersleigh.

B OPPOSITE SEX

Nick's pig ignorance embraces girls. Or rather, fails to embrace them. He cannot believe that any girl he admires could possibly admire him. And when, by chance, he finds himself in the right place at the right time with the right girl, he is baffled by her behaviour.

Rita, over there, standing alone by the bar of the Jive Club … Just look at her! The red of her lips, the flash of her eyes, the roll of her hips, the curve of her thighs (Nick often finds himself thinking in bad verse) – it isn't fair to make them like that, sugar and spice and all things nice, oh, you beautiful doll, you small, sweet beautiful doll, let me put my arms around you …

10 Some hope. She goes with Rex, a jazz journalist, an ancient man of thirty-something, a man who buys her things and takes her about in his Railton car. It isn't fair, it isn't fair.

Rita is bored out of her mind. She drinks a gin-and-something that Rex will pay for later. But Rex is late, Rita needs amusement. She flashes her eyes at Nick! And again! And she's smiling at him, a slight and secret smile, surely she can't mean …?

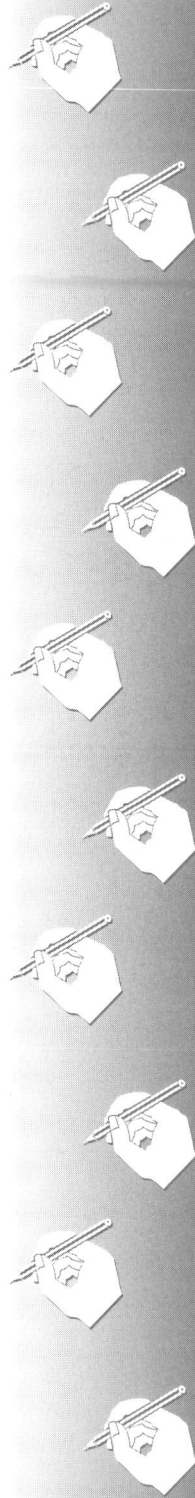

He goes across to her, smiles shakily and says, 'I say … hello … not many people here yet.' A brilliant opening **gambit**.

20   Yet she replies! She even smiles! 'You haven't got a drink,' she says. 'You're Nick, aren't you? Guitarist, right? Mmmm … I love guitar players.' Wisps of steam curl upwards from Nick's ears.

Rita has a new flat. It is near Notting Hill Gate. 'Oh, but I'd love you to see it,' she says. 'And bring your guitar, if you feel like playing. Do you like to play? I do.'

Then Rex is pushing through the crowd round the bar, grinning, slapping backs, catching the barman's eye, being Well Known and Popular. 'Cripes, kid,' he says to Rita, 'bloody BBC, they'll drive me mad, won't make up their minds. Who's this?'

'Nick,' says Rita. 'Nick Thing. Bloody BBC, poor you.'

30   Now their backs are turned to Nick. Rex's back is glaring **windowpane check** with padded shoulders. Hers is creamy, warm, silken flesh.

'Let's scram,' Rita says to Rex. 'Take me somewhere *interesting*.'

They go without a backward glance.

It isn't fair.

From N. Fisk, *Pig Ignorant*, Walker Books, 1992

DICTIONARY

conical cone-shaped
trike tricycle
derailleur the mechanism for changing gear
butt push
Players Navy Mixture a brand of tobacco
gambit tactic or strategy
windowpane check the large check pattern of his jacket

CLOSER READING

Questions 1–4 refer to extract A.

1 In the opening paragraph (lines 1–4), Fisk describes what it is like to write about one's own life. Pick out **three** key phrases which describe his feelings and explain what they mean.

2 Autobiographies are usually written in the *first person* ('I'). Why do you think Fisk has chosen to write about himself in the *third person* ('he')?

3 With what moment in his life has he chosen to begin his autobiography? (Look at lines 7–10.) Why is this an important stage in someone's life?

4 Look at the section beginning *'Wait! Suddenly ...'* (lines 33–57). Fisk describes how he feels when he sees the errand boys.
  - How did they treat him when he was younger?
  - How does he feel he had changed by the time he was 16?

5 Re-read extract B.

This extract describes his relationships with women. How does he show in this extract that at 16 he still felt and behaved like a boy, even though he would like to have been a man?

2 | Uncle Willie

The following extract is taken from *I Know Why the Caged Bird Sings* by Maya Angelou. The book, the first of five which make up her autobiography, describes her experiences as a young black child growing up in the American South in the 1930s. This extract describes someone who was one of the earliest influences in her life.

(Some words are highlighted in the text. You will find further information about these words at the end of the passage.)

When Bailey was six and I a year younger, we used to rattle off the times tables with the speed I was later to see Chinese children in San Francisco employ on their abacuses. Our summer-gray pot-bellied stove bloomed rosy red during winter, and became a severe disciplinarian threat if we were so foolish as to indulge in making mistakes.

Uncle Willie used to sit, like a giant black Z (he had been crippled as a child), and hear us **testify to** the Lafayette County Training Schools' abilities. His face pulled down on the left side, as if a pulley had been attached to his lower teeth, and his left hand was only a mite bigger than Bailey's, but on the
10   second mistake or on the third hesitation his big overgrown right hand would catch one of us behind the collar, and in the same moment would thrust the culprit toward the dull red heater which throbbed like a devil's toothache. We were never burned, although once I might have been when I was so terrified I tried to jump onto the stove to remove the possibility of its remaining a threat. Like most children, I thought if I could face the worst danger voluntarily, and *triumph*, I would forever have power over it. But in my case of sacrificial effort I was thwarted. Uncle Willie held tight to my dress and I only got close enough to smell the clean dry scent of hot iron. We learned the times tables without understanding their grand principle, simply
20   because we had the capacity and no alternative.

The tragedy of lameness seems so unfair to children that they are embarrassed in its presence. And they, **most recently off nature's mold**, sense that they have only narrowly missed being another of her jokes. In relief at

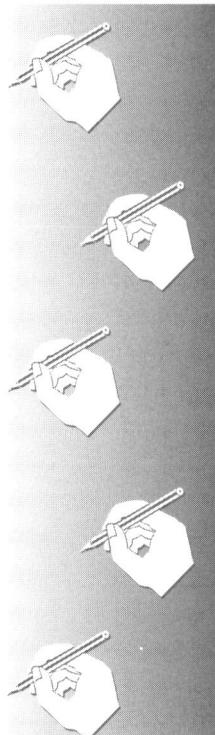

the narrow escape, they vent their emotions in impatience and criticism of the unlucky cripple.

Momma related times without end, and without any show of emotion, how Uncle Willie had been dropped when he was three years old by a woman who was minding him. She seemed to hold no rancour against the baby-sitter, nor for her just God who allowed the accident. She felt it necessary to explain
30 over and over again to those who knew the story by heart that he wasn't 'born that way'.

In our society, where two-legged, two-armed strong Black men were able at best to **eke out** only the necessities of life, Uncle Willie, with his starched shirts, shined shoes and shelves full of food, was the **whipping boy** and butt of jokes of the underemployed and underpaid. Fate not only disabled him but laid a **double-tiered barrier** in his path. He was also proud and sensitive. Therefore he couldn't pretend that he wasn't crippled, nor could he deceive himself that people were not repelled by his defect.

Only once in all the years of trying not to watch him, I saw him pretend to
40 himself and others that he wasn't lame.

Coming home from school one day I saw a dark car in our front yard. I rushed in to find a strange man and woman (Uncle Willie said later they were schoolteachers from Little Rock) drinking Dr Pepper in the cool of the Store. I sensed a wrongness around me, like an alarm clock that had gone off without being set.

I knew it couldn't be the strangers. Not frequently, but often enough, travellers pulled off the main road to buy tobacco or soft drinks in the only Negro store in Stamps. When I looked at Uncle Willie, I knew what was pulling my mind's coattails. He was standing erect behind the counter, not
50 leaning forward or resting on the small shelf that had been built for him. Erect. His eyes seemed to hold me with a mixture of threats and appeal.

I dutifully greeted the strangers and roamed my eyes around for his walking stick. It was nowhere to be seen. He said, 'Uh … this this … this … uh, my niece. She's … uh … just come from school.' Then to the couple – 'You know … how, uh, children are … th-th-these days … they play all d-d-day at school and c-c-can't wait to get home and pl-play some more.'

The people smiled, very friendly.

He added, 'Go on out and pl-play, Sister.'

The lady laughed in a soft Arkansas voice and said, 'Well, you know, Mr
60 Johnson, they say, you're only a child once. Have you children of your own?'

Uncle Willie looked at me with an impatience I hadn't seen in his face even when he took thirty minutes to loop the laces over his high-topped shoes. 'I … I thought I told you to go … go outside and play.'

Before I left I saw him lean back on the shelves of Garret Snuff, Prince Albert and Spark Plug chewing tobacco.

'No, ma'am … no ch-children and no wife.' He tried a laugh. 'I have an old m-m-mother and my brother's t-two children to l-look after.'

I didn't mind his using us to make himself look good. In fact, I would have pretended to be his daughter if he wanted me to. Not only did I not feel any

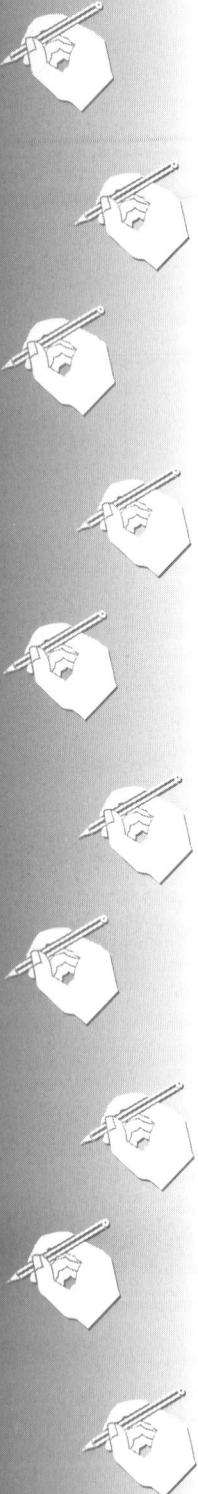

70 loyalty to my own father, I figured that if I had been Uncle Willie's child I would have received much better treatment.

The couple left after a few minutes, and from the back of the house I watched the red car scare chickens, raise dust and disappear toward Magnolia.

Uncle Willie was making his way down the long shadowed aisle between the shelves and the counter – hand over hand like a man climbing out of a dream. I stayed quiet and watched him lurch from one side, bumping to the other, until he reached the coal-oil tank. He put his hand behind that dark recess and took his cane in the strong fist and shifted his weight on the wooden support. He thought he had pulled it off.

80 I'll never know why it was important to him that the couple (he said later that he'd never seen them before) would take a picture of a whole Mr Johnson back to Little Rock.

He must have tired of being crippled, as prisoners tire of **penitentiary** bars and the guilty tire of blame. The high-topped shoes and the cane, his uncontrollable muscles and thick tongue, and the looks he suffered of either contempt or pity had simply worn him out, and for one afternoon, one part of an afternoon, he wanted no part of them.

I understood and felt closer to him at that moment than ever before or since.

From M. Angelou, *I Know Why the Caged Bird Sings*, Virago, 1969

DICTIONARY

testify to account for
most recently off nature's mould most recently born
eke out to make the best of
whipping boy scapegoat, person always blamed for things that go wrong
double-tiered barrier double block
penitentiary prison

CLOSER READING

1 There are two main characters in this extract – Maya Angelou as a child and Uncle Willie. Look at the way the young Angelou describes Uncle Willie's appearance. Write down key words and phrases from the second paragraph (lines 6–20). What makes you feel that this is written from the point of view of a child?

2 This extract is about learning lessons. The first lesson she learns is one that will be useful in school. Describe Uncle Willie's 'teaching methods'. What do you think of them? What does Angelou learn about education?

3 In the fourth and fifth paragraphs (lines 26–38) Angelou shows her sympathy for Uncle Willie. This balances out the negative impression we are given at the start of the extract. Explain why Angelou feels that he had a particularly hard life.

4 This incident when Willie pretended he had no disability was chosen by Angelou because it stood out in her memory.

   a Explain how she shows that, as a child, she couldn't always understand Willie's behaviour.

   b What valuable lesson did she learn from the incident?

   c How might the title of the book relate to Uncle Willie?

3 Earliest experiences

This extract is taken from the opening to *My Childhood* by Maxim Gorky, a writer who grew up in late 19th-century Russia. Gorky was a highly regarded figure in both literature and politics, and his writing was famous for its description of the daily life of ordinary people. This extract describes one of his earliest memories as a child, when he witnessed some very dramatic family events.

(Some words are highlighted in the text. You will find further information about these words at the end of the passage.)

Father lay on the floor, by the window of a small, darkened room, dressed in white, and looking terribly long. His feet were bare and his toes were strangely **splayed out**. His gentle fingers, now peacefully resting on his chest, were also distorted, and the black disks of copper coins firmly sealed his once shining eyes. His kind face had darkened and its nastily bared teeth frightened me.

Mother, half naked in a red skirt, was kneeling beside him combing his long soft hair down from the forehead to the nape of his neck with the black comb I loved to use as a saw for melon rinds. She kept muttering something in a
10 hoarse, deep voice. Her grey eyes were swollen and seemed to be dissolving in a flood of tears.

Grandmother was holding me by the hand. She was a fat, round woman with a large head, enormous eyes and a funny, puffy nose. All black and soft, she was terribly fascinating. She was crying as well, her voice pitched differently from Mother's but in a way that perfectly harmonized with it. Shaking all over, she pulled and pushed me over to Father. I stubbornly resisted and tried to hide behind her, for I felt frightened and out of place there.

I'd never seen grown-ups crying before and couldn't make head or tail of the words Grandmother repeated again and again:

20 'Say goodbye to your father. You won't ever see him again, dear. He died too young, before his time …'

I'd been very ill and had only just started walking again. During my illness – and this I remember very clearly – Father had lightheartedly played games with me and kept me amused. And then he suddenly disappeared and a new person, Grandmother, took his place.

'Where did you walk down from?' I asked her.

She answered: 'From up the river, from Nizhny. But I didn't walk – I came by boat! You can't walk on water! Enough of your questions now!'

This I found both funny and puzzling. Upstairs in the house lived two
30 bearded Persians, while the cellar was occupied by an old, **sallow-faced** Kalmuck who sold sheep-skins. I could slide down the banisters or somersault down if I fell off – that was an accepted fact. But what did water have to do with it?

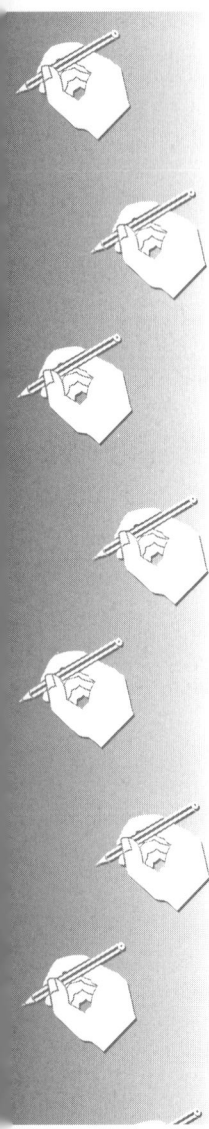

It all seemed wrong and **ludicrously** mixed up.

'And why should I be quiet?'

'Because you've always too much to say for yourself,' she said, laughing.

The way she spoke was warm, cheerful, rhythmical. We became firm friends from the very first day, and now I wanted both of us to get out of that room as soon as possible.

40 Mother's presence had a **stifling** effect on me and her tears and wailing awakened an unfamiliar feeling of anxiety in me. I'd never seen her like that before: she had always been stern with me and was given to few words. She was a clean, smooth, large person, like a horse. She had a firm body and extremely strong hands. And now she looked unpleasantly swollen and **dishevelled**. All her clothes were torn. Her hair, which was usually neatly combed into place like a large gay hat, was scattered over her bare shoulders, and hung over her face, and some of it, in the form of a large plait, dangled about, touching Father's sleeping face. For all the time I'd been standing in that room, not once did she so much as look at me, but just went on combing Father's hair, choking with tears and howling continually.

50 Some dark-skinned peasants and a local constable peered round the door. 'Hurry up and get him out of here!' the constable shouted angrily.

A dark shawl had been used as a curtain over the window and it swelled out like a sail. Once Father had taken me sailing and suddenly there was a thunderclap. Father had laughed, pressed me firmly between his knees and shouted: 'It's nothing, don't be frightened, Alex!'

Suddenly Mother lifted herself heavily from the floor, then fell down on her back, so that her hair brushed over the floor. Her unseeing, pale face had gone blue. Baring her teeth like Father's, she said in a terrifying voice: 'Close the door. Get Alexei out of here!'

60 Grandmother pushed me aside as she made for the door.

'Friends, don't be afraid,' she cried. 'Don't touch her. And go away, for Christ's sake! It's not cholera. She's in labour – please go away!'

I hid in a dim corner behind a trunk and looked from there at Mother writhing over the floor, groaning and gnashing her teeth, while Grandmother crawled round her and said in a gentle, joyful voice:

'In the name of the Son and the Holy Ghost! Try and bear the pain, Varyusha! Holy Mother of God who prays for us …'

I was frightened out of my wits: there they were rolling over the floor, knocking up against Father's body, groaning and shouting; he didn't move 70 and seemed to be laughing. This went on for a long time, and several times Mother got to her feet only to fall down again.

Grandmother kept rolling in and out of the room like a big black soft ball. Suddenly a baby cried in the darkness.

'God be praised!' said Grandmother. 'A boy!' And she lit a candle.

I must have dozed off in a corner as I don't remember anything more.

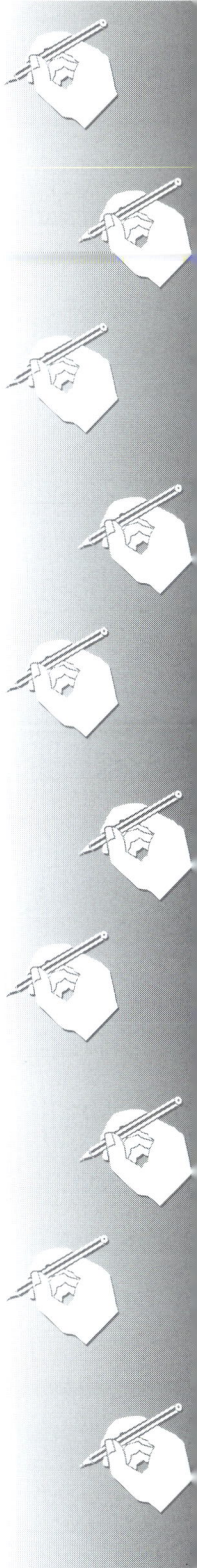

From M. Gorky, *My Childhood*, trans. R. Wilks, Penguin Books, 1966

DICTIONARY

splayed out spread out

sallow-faced unhealthily pale

ludicrously ridiculously

stifling suffocating

dishevelled untidy

CLOSER READING

1 Look at the very powerful descriptions of the three family members. Find phrases that describe what they looked like, how they behaved, how this was different from usual, and what feelings Gorky had about them. You may find it easier to set out your responses using the following table:

family member	appearance	behaviour	change from the usual	Gorky's feelings
Mother Father Grandmother				

2 What is the effect of the 'dark-skinned peasants' and the police officer in adding to the chaos of the scene?

3 Why does Gorky keep from the reader the fact that his mother was pregnant until near the end of the extract?

4 This is a very dramatic opening as it focuses on a child's first experiences of birth (a beginning) and death (an ending) simultaneously. How does Gorky convey a child's confusion and incomprehension in the face of these events?

4 Kidnapped

The following extracts are taken from *The Interesting Narrative of the Life of Olaudah Equiano, or Gustavas Vassa, the African*, published in 1791. Equiano's autobiography describes his experiences as a slave and then as a freed man, still suffering racial prejudice. It eventually became a bestseller. The first extract explains his feelings about writing an autobiography, and the second describes the time when he and his sister were kidnapped and his time of slavery began.

(Some words are highlighted in the text. You will find further information about these words at the end of the passages.)

A

I believe it is difficult for those who publish their own memoirs to escape the **imputation** of vanity; nor is this the only disadvantage under which they labour: it is also their misfortune, that what is uncommon is rarely, if ever, believed, and what is obvious we are apt to turn from with disgust and to charge the writer with impertinence. People generally think those memoirs only worthy to be read or remembered which abound in great or striking events; those, in short, which in a high degree excite either admiration or pity: all others they **consign to contempt and oblivion**. It is therefore, I confess, not a little hazardous in a private and **obscure** individual, and a

10   stranger too, thus to **solicit** the **indulgent** attention of the public; especially when I **own** I offer here the history of neither a saint, a hero, nor a tyrant. I believe there are few events in my life, which have not happened to many: it is true the incidents of it are numerous; and, did I consider myself an European, I might say my sufferings were great: but when I compare my lot with that of most of my countrymen, I regard myself as a particular favourite of Heaven, and acknowledge the mercies of **Providence** in every occurrence of my life. If, then, the following narrative does not appear sufficiently interesting to engage general attention, let my motive be some excuse for its publication. I am not so foolishly vain as to expect from it either immortality

20   or literary reputation. If it affords any satisfaction to my numerous friends, at whose request it was written, or in the smallest degree promotes the interests of humanity, the ends for which it was undertaken will be fully attained, and every wish of my heart gratified. Let it therefore be remembered, that, in wishing to avoid **censure**, I do not aspire to praise.

B

I hope the reader will not think I have trespassed on his patience in introducing myself to him, with some account of the manners and customs of my country. They had been implanted in me with great care, and made an impression on my mind, which time could not erase, and which all the adversity and variety of fortune I have experienced, served only to **rivet and record**; for, whether the love of one's country be real or imaginary, or a lesson of reason, or an instinct of nature, I still look back with pleasure on the first scenes of my life, though that pleasure has been for the most part mingled with sorrow.

10   I have already acquainted the reader with the time and place of my birth. My father, besides many slaves, had a numerous family, of which seven lived to grow up, including myself and a sister, who was the only daughter. As I was the youngest of the sons, I became, of course, the favourite with my mother, and was always with her; and she used to take particular pains to form my mind. I was trained from the earliest years in the art of war: my daily exercise was shooting and throwing javelins; and my mother adorned me with **emblems**, after the manner of our greatest warriors. In this way I grew up till I was turned the age of eleven, when an end was put to my happiness in the following manner: – generally when the grown people in the neighbourhood

20   were gone far in the fields to labour, the children assembled together in some

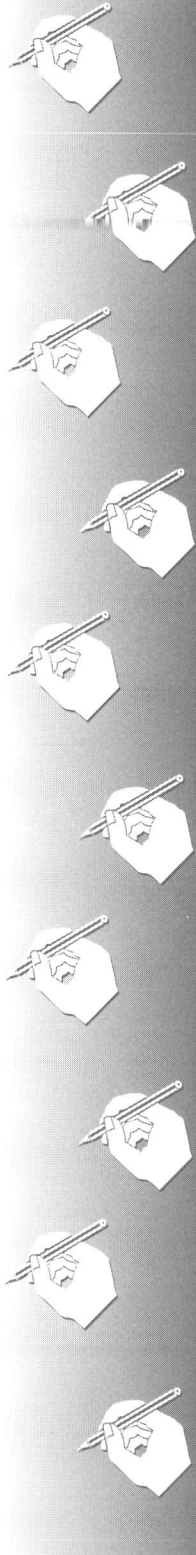

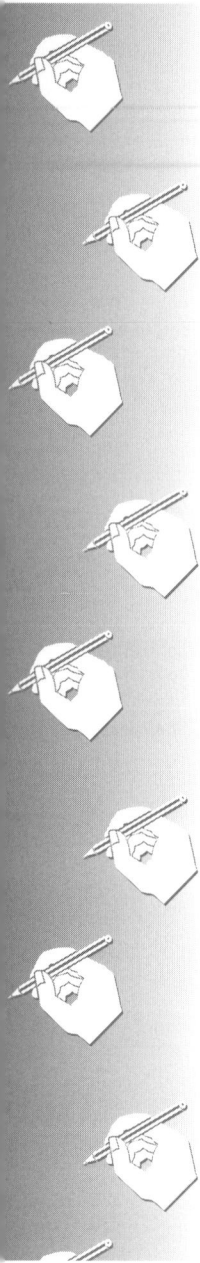

of the neighbouring premises to play; and commonly some of us used to get up a tree to look out for any **assailant**, or kidnapper, that might come upon us – for they sometimes took those opportunities of our parents' absence, to attack and carry off as many as they could seize. One day as I was watching at the top of a tree in our yard, I saw one of those people come into the yard of our next neighbour but one to kidnap, there being many **stout** young people in it. Immediately on this I gave the alarm of the rogue, and he was surrounded by the stoutest of them, who tangled him with cords, so that he could not escape till some of the grown people came and secured him. But,

30   alas! ere long it was my fate to be thus attacked, and to be carried off, when none of the grown people were nigh. One day, when all our people were gone out to their works as usual, and only I and my dear sister were left to mind the house, two men and a woman got over our walls, and in a moment seized us both, and, without giving us time to cry out, or make resistance, they **stopped our mouths**, and ran off with us into the nearest wood. Here they tied our hands, and continued to carry us as far as they could, till night came on, when we reached a small house, where the robbers halted for refreshment, and spent the night. We were then unbound, but were unable to take any food; and being quite overpowered by fatigue and grief, our only

40   relief was some sleep, which **allayed** our misfortune for a short time. The next morning we left the house, and continued travelling all the day. For a long time we had **kept the woods**, but at last we came into a road which I believed I knew. I had now some hopes of being delivered; for we had advanced but a little way before I discovered some people at a distance, on which I began to cry out for their assistance; but my cries had no other effect than to make them tie me faster and stop my mouth, and then they put me into a large sack. They also stopped my sister's mouth, and tied her hands; and in this manner we proceeded till we were out of sight of these people. When we went to rest the following night, they offered us some **victuals**, but

50   we refused it; and the only comfort we had was in being in one another's arms all that night, and bathing each other with our tears. But alas! we were soon deprived of even the small comfort of weeping together. The next day proved a day of greater sorrow than I had yet experienced; for my sister and I were then separated, while we lay clasped in each other's arms. It was in vain that we **besought** them not to part us; she was torn from me, and immediately carried away, while I was left in a state of distraction not to be described. I cried and grieved continually; and for several days did not eat any thing but what they forced into my mouth.

From O. Equiano, *The Interesting Narrative of the Life of Olaudah Equiano*, ed. N. Baym,
The Norton Anthology of American Literature, 1994

> **DICTIONARY**
>
> **imputation** accusation
> **consign to contempt and oblivion** forget about and treat as worthless
> **obscure** unknown
> **solicit** request
> **indulgent** sympathetic
> **own** acknowledge, admit
> **Providence** God's care
> **censure** disapproval

rivet and record fix very firmly

emblems trophies

assailant attacker

stout strong

stopped our mouths put a hand over our mouths to stop us making a noise

allayed eased

kept the woods stayed in the woods (to keep hidden)

victuals food

besought pleaded with

DICTIONARY

CLOSER READING

Questions 1–2 refer to extract A.

1 In this extract Equiano describes the concerns he had when he was putting together his autobiography.

  a What are the *general* problems that he claims all autobiographers face?

  b What are the *specific* problems he faced as a result of who he is?

2 Why did he write his autobiography despite these problems?

Questions 3–4 refer to extract B.

3 What does Equiano think have been the greatest influences on his life?

4 The episode he describes is a very traumatic one. Like all the writers in this section, he has explored a crucial event in his life in vivid detail.

- Why do you think he describes the event in so much detail?
- What effect does it have on you as the reader?

FURTHER ACTIVITIES

The following are all activities which aim to guide you in your own autobiographical writing. You could choose to focus on one in particular, or use all of them to produce a sustained autobiographical piece of writing.

1 Select the most important events in your life so far. The following are suggestions of some of the things that you may choose to focus on:

- beginnings, for example births, a new school, job, home or friendship;
- endings, for example leaving primary school, the end of a friendship, the death of someone close;
- significant events, for example birthdays, weddings, winning, losing, accidents, holidays.

It may be helpful to produce a time-line marking the main events of your life so far. There is an example of one below.

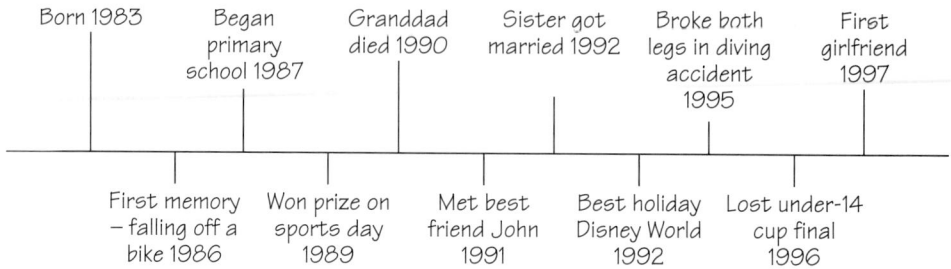

Born 1983	Began primary school 1987	Granddad died 1990	Sister got married 1992	Broke both legs in diving accident 1995	First girlfriend 1997

First memory – falling off a bike 1986	Won prize on sports day 1989	Met best friend John 1991	Best holiday Disney World 1992	Lost under-14 cup final 1996

Choose the event or events that you remember most clearly, and that would be interesting for someone else to read. You need to describe the event or events in detail to hold the reader's attention. You should describe the following things:

- what actually happened;
- where it happened;
- the people involved, including their behaviour;
- your feelings at the time;
- your feelings about the event now;
- why the event was important to you.

2 Many autobiographers focus on the important people in their life. They then describe events involving these people which demonstrate something about their character.

List the people who are or have been important in your life. Choose one that you would like to write about and brainstorm (using a spider diagram) everything you know about them.

Selecting from your notes, produce a piece of writing including the following things:

- one or two incidents involving this person which you witnessed personally and which show something important about them;
- your feelings at the time of the events and your feelings now;
- the influence this person has had on you (good or bad).

3 Most autobiographers include some of their earliest memories. These may not always be important in themselves, but are fascinating because they are the first events of their lives that they can remember.

- This activity should be carried out in pairs. But first, on your own, write down the things you remember that happened before you were seven. (Don't write them out in full; use headings such as 'Fell off my bike' or 'Ill with measles'.)
- Now in pairs, take turns to describe to each other your earliest memories, including as much detail as possible.

- The partner who is listening should ask questions to help you include the detail a reader would need if your memories were to be written down.
- Now write about your very earliest memories – they may be a mixture of 'snapshots' and detailed accounts. When describing these memories, try to show how you viewed the events as a small child and how you now view them as a teenager.

4 Write a piece entitled 'Regrets', in which you describe moments in your life which you wish could have turned out differently. You could look at occasions when you or someone else made a mistake or behaved badly. Or you could describe something that happened due to bad luck or unfortunate circumstances.

In your piece you should aim to describe:

- what happened;
- what were the causes;
- what your feelings were;
- how things could have turned out differently;
- what you learned from the occasion.

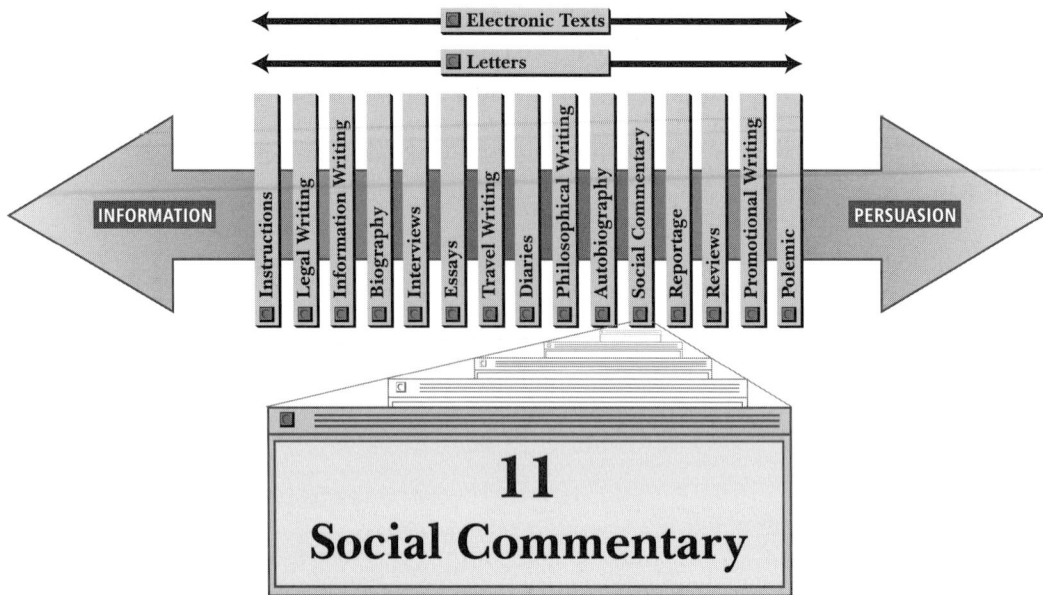

```
◄────────────■ Electronic Texts ■────────────►
◄────────────■ Letters ■────────────►
```

INFORMATION — Instructions · Legal Writing · Information Writing · Biography · Interviews · Essays · Travel Writing · Diaries · Philosophical Writing · Autobiography · Social Commentary · Reportage · Reviews · Promotional Writing · Polemic — PERSUASION

11
Social Commentary

Throughout the ages people have expressed their views about their society. This often starts with observations about what they see around them, and then develops into a challenge to the way things are in the belief that their society can be improved. This type of writing can range over a whole variety of issues, including the state of the environment, relationships between adults and teenagers or men and women, the problems faced by the unemployed, the effects of AIDS and drug abuse on society and the significance of the information super-highway. Some issues, such as the revolution in information technology, are new, while others, such as the problem of poverty and relationships between men and women, are returned to by each generation.

This type of writing, therefore, expresses feelings and opinions on those things that directly affect our day to day lives. It is about people trying to understand what and who influences their quality of life and their behaviour, as well as about the contribution they can make to changing those influences through writing it down and bringing the issue to the attention of as many people as possible.

If you look at the continuum at the top of this page, you can see that this type of writing conveys information about a subject, but usually so that it persuades its reader that there are alternatives to the ways in which people currently conduct their lives. If a writer wants to persuade people, they need to think of the ways in which they write as well as what they write. In this chapter you will be looking at how some writers have tried to gain the interest of their readers so that they can influence their views.

1 | Eating disorders

The following passage, written by a teenage girl, looks at how the pressures of society can cause some teenagers, particularly girls, to suffer serious physical and emotional damage. It presents one view on what is a very complex issue.

(Some words are highlighted in the text. You will find further information about these words at the end of the passage.)

IT is one of the most exploited products on the market. Millions of pounds are made from it each week. IT has possibly caused more tragedies than any other product. IT is Slimming …

'I want to lose weight for Summer, something simple but with quick results.' The girl who made this statement to her friend was unknowingly stepping into danger when she decided to go on a fasting diet. A fasting diet is when you stop eating food for several days, then, drinking only the minimum of liquids, you eat a small amount of food. This is carried on until you have lost the required amount of weight. The girl eventually found that when she
10   started to eat food again, after losing over two stone in under two months, she was vomiting violently after each meal. She couldn't control her weight loss, she was feeling constantly light-headed, her periods were irregular, and after a while she couldn't bear to look at food.

Luckily for her, her mother insisted on her going to the doctor. He admitted her into hospital where they **drop fed her**. It sounds pretty gruesome but after a few weeks she was of normal, healthy weight again. Their therapists soon had her muscles toned up and the rest did her good.

The story I've just told you is a happy ending one. It's a pity that all anorexic girls' stories can't end like it. Some girls can't speak to their parents. They
20   can't relate, for one reason or another. The girls keep their complaint hidden and bluff it over when somebody enquires. This is when trouble begins. Anorexia somehow can affect the person's way of thinking. A severely underweight girl could look in the mirror and see a grossly overweight reflection.

When you diet to extreme extents you are literally taking your life into your own hands. But why do we diet? A stroll down the High Street will reveal chemists and beauty shops packed with **appetite suppressers** and wonder potions promising weight loss; clothes shops bulging with lovely styled fashion clothes but all in tiny sizes; tight fitted 'second skin' jeans in various bright
30   colours, bill board posters advertising the so-called 'ideal woman'. How many times have you seen a group of teenage boys splitting their sides laughing at a fat woman struggling with heavy shopping bags? Or a man literally undressing a pretty girl with his eyes? Plenty, I can bet.

Women, girls, females alike have been brainwashed, through the media and health fanatics, into thinking that 'thin is beautiful and fat is to be laughed

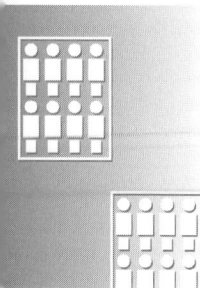

at'. It's very sad indeed. Everybody has a picture in their mind's eye of how they want their bodies to look, an image if you want. Some don't achieve that image, but stay contented and happy with life. Some don't achieve it and stay miserable and suicidal. Others do, and decide they were happier to begin
40   with, and a minority go over the top and end up anorexic.

Which one are you? What is your image? Do you want to be blonde and tall or brunette and chubby? Are you satisfied with your life?

From E. D. Vincent, 'Slimming', in *True to Life Writings by Young Women*, ed. S. Hemmings, Sheba Feminist Publishers, 1966

DICTIONARY

drop fed her fed her through a tube into a vein

appetite suppressers drugs that remove feelings of hunger

CLOSER READING

1 The girl described at the beginning of the extract goes on a 'fasting diet'. What were the effects of this (lines 4–13)?

2 Why is the girl described as 'lucky' (lines 14–24)?

3 List the causes of anorexia given by the writer (lines 25–40). Would you add any to this list?

4 Copy and complete the grid below. For each of the items in the left-hand column you need to find a phrase or sentence from the text.

a) the danger of slimming	
b) the worst effects of becoming anorexic	
c) the girl's experience in hospital	
d) the mental condition of someone with anorexia	
e) the main causes of anorexia	
f) the view some boys have of what a young woman should look like	

Using this grid, write about whether you agree with the writer and explain your own views about the subject of weight.

2 | Children of the Eighties

This is an extract from an article, written by Linda Grant, that appeared in the *Guardian* newspaper. It looks at the lives of a group of teenagers, using this information to make general comments about how teenage life has changed over the last forty years

(Some words are highlighted in the text. You will find further information about these words at the end of the passage.)

The selected 10 come into the classroom and ask urgently, 'Miss, miss, is it all right to sit on the desks?' From **time immemorial** this has been the true cool way for a schoolchild to demonstrate her or his sophistication, by breaking ranks from the orderly rows of daily school life. I say yes, it's okay, and they sit on the desks, dead grown-up. Feet dangling, nine pairs of trainers and one set of Doc Martens wave about before my eyes. The girl in the **clodhoppers** is not a lone **individualist**; her parents have never allowed her to wear trainers and, as a result, she moves in her own, externally enforced world of old-for-her-age hipness. On their chests are 10 'tops'

10 (that's the right word), each bearing a logo: Blue Jeans, Giorgio, Levi, Timberland, Aramis, Official Bison. What would happen if you didn't have a logo on your clothes? Don't ask. And if it was the wrong logo? Well, there are worse things that could happen to you. Like what? You could have Fred and Rosemary West for your Mum and Dad.

Here are ten 12- and 13-year-olds at Highgate Wood Comprehensive in north London. They come from Finsbury Park and Hornsey and Crouch End and Wood Green. The word Highgate may be in the school's name but Highgate residents don't, on the whole, send their children to the local state comprehensives. I ask them what they wanted for Christmas. These are their

20 lists: 1. Leather jacket, Sony Playstation, money. 2. Bike, Sony Playstation. 3. Money, clothes. 4. 'Just money because then you can get what you want.' 5. Jewellery, money, clothes. 6. Money, camera with a zoom lens. 7. Clothes. 8. Jewellery, clothes. 9. Money, a computer. 10. Music, tapes, CDs.

They like: swing, jungle, hip-hop, soul, indie, garage, house, socca and Brit pop. Someone tentatively suggests that he likes Oasis but is barracked. You aren't allowed to like Oasis. This, I am later told, is because the majority of kids in the class are Rudes. You can be a Rude or a Grunge or an Independent in-betweeny. Their pocket money runs at between £2.50 and £5 a week. They read the *Sun*, the *Express*, the *Mirror* and *Melody Maker*. They

30 watch on TV: The *X Files*, *Fresh Prince Of Bel Air*, *Heartbreak High*, *Beverly Hills 90210* and *EastEnders*. The average age at which they first knew about sex was six; about Aids, a couple of years later. Tactfully, I don't ask them if they have taken drugs, just if they would know where to get hold of them. 'Ye-es' they cry in **derision**.

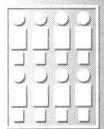

We move on down through my list of questions. What foreign holidays have you had? 1. France, Belgium, USA. 2. South Africa. 3. Cyprus and Spain. 4. Trinidad. 5. Canada, Canaries, USA, Lanzarotte, Majorca, Turkey. 6. USA, Spain, France, Italy, Greece, Ireland. 7. Greece, Cyprus, USA, France. 8. Trinidad and Canada. 9. Cyprus, France, Germany, Italy. (Their teacher, **40** Karen Field, will later listen in awe as I read this list. 'When I was a child,' she says, 'holidays were a caravan in Devon.') Five have their own PC, four have divorced or separated parents. All of them have seen some kind of pornography.

When I was their age, back during the **Palaeolithic Era**, a group of us gathered at a bus stop and a girl said: 'Only six months ago I still thought that a girl just had to sleep in the same bed as a boy she'd get pregnant.' So we all laughed. Nervously. And went home and went to bed and stared out into the darkness, never connecting those dutifully-copied **anatomical diagrams** of the reproductive cycles of fruit flies with our own flushed faces as **50** we watched the Rolling Stones on *Top Of The Pops*. I had been abroad once, to Ostend, had never heard of drugs or pornography or the word f*** and I did not know anyone whose parents were divorced. I wanted a framed ballet picture for Christmas to hang on my bedroom wall.

We have never seen anything like them before, the teens and pre-teens of today, if that's what they still are. If the Fifties created the teenager, the Nineties seems to have destroyed that infant **phenomenon**. A spokesman at Sony confirms that, apart from computer games, it does not create and market electronic products specifically for teenagers. Teenagers want what their parents have, at prices that have nothing to do with what their pocket **60** money can buy – or even within the long-term range of pocket money to save for – and they make their choices with advanced adult consumer skills. You can barely distinguish their Christmas lists from those of their twentysomething older brothers and sisters. Every year the ad agency J Walter Thompson interviews a panel of children aged between four and 13. For the first time this year clothes topped the Christmas present list for all ages and both sexes.

From L. Grant, 'Children of the Eighties', *The Guardian*, 6 Jan 1966

DICTIONARY

time immemorial ancient times

clodhoppers large, heavy boots (i.e. the Doc Martens)

individualist someone with their own opinions

derision mockery

Palaeolithic Era ancient time

anatomical diagrams drawings of bodies

phenomenon type

C LOSER READING

1 The children's experiences and tastes are listed in this extract.

   a Write your own lists in the same areas:
   - fashion – your favourite clothes
   - Christmas presents
   - musical tastes
   - holidays you have been on
   - television programmes.

   b Are these similar to those in the passage?

   c Compare your lists with those of a friend and others in the class. Are they quite similar? If so, why do you think this is? Is it possible to divide the class into different 'groups' with different tastes?

2 What problems do these children face? Look at the pressures on them and the things that they might worry about.

3 a How are the children's experiences different from the writer's teenage years?

   b How do your experiences differ from your parents'? Think of the times when they compare their lives as young people with yours.

4 Look at the final paragraph (lines 54–66). Why does the writer feel that children today miss out on childhood?

5 What do you think is the writer's attitude towards teenage life today? Find examples, looking at what she says and how she says it.

3 Violence in society

The following passage is an extract from 'Violent Anxiety', an article by the same author as Text no. 2. It claims that we live in a society that is obsessed with violence, and questions some of the attitudes that people have.

(Some words are highlighted in the text. You will find further information about these words at the end of the passage.)

I want to ask whether it is true that there is more violence in society than there used to be, or if it is just that everyone feels this to be the case. Sections of the media feed the idea that there once was a golden age which was crime-free, when you could go down to your local and leave the back door open and when you got home everything was just as you left it. It is probably true that there was far less burglary and car theft during the Thirties and Forties because there was far less to nick, particularly from the homes of the poor, whereas nowadays a thief can more or less rely on there being a colour television anywhere he (or, extremely rarely, she) breaks into.

10   But we are not the first generation to be fearful of walking the streets. A very early moral panic about violence occurred in the 1860s when there was an outbreak of **garrotting**. The population of the **metropolis** lived in so much terror that advertisements began to appear for special anti-garrotting collars. 'Garrotting is the talk of the town, **penal jurisprudence** the favourite after-dinner topic,' a journalist wrote in the *Illustrated London News* for November 29, 1862. Were the men and women of the 1860s right to believe that there was more violent crime about then than in the past? Actually, yes. The highest ever recorded figure for homicide occurred in 1865 – 414 or 19.6 per million of the British population, compared with the all-time low in

20   1918, when murders accounted for only 6.1 per million, perhaps because those with a **penchant** for killing had signed up early for the mass **carnage** and were already dead. Homicide rates were low between the wars and during the Fifties, and did not begin to rise until the Seventies, doing so slowly, rather than alarmingly, reaching 14.1 per thousand of the population in 1994, the last year for which the Home Office has figures. So yes, there is more violent crime now than there has been in living memory, though whether we are right to panic is another matter.

What was the actual number of murders in 1994? It was 729. That is how many people were murdered in England and Wales. It isn't a lot. What is the

30   likelihood of a reader of this sentence having known anyone who has been murdered? How many people do you know who know someone who has murdered? On the whole, murder barely touches our lives, like the jackpot on the National Lottery. The two are similar in their randomness: it could be you. But it's unlikely.

So why are we so worried, and who is doing the worrying? We can correctly deduce that we worry more about crime because we are more aware of it. The part of London in which I live has a local paper which displays a **hoarding** outside all the local newsagents. Virtually every single week the headline is a crime story – a rape, a mugging, an armed robbery or a murder – even when

40   that story may be found in the actual paper buried away in one paragraph at the bottom of page two. A friend who has lived in the area longer than I have pointed out that, ten years ago, week after week the hoarding displayed 'loony left' local government stories. Perhaps they became more responsible, perhaps the loony left story went out of fashion. **Unerringly**, the editors knew that beneath this brief interest in how ratepayers' money was being spent was a reserve of **preoccupation** with crime that could always be tapped when nothing else very interesting was going on. So are the media to blame for **exacerbating** our fear of crime? If so, newspaper bosses have a great deal of **previous**. In 1866, 50 per cent of the content of a London newspaper

50   called *Lloyd's Weekly News* dealt with crime. Crime stories are those which carry a high 'through reading score', that is, readers carry on to the end rather than skimming the first paragraph. So editors are not exactly force-feeding us material we would rather run away from.

I want to suggest that violence forms our greatest anxiety now because the crimes we currently fear strike at the heart of our private lives. Unlike the anxiety of the Victorians, which was directed to street crime, we fear what might happen in the **sanctuary** of our own homes. A number of murders in the past quarter of a century have had a particular and peculiar effect on **the**

public psyche. They fall into three categories: the murder of women, the
60 murder of children and murders by children. I do not believe that the
population is **unduly exercised** by fatalities outside pubs in which both parties
are drunk, or by gangland shootings between different Yardie factions.
There have always been gangsters at the movies; we know all about them.
They are organised. Let them shoot each other to death if they like, as in the
last scene of *Reservoir Dogs* (a Tarantino film I did laugh at) in which a circle
of hoodlums each has a gun pointed at another's head. They all fire
simultaneously and that's the end of them. Rather quarrelsome gangsters
than lone woman-hating psychos of whom the neighbours ritually say, 'he
kept himself to himself'.

From L. Grant, 'Violent Anxiety', *The Guardian*, 28 Sept 1996

DICTIONARY

garrotting strangling, usually using an iron collar
metropolis city, i.e. London
penal jurisprudence the branch of law dealing with punishment
penchant tendency, liking
carnage slaughter
hoarding display board
Unerringly making no mistake
preoccupation obsession
exacerbating making more intense
previous previous convictions
sanctuary safety
the public psyche the public's mental state
unduly exercised particularly concerned

CLOSER READING

1 a The opening sentence sets up the argument that the piece is going to debate.
   What is the argument going to be about?

  b The writer then looks at two different views of the past in the first two
    paragraphs of the extract (lines 1–27). Describe these two views.

2 Find all the statistics used by the writer.
  • How do these statistics make the argument sound more convincing?
  • Could any of them be given a different interpretation from the writer's?

3 In the third paragraph (lines 28–34), the writer stresses that the murder rate in
  Britain is very low. Find evidence to show that she does this by:
  • a direct appeal to the reader's experience;
  • a comparison with another national 'obsession'.

4 In the fourth paragraph (lines 35–53) she uses anecdotal evidence (personal
  experience rather than large-scale research) to support her argument.
  • What point is she making?
  • Is this use of anecdotes effective in an argument?

5 The last paragraph (lines 54–69) contains the writer's opinion on what she feels is
  the real reason for the increase in our fear of violence. What is it?

4 The Condition of the Working Class in England

This is a passage from a book published in 1845. It was written by a German called Friedrich Engels after a long visit to England. During this visit he toured round the major cities of Britain, looking at the effects of the Industrial Revolution on the poorest people. This passage describes the living conditions of the poor in London, using the reports of various court cases.

(Some words are highlighted in the text. You will find further information about these words at the end of the passage.)

On the occasion of an **inquest** held on 14 November 1843 by Mr Carter, **coroner** for Surrey, upon the body of Ann Galway, aged 45 years, the newspapers related the following **particulars** concerning the deceased: She had lived at No. 3 White Lion Court, Bermondsey Street, London, with her husband and a 19-year-old son in a little room, in which neither a bedstead nor any other furniture was to be seen. She lay dead beside her son upon a heap of feathers which were scattered over her almost naked body, there being neither sheet nor coverlet. The feathers stuck so fast over the whole body that the physician could not examine the corpse until it was cleansed,
10 and then found it starved and scarred from the bites of vermin. Part of the floor of the room was torn up, and the hole used by the family as a **privy**.

On Monday, 15 January 1844 two boys were brought before the police magistrate because, being in a starving condition, they had stolen and immediately devoured a half-cooked calf's foot from a shop. The magistrate felt called upon to investigate the case further, and received the following details from the policeman: The mother of the two boys was the widow of an ex-soldier, afterwards policeman, and had had a very hard time since the death of her husband, to provide for her nine children. She lived at No. 2 Pool's Place, Quaker Court, Spitalfields, in the utmost poverty. When the
20 policeman came to her, he found her with six of her children literally huddled together in a little back room, with no furniture but two old **rush-bottomed chairs** with the seats gone, a small table with two legs broken, a broken cup, and a small dish. On the **hearth** was scarcely a spark of fire, and in one corner lay as many old rags as would fill a woman's apron, which served the whole family as a bed. For bed clothing they had only their scanty day clothing. The poor woman told him that she had been forced to sell her bedstead the year before to buy food. Her bedding she had pawned with the **victualler** for food. In short, everything had gone for food. The magistrate ordered the woman a considerable provision from the poor-box.

30 In February 1844 Theresa Bishop, a widow 60 years old, was recommended, with her sick daughter, aged 26, to the compassion of the police magistrate in Marlborough Street. She lived at No. 5 Brown Street, Grosvenor Square, in a small back room no larger than a closet, in which there was not one single piece of furniture. In one corner lay some rags upon which both slept;

a chest served as table and chair. The mother earned a little by **charring**. The owner of the house said that they had lived in this way since May 1843, had gradually sold or **pawned** everything that they had, and had still never paid any rent. The magistrate assigned them £1 from the poor-box.

40 I am far from asserting that *all* London working people live in such want as the **foregoing** three families. I know very well that ten are somewhat better off, where one is so totally trodden under foot by society; but I assert that thousands of industrious and worthy people – far worthier and more to be respected than all the rich of London – do find themselves in a condition unworthy of human beings; and that every **proletarian**, everyone, without exception, is exposed to a similar fate without any fault of his own and in spite of every possible effort.

But in spite of all this, they who have some kind of a shelter are fortunate, fortunate in comparison with the utterly homeless. In London 50,000 human beings get up every morning, not knowing where they are to lay their heads
50 that night. The luckiest of this multitude, those who succeed in keeping a penny or two until evening, enter a lodging-house, such as abound in every great city, where they find a bed. But what a bed! These houses are filled with beds from cellar to **garret**, four, five, six beds in a room; as many as can be crowded in. Into every bed four, five, or six human beings are piled, as many as can be packed in, sick and well, young and old, drunk and sober, men and women, just as they come, **indiscriminately**. Then come strife, blows, wounds, or, if these bedfellows agree, so much the worse; thefts are arranged and things done which our language, grown more humane than our deeds, refuses to record.

From F. Engels, *The Condition of the Working Class in England*,
trans. F. Kelley-Wischnewtsky, Penguin, 1993

DICTIONARY

inquest official investigation of a death

coroner the official in charge of an inquest

particulars details

privy toilet

rush-bottomed chairs chairs with seats made from rushes

hearth the floor of a fireplace

victualler food supplier

charring house cleaning

pawned gave belongings in exchange for money

foregoing mentioned earlier

proletarian working-class person

garret attic

indiscriminately regardless of who they were

CLOSER READING

1 Engels quotes from various court cases or coroner reports, giving precise details of times, places and events. How does this make the picture painted more convincing?

2 Look at the ages and sexes of the people described in the first three paragraphs (lines 1–38). What point might Engels be making by choosing this selection of people?

3 The first three paragraphs are harrowing descriptions of the conditions in which these people lived.

   a Summarise what each of these cases has in common.

   b In these paragraphs, Engels does not state directly his view of what is described. Instead, he picks out what he thinks are the most important details, showing us rather than telling us.

   Do you think this method is effective? Give reasons for you answer.

4 In the fourth paragraph (lines 39–46) Engels does begin to tell us his views.

   • What is his view of the people he has described?

   • Why does this make their poverty all the worse?

5 The final paragraph (lines 47–59) is effective because it takes us one step further than we imagined: there are people who are even worse off than the cases described. In what ways do they suffer more?

FURTHER ACTIVITIES

1 The first two passages in this chapter point to the influence of the media on our lives. One area of our lives that might be influenced is our view of men and women. The following activity should be carried out in groups.

Collect together a range of newspapers and magazines – the more you have, the easier it will be to carry out the task!

• Find and cut out all the pictures of men and women.

• Find and cut out all the words that are used in headlines that describe men or women, for example 'Sexy Samantha' or 'Hunk saves dog from drowning'.

• When you have done this, see if you can discover any pattern in the appearances of the people who feature most commonly in your selection. Then, create two collages, one with images of men and one with images of women.

• Now look for patterns in the words used to describe men and women. Add these to the collage, matching them with the images wherever possible.

• Present your collages to the rest of the class, explaining what you think they show about society's view of the ideal man and woman.

2 The piece of writing on slimming (Text no. 1) has a particular structure which makes it effective.

- It has a dramatic opening which gains the reader's interest through the air of mystery over what 'IT' is, and through the use of high numbers ('millions') and words such as 'most' and 'more', which help to make this sound the most important issue of the moment.
- The story of a particular girl helps to bring home how dieting affects people in every day life. Because the reader feels sympathy for the girl, they are more likely to feel sympathy for the issue the writer is addressing. Also, the list of the things she suffers makes the reader feel the horror of the illness.
- This story, bad as it is, has a happy ending – others are much worse. This makes the reader feel that this is a common problem. We are left to imagine for ourselves the desperate position of girls with unsupportive parents.
- The last two paragraphs (lines 34–42) examine the causes of the problems. These opinions are presented as facts and, following a story which has gained the reader's sympathy, they seem difficult to contradict.

Choose another aspect of the relationship between men and women which you find interesting. You could, for example, look at the kind of jobs men and women can and should do, or the responsibilities that men and women have for their children. Whatever you choose, you should try to use the same structure as the writer of the piece on slimming.

3 All the pieces in this chapter use evidence to support their views, whether this is in the form of statistics, news reports or personal experiences. The writers do this to make their arguments more interesting and convincing.

In pairs, you are going to produce a speech on a topic which you feel strongly about – a number of subjects are mentioned in the introduction to this chapter which you could choose from. When you have made a decision about your subject, collect as much evidence as possible to support your views. Alternatively, you could keep an open mind and base your views on what your research has shown (a much more honest approach!).

There are a number of places which you can go to for evidence, depending on your subject. Some suggestions are:

- reference books and other non-fiction in your school or local library;
- the media: newspapers, magazines, television etc.;
- IT: CD-ROM or the Internet;
- other people: experts, people with personal experiences, organisations related to your subject;
- your own questionnaire;
- your own personal experiences!

From this research you should select the evidence that is likely to have the greatest impact on your listeners. For example, Engels (Text no. 4) chose to describe only those cases that would make his point effectively. When writing the speech you could use the structure described in Activity 2 – this would help to make your speech hard-hitting.

Now think about how you will present your speech as a pair. Here are some suggestions:

- Alternate who is speaking frequently during the speech – the change and variety in voice helps to keep your audience interested.
- Take opposing views, each giving a different side of the argument.
- Role play scenes that are examples of the points you are trying to get across – this would be like using anecdotes in a piece of writing.

4 Many writers feel that they can comment best on their society through describing it in detail rather than just stating their views. In this way they can appeal to the reader's feelings and imagination as well as to their minds. They *show* rather than *tell* their message.

This exercise is best done individually, although it could be done with a close friend with whom you share similar ideas and experiences. Focus on an issue that affects you personally on a day to day basis. It might be one of the following:

- your relationship with your parents or teachers
- pressures of schoolwork
- bullying
- society's view of teenagers
- peer pressure – to do things that you would rather not do
- the lack of things to do for young people.

When you have chosen your issue, describe *in detail* your experiences – things that have happened to you or things that you have seen. These descriptions should be so colourful that they make your point for you. You should save any direct expression of your views for the final paragraph.

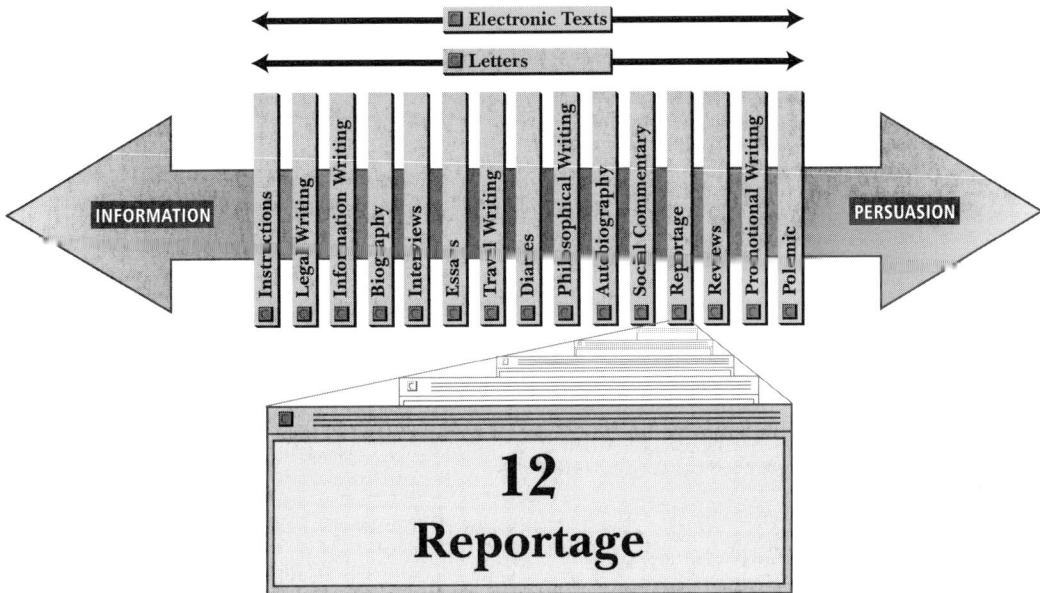

Electronic Texts
Letters

INFORMATION — Instructions · Legal Writing · Information Writing · Biography · Interviews · Essays · Travel Writing · Diaries · Philosophical Writing · Autobiography · Social Commentary · Reportage · Reviews · Promotional Writing · Polemic — PERSUASION

12
Reportage

This type of writing is about recording significant events in the world as they happen. It is now most commonly found in newspapers, although people have always felt the need to write down their view of events as they saw them. The aspect of reportage that distinguishes it from other types of writing is its sense of immediacy: the reader feels that they are reliving the event as it is described. This is usually because the writer was an eye-witness who was either a close observer or a participant.

This writing has similarities with other types in this book. The event being described by the 'reporter' often happens in different parts of the world and therefore there is a cross-over with travel writing (see pages 77–88) as the writer tries to explain events clearly to their home audience. Much reportage comes in the form of diaries (see pages 89–100), particularly when the diarist is keen to record events happening outside their own personal life (compare Samuel Pepys, writing in the 'Diaries' chapter). Some reporters also have an element of social commentary (see pages 128–140) in that they have an opinion about what they describe.

The main purpose of reportage is to paint a clear picture for the reader, and to do this it must describe the event with an eye for detail. The reader must remember, however, that the writer may have selected details that reflect their own views about what they have observed.

1 Evacuation

The following passage, written by a journalist called Hilde Marchant, describes a group of London children being sent to the countryside at the beginning of the Second World War. This was to protect them from the air-raids that were expected.

(Some words are highlighted in the text. You will find further information about these words at the end of the passage.)

It was not until Friday morning, September 1st, that I really took the sharp, agonised breath of war. That day it began, in a slum in London.

The office had told me to cover the evacuation of some of London's schoolchildren. There had been great preparations for the scheme – preparations that raised strong criticism. Evacuation would split the British home, divide child and parent, break that **domestic background** that was our strength.

I went to a block of working-class flats at the back of Gray's Inn Road and in the early morning saw a tiny, frail, Cockney child walking across to school.
10   The child had a big, brown-paper parcel in her hand and was dragging it along. But as she turned I saw a brown box banging against her thin legs. It bumped up and down at every step, slung by a thin string over her shoulder.

It was Florence Morecambe, an English schoolchild, with a gas mask instead of a satchel over her shoulder.

I went along with Florence to her school. It was a big Council school and the classrooms were filled with children, parcels, gas masks. The desks and blackboards were piled up in a heap in one corridor. They were not going to school for lessons. They were going on a holiday. The children were excited and happy because their parents had told them they were going away to the
20   country. Many of them, like my little Florence, had never seen green fields. Their playground was the tarmac or a sandpit in the concrete square at the back.

I watched the schoolteachers calling out their names and tying luggage labels in their coats, checking their parcels to see there were warm and clean clothes. On the gates of the school were two fat policemen. They were letting the children through but gently asking the parents not to come farther. They might disturb the children. So mothers and fathers were saying goodbye, straightening the girls' hair, getting the boys to blow their noses, and lightly and quickly kissing them. The parents stood outside while the children went
30   to be registered in their classrooms. There was quite a long wait before this small army got its orders through from the **LCC** to move off. In the meantime I sat in the school playground watching these thin, wiry little Cockneys playing their rough-and-push games on the faded netball pitch. It was disturbing, for through the high **grille** their mothers pressed their faces,

trying to see one child that resembled them. Every now and then the policeman would call out a child's name and a mother who had forgotten a bar of chocolate or a toothbrush had a last chance to tell a child to be good, to write and to straighten her hat.

40 Labelled and lined up, the children began to move out of the school. I followed Florence, her live tiny face bobbing about, white among so many navy-blue school caps. She was chattering away to an older schoolgirl, wanting to know what the country was like, where they were going, what games they would play on the grass.

On one side of Gray's Inn Road this ragged crocodile moved towards the tube station. On the other, were mothers who were waving and running along to see the last of their children. The police had asked them not to follow, but they could not resist.

The children scrambled down into the tube.

From H. Marchant, *Women and Children Last*, Gollancz, 1941

DICTIONARY

domestic background home life
LCC London County Council
grille barrier made of metal bars

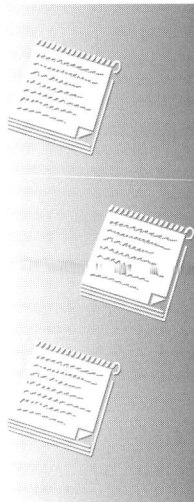

C LOSER READING

1 Re-read the first two paragraphs (lines 1–7). What do you think is Hilde Marchant's view of evacuation?

2 Marchant focuses on one child in particular: Florence Morecambe. Look at the description of Florence in the third, fourth and fifth paragraphs (lines 8–22) and pick out the details that make us feel sympathy for her.

3 Re-read the sixth paragraph (lines 23–38). What evidence is there that the people in charge, the teachers and the police, are trying to make the evacuation as painless as possible?

4 The rest of the passage describes the difference between the parents' feelings and the children's. Give as many examples as you can from the passage which show the differences between their feelings. Remember that feelings are shown through what each group does, not just through what the writer tells us. You might wish to set your examples out in the following way:

Examples of children's feelings	Examples of parents' feelings
1 They were excited and happy – 'They were not going to school for lessons. They were going on a holiday.'	

Using your answers in the second column, write a short piece from the point of view of one of the parents, describing your feelings as you say goodbye to your child.

2 Force-feeding

This passage was written in 1910 by a woman called Lady Constance Lytton. She was a suffragette, a campaigner for a woman's right to vote. Many suffragettes were arrested for their activities and put in prison, where some went on hunger-strike in protest at the way they were being treated. Lytton disguised herself as a working-class woman called Jane Warton so that she could experience what hunger-strikers had to go through.

(Some words are highlighted in the text. You will find further information about these words at the end of the passage.)

I was visited again by the Senior Medical Officer, who asked me how long I had been without food. I said I had eaten a buttered scone and a banana sent in by friends to the police station on Friday at about midnight. He said, 'Oh, then, this is the fourth day; that is too long, I shall feed you, I must feed you at once,' but he went out and nothing happened till about six o'clock in the evening, when he returned with, I think, five **wardresses** and the feeding apparatus. He urged me to take food voluntarily. I told him that was absolutely out of the question, that when our **legislators** ceased to resist **enfranchising** women then I should cease to resist taking food in prison. He

10 did not examine my heart nor feel my pulse; he did not ask to do so, nor did I say anything which could possibly induce him to think I would refuse to be examined. I offered no resistance to being placed in position, but lay down voluntarily on the plank bed. Two of the wardresses took hold of my arms, one held my head and one my feet. One wardress helped to pour the food. The doctor leant on my knees as he stooped over my chest to get at my mouth. I shut my mouth and clenched my teeth. I had looked forward to this moment with so much anxiety lest my identity should be discovered beforehand, that I felt positively glad when the time had come. The sense of being overpowered by more force than I could possibly resist was complete,

20 but I resisted nothing except with my mouth. The doctor offered me the choice of a wooden or steel gag; he explained **elaborately**, as he did on most subsequent occasions, that the steel gag would hurt and the wooden one not, and he urged me not to force him to use the steel gag. But I did not speak nor open my mouth, so that after playing about for a moment or two with the wooden one he finally **had recourse** to the steel. He seemed annoyed at my resistance and he broke into a temper as he **plied** my teeth with the steel implement. He found that on either side at the back I had false teeth mounted on a bridge which did not take out. The superintending wardress asked if I had any false teeth, if so, that they must be taken out; I made no

30 answer and the process went on. He dug his instrument down on to the sham tooth, it pressed fearfully on the gum. He said if I resisted so much with my teeth he would have to feed me through the nose. The pain of it was intense and at last I must have given way for he got the gag between my teeth, when he proceeded to turn it much more than necessary until my jaws were

fastened wide apart, far more than they could go naturally. Then he put
down my throat a tube which seemed to me much too wide and was
something like four feet in length. The irritation of the tube was excessive. I
choked the moment it touched my throat until it had got down. Then the
food was poured in quickly; it made me sick a few seconds after it was down
40   and the action of the sickness made my body and legs double up, but the
wardresses instantly pressed back my head and the doctor leant on my knees.
The horror of it was more than I can describe. I was sick over the doctor and
wardresses, and it seemed a long time before they took the tube out. As the
doctor left he gave me a slap on the cheek, not violently, but, as it were, to
express his contemptuous disapproval, and he seemed to take for granted
that my distress was **assumed**. At first it seemed such an utterly contemptible
thing to have done that I could only laugh in my mind. Then suddenly I saw
Jane Warton lying before me, and it seemed as if I were outside of her. She
was the most despised, ignorant and helpless prisoner that I had seen. When
50   she had served her time and was out of the prison, no one would believe
anything she said, and the doctor when he had fed her by force and tortured
her body, struck her on the cheek to show how he despised her! That was
Jane Warton, and I had come to help her.

When the doctor had gone out of the cell, I lay quite helpless. The
wardresses were kind and knelt round to comfort me, but there was nothing
to be done, I could not move, and remained there in what, under different
conditions, would have been an intolerable mess. I had been sick over my
hair, which, though short, hung on either side of my face, all over the wall
near my bed, and my clothes seemed **saturated** with it, but the wardresses
60   told me they could not get me a change that night as it was too late, the
office was shut. I lay quite motionless, it seemed paradise to be without the
suffocating tube, without the liquid food going in and out of my body and
without the gag between my teeth. Presently the wardresses all left me, they
had orders to go, which were carried out with the usual promptness. Before
long I heard the sounds of the forced feeding in the next cell to mine. It was
almost more than I could bear, it was Elsie Howey, I was sure. When the
ghastly process was over and all quiet, I tapped on the wall and called out at
the top of my voice, which wasn't much just then, 'No surrender,' and there
came the answer past any doubt in Elsie's voice, 'No surrender.'

From C. Lytton, *Prisons and Prisoners*, 1914

DICTIONARY

wardresses female prison officers
legislators law-makers, that is, Parliament
enfranchising giving the vote to
elaborately in great detail
had recourse to resorted to
plied pressed open
assumed a pretence
saturated soaked

CLOSER READING

1 Lytton describes her experience in great detail, reporting exactly what happened to her so as to bring home the horror of it to her readers. List all the details she gives which make this seem such a degrading incident.

2 Re-read the long first paragraph (lines 1–53). The doctor is seen by Lytton as a representative of the government, dealing with the protesters. What is the doctor's attitude towards Lytton? List as many details as you can about his behaviour and what he says.

3 At the end of the first paragraph and the beginning of the second, Lytton realises what other protesters must feel after being force-fed. Describe in your own words what she has learnt.

4 Despite the horrific nature of what she has undergone, the passage ends on a note of hope. How?

5 There are details in the passage which show that the wardresses are uncomfortable with what they have to do. Re-write the incident from the point of view of one of them, describing how they are torn between doing their duty and their sympathy for the prisoners.

3　Visiting Hiroshima

The following passage by Marcel Junod reports his encounter with a Japanese journalist. The journalist is describing the moment when an atomic bomb was dropped on Hiroshima in 1945 at the end of the Second World War.

(Some words are highlighted in the text. You will find further information about these words at the end of the passage.)

'The town was not much damaged,' he explained. 'It had suffered very little from the bombing. There were only two minor raids, one on March 19th last by a squadron of American naval planes, and one on April 30th by a Flying Fortress.

'On August 6th there wasn't a cloud in the sky above Hiroshima, and a mild, **hardly perceptible** wind blew from the south. Visibility was almost perfect for ten or twelve miles.

'At nine minutes past seven in the morning an air-raid warning sounded and four American B-29 planes appeared. To the north of the town two of them
10　turned and made off to the south and disappeared in the direction of the Shoho Sea. The other two, after having circled the neighbourhood of Shukai, flew off at high speed southwards in the direction of the Bingo Sea.

'At 7.31 the all-clear was given. Feeling themselves in safety people came out of their shelters and went about their affairs and the work of the day began.

'Suddenly a glaring whitish pinkish light appeared in the sky accompanied by an unnatural tremor which was followed almost immediately by a wave of suffocating heat and a wind which swept away everything in its path.

'Within a few seconds the thousands of people in the streets and the gardens in the centre of the town were scorched by a wave of searing heat. Many were
20 killed instantly, others lay writhing on the ground screaming in agony from the intolerable pain of their burns. Everything standing upright in the way of the blast, walls, houses, factories and other buildings, was annihilated and the debris spun round in a whirlwind and was carried up into the air. Trams were picked up and tossed aside as though they had neither weight nor solidity. Trains were flung off the rails as though they were toys. Horses, dogs and cattle suffered the same fate as human beings. Every living thing was **petrified** in an attitude of indescribable suffering. Even the vegetation did not escape. Trees went up in flames, the rice plants lost their greenness, the grass burned on the ground like dry straw.

30 'Beyond the zone of utter death in which nothing remained alive houses collapsed in a whirl of beams, bricks and girders. Up to about three miles from the centre of the explosion lightly built houses were flattened as though they had been built of cardboard. Those who were inside were either killed or wounded. Those who managed to **extricate** themselves by some miracle found themselves surrounded by a ring of fire. And the few who succeeded in making their way to safety generally died twenty or thirty days later from the delayed effects of the deadly **gamma rays**. Some of the reinforced concrete or stone buildings remained standing but their interiors were completely gutted by the blast.

40 'About half an hour after the explosion whilst the sky all around Hiroshima was still cloudless a fine rain began to fall on the town and went on for about five minutes. It was caused by the sudden rise of over-heated air to a great height, where it condensed and fell back as rain. Then a violent wind rose and the fires extended with terrible rapidity, because most Japanese houses are built only of timber and straw.

'By the evening the fire began to die down and then it went out. There was nothing left to burn. Hiroshima had ceased to exist.' …

We got out of the car and made our way slowly through the ruins into the centre of the dead city. Absolute silence reigned in the whole **necropolis**.

From M. Junod, *Warrior Without Weapons*, Cape, 1951

DICTIONARY

hardly perceptible barely noticeable

petrified frozen, fossilised

extricate remove

gamma rays radioactive rays

necropolis city of the dead, large graveyard

⊙LOSER READING

1   In the opening four paragraphs (lines 1–14) the journalist describes the 'calm before the storm', explaining how the bomb came as a total shock. Pick out a detail from each paragraph which helps build the atmosphere of unsuspecting calm.

2   In the next three paragraphs (lines 15–39) the impact of the bomb is described as a destructive monster. Find at least four examples that give this impression.

3   The passage finishes by describing the overall effect of the bomb. Find words and phrases that underline the sense of total destruction.

4   At a number of points in the passage the journalist gives precise dates, times and measurements. What effect does this have on you as a reader?

4 Famous deaths

The first passage below, written in 1586, describes one man's view of how Mary, Queen of Scots, prepared herself for execution. She had fled to England when she had been forced from the throne in Scotland. She was imprisoned by Elizabeth I and then beheaded for plotting against the English crown.

The second passage is a detailed account, written in 1805, of how Lord Nelson, the British naval commander, faced his imminent death on board ship at the end of the Battle of Trafalgar. Lady Hamilton was his mistress who had had a child by him five years earlier.

(Some words are highlighted in the text. You will find further information about these words at the end of the passages.)

A

Her prayers being ended, the executioners, kneeling, desired her Grace to forgive them her death: who answered, 'I forgive you with all my heart, for now, I hope, you shall make an end of all my troubles.' Then they, with her two women, helping her up, began to **disrobe her of her apparel**: then she, laying her crucifix upon the stool, one of the executioners took from her neck the **Agnus Dei**, which she, laying hands off it, gave to one of her women, and told the executioner he should be answered money for it. Then she **suffered** them, with her two women, to disrobe her of her **chain of pomander beads** and all other her apparel most willingly, and with joy rather than

10   sorrow, helped to make unready herself, putting on a pair of sleeves with her

own hands which they had pulled off, and that with some haste, as if she had longed to be gone.

All this time they were pulling off her apparel, she never changed her **countenance**, but with smiling cheer she uttered these words, 'that she never had such **grooms** to make her unready, and that she never put off her clothes before such a company'.

Then she, being stripped of all her apparel saving her petticoat and **kirtle**, her two women beholding her made great lamentation, and crying and crossing themselves prayed in Latin. She, turning herself to them, embracing

20   them, said these words in French, **'Ne crie vous, j'ay promé pour vous'**, and so crossing and kissing them, bade them pray for her and rejoice and not weep, for that now they should see an end of all their mistress's troubles.

Then she, with a smiling countenance, turning to her men servants, as Melvin and the rest, standing upon a bench nigh the scaffold, who sometime weeping, sometime crying out aloud, and continually crossing themselves, prayed in Latin, crossing them with her hand bade them farewell, and wishing them to pray for her even until the last hour.

From R. Wynkfielde, *Original Letters*, ed. H. Ellis, 1824–46

B

Captain Hardy now came to the **cockpit** to see his Lordship a second time, which was after an interval of about fifty minutes from the conclusion of his first visit. Before he quitted the deck, he sent Lieutenant Hills to acquaint Admiral Collingwood with the **lamentable circumstance** of Lord Nelson's being wounded. Lord Nelson and Captain Hardy shook hands again: and while the Captain retained his Lordship's hand, he congratulated him, even in the arms of death, on his brilliant victory; 'which', said he, 'was complete'; though he did not know how many of the Enemy were captured, as it was impossible to perceive every Ship distinctly. He was certain however of

10   fourteen or fifteen having surrendered. His Lordship answered, 'That is well, but I bargained for twenty': and then **emphatically** exclaimed, '*Anchor, Hardy, anchor!*' To this the Captain replied: 'I suppose, my Lord, Admiral Collingwood will now take upon himself the direction of affairs.' 'Not while I live, I hope, Hardy!' cried the dying Chief; and at that moment **endeavoured ineffectually** to raise himself from the bed. 'No' added he; 'do *you* anchor, Hardy.' Captain Hardy then said: 'Shall *we* make the signal, Sir?' 'Yes,' answered his Lordship, 'for if I live, I'll anchor.' The energetic manner in which he uttered these his last orders to Captain Hardy, accompanied with his efforts to raise himself, **evinced** his determination never to resign the

20   Command while he retained the exercise of his **transcendent faculties**, and that he expected Captain Hardy still to carry into effect the suggestions of his **exalted** mind; a sense of his duty overcoming the pains of death. He then told Captain Hardy, he felt that in a few minutes he should be no more;

adding in a low tone, 'Don't throw me overboard, Hardy.' The Captain answered: 'Oh! no, certainly not.' 'Then,' replied his Lordship, 'you know what to do: and', continued he, 'take care of my dear Lady Hamilton, Hardy: take care of poor Lady Hamilton. Kiss me, Hardy.' The Captain now knelt down, and kissed his cheek; when his Lordship said, 'Now I am satisfied. Thank God, I have done my duty.' Captain Hardy stood for a minute or two
30 in silent contemplation: he knelt down again, and kissed his Lordship's forehead. His Lordship said: 'Who is that?' The Captain answered: 'It is Hardy'; to which his Lordship replied, 'God bless you, Hardy!' … His thirst now increased; and he called for 'drink, drink,' 'fan, fan,' and 'rub, rub,' addressing himself in the last case to Doctor Scott, who had been rubbing his Lordship's breast with his hand, from which he found some relief. These words he spoke in a very rapid manner, which **rendered his articulation difficult**: but he every now and then, with evident increase of pain, made a greater effort with his vocal powers, and pronounced distinctly these last words: 'Thank God, I have done my duty'; and this great sentiment he
40 continued to repeat as long as he was able to give it utterance.

From W. Beatty, *Despatches and Letters of Nelson*, 1845

DICTIONARY

disrobe her of her apparel undress her

Agnus Dei a religious medallion

suffered allowed

chain of pomander beads sachets of perfumes

countenance face, expression

grooms servants

kirtle skirt or dress

'Ne crie vous, j'ay promé pour vous' 'Don't cry. I pray for you'

cockpit the quarters of the junior officers and the first aid station

lamentable circumstance unfortunate event

emphatically forcefully

endeavoured ineffectually tried without success

evinced made clear

transcendent faculties mental abilities

exalted excited

rendered his articulation difficult made understanding him difficult

CLOSER READING

1 Both of these passages show how a famous person faced death. Both are concerned to show the central character in a very favourable light. However, these people are not praised directly by the writers, but instead details are given of what they say and do and of the response of those around them. Find these details in the passages. You might choose to record them using the table below.

Historical character	What they say	What they do	How others respond to them
Mary			
Nelson			

2 Both of these accounts aim to show the central character as heroic, using the way they died to state something about their personality. Imagining yourself as the observer, write a fictional account of the death of someone in heroic circumstances. It could be about a soldier, a fire-fighter or mountain-rescuer. Think about which details you are going to record to bring out what was special about this person.

FURTHER ACTIVITIES

1 In groups, collect together as many examples of reportage as you can. You should find examples in daily and weekend newspapers and magazines. Remember, you are looking for writing that describes a particular event in great detail, and that makes you feel that you were present.

As a group, decide on two pieces that you think are effective and two that are less so. Then, using a large sheet of paper (flip-chart or display paper will be the right size), copy out and complete the following grid:

Subject	Is the writer an observer or a participant?	How does the writer make you feel as though you are present?	Describe people in the report that you either dislike or sympathise with	Does the writer communicate feelings to you directly or through the way things are described?
1.				
2.				
3.				
4.				

Now, on your own, use this information and the notes you have made throughout this chapter to write about what makes successful reportage. Give examples from all the texts you have studied to support your points.

2 Although reportage is usually about major events, it is a style that can be used to record small-scale events too. Choose an event that has happened in your life recently, which you feel was important and which you remember in great detail. Produce a piece of reportage based on this event. Before you begin make notes on the following areas:

- Were you an eye-witness or were you personally involved? Will this affect the way you report the incident?

- What happened exactly? Make a note of important times, dates, numbers, places etc., which you can use to make the reader feel the event is unfolding before their eyes.

- What were the most important moments in the event? Choose the most interesting and dramatic details and record them carefully, describing sights, sounds and smells so that the reader feels that they are present.

- Who were the key figures in the event? How do you want your reader to feel about these people? Can you do this through describing what these people do and say rather than by telling us directly?

- Can you use language to appeal to the reader's imagination? If you compare people or events to other things (like the Hiroshima bomb being compared to a destructive beast) you will bring your report alive.

- The opening and closing paragraphs will be very important in directing the reader's feelings. What mood do you want to convey in these two paragraphs? How will you put this across dramatically?

3 This task should be done in pairs.

Imagine a situation where a woman walking home one night sees a group of men across the road break down the door to a house and pull out two teenage boys. There is a lot of shouting between the boys and the men and some of the boys' friends arrive on the scene. Eventually a fight breaks out. At this point the woman rushes off to phone the police.

Each of you should write a report on the event, one by the woman and one by one of the men involved in the incident.

- The person writing as the woman should select details and interpret them in such a way as to present the men who break into the house in the worst possible light.

- The person writing as the man, however, wishes to justify his actions and explains what happens from his own point of view.

Remember to consider the details listed in Activity 2 before writing your reports.

When you have completed your report, swap with your partner and read their account. Discuss how the same events can be portrayed in very different ways. What could this tell you about reports in the daily newspapers?

INFORMATION ←→ PERSUASION

Electronic Texts
Letters

Instructions · Legal Writing · Information Writing · Biography · Interviews · Essays · Travel Writing · Diaries · Philosophical Writing · Autobiography · Social Commentary · Reportage · Reviews · Promotional Writing · Polemic

13
Reviews

Reviews can be about virtually anything: television programmes, videos, CDs, films, books, computer games, plays, comedy shows and art exhibitions are some examples. All reviewers aim to give their opinion about what they are reviewing, and they often give the reader advice about whether they think the thing that they are reviewing is worth taking notice of.

Reviews can sometimes be very brief, no more than a few lines which direct the reader to a particular view. Other reviews are very detailed, offering a full analysis. The nature of the review depends largely on the audience it is aimed at. For example, a film review in a specialist magazine aimed at film enthusiasts would assume that the reader knows a great deal about cinema and therefore would expect a detailed analysis of the plot, characters and style of the film.

Many reviews appear in newspapers and will adopt the style of that newspaper. So, reviews in tabloid newspapers like the *Sun* will be brief, chatty and focus on personalities. However, in broadsheet newspapers like *The Times*, reviews will be more detailed, discussing themes and styles.

Reviewers may also be biased. Their own individual taste and preferences will influence the opinions they give. They may choose to focus on some aspects while ignoring others. When reading reviews it is important to distinguish between facts and opinions – how does the reviewer support his or her views?

1 Television reviews

Read these two reviews of television programmes, the first from the *Radio Times*, the second from the *Guardian*.

(Some words are highlighted in the text. You will find further information about these words at the end of the passages.)

A LONDON'S BURNING

THIS WEEK

GOING OUT IN A BLAZE OF GLORY

London's Burning star Sean Blowers leaves behind his firefighting career for a life on the ocean wave

am going out with a bang,' says Sean Blowers as he prepares to say an explosive farewell to sub-officer John Hallam, the character he first created ten years ago In Jack Rosenthal's original TV play of *London's Burning*.

Hallam has seen Blowers through nine series of the firefighting drama, but the time has come for him to go out in a blaze of glory. And it's no coincidence that Hallam's demise coincides with the start of a seven-month round-the-world **odyssey**. An enthusiastic amateur sailor, he is taking part in four **arduous** legs of the BT Global Challenge, helping to crew a racing yacht from Southampton to Cape Town. The progress of the race, which starts next week, will be followed on BBC2, beginning on 29 September.

'I've felt the urge to move on for some time now and this was just something I couldn't miss – the chance of a lifetime,' he says. 'But I shall certainly miss the *London's Burning* team and it's like being divorced from the Fire Brigade. We've always had a fantastic relationship with them.'

Blowers won't, however, miss the all-enveloping stench of smoke after a shoot – 'it lingers on your body for hours' – or the occasionally unpredictable bursts of flame. 'Last year my ear was quite badly burned because I didn't duck quickly enough.'

There are already new horizons. He's planning a new environmentally slanted drama series with his old drama school mate Jerome Flynn, and we'll soon see him in a very different role – as a brutal wife-beater in LWT's new medical thriller *Staying Alive*. 'He's a policeman with a drink problem and his violence against his wife is quite calculated – body blows, never in the face,' says Blowers. 'Not a pleasant character. After a day with him it was very nice to get the train home.'

From *Radio Times*, 21 Sept 1996

B CAROLINE IN THE CITY

Caroline in the City 9 p.m., C4

A young, attractive woman in a **nominally** glamorous media job can't seem to find the right man, but gains solace from her kooky but loyal friends. Sound familiar? Yes, it is *The Naked Truth*, only with a newspaper cartoonist instead of a newspaper photographer. While Lea Thompson could never aspire to the heights of cuteness occupied by Tea Leoni, her slightly more presentable CV (*Back To The Future*, *Red Dawn*, *Howard The Duck*) seems to have earned her a higher-grade supporting cast; in particular, Malcolm Gets, as **deadpan** colourist Richard, gets some joyously **scathing** lines. Otherwise, the jokes in this pilot rarely rise above **mediocre**, but the fact that later episodes regularly leapfrogged *Friends* to make the US top five bodes well for the future.

A. Bodle, *The Guardian*, 14 Sept 1996

DICTIONARY

odyssey journey
arduous tiring
nominally supposedly
deadpan expressionless
scathing severe, cutting
mediocre average

C LOSER READING

1 Re-read the first fourteen lines of the review of *London's Burning*. The reviewer plays on the idea of firefighting in the language he uses. Find three examples of language which are related to the job of a firefighter.

2 Find at least three reasons Sean Blowers gives for leaving the series.

3 The review of *Caroline in the City* is mixed. Find three reasons given by the reviewer for the reader to miss the programme and two reasons for watching it.

4 These two reviews take very different approaches to the television programmes they are discussing. Which review fits each of the descriptions below?
   • The focus is on personalities;
   • The focus is on characters;
   • Little details and stories are important;
   • Originality is important;
   • The quality of the script is important;
   • Viewers wish to identify with the people they see on television;
   • The popularity of a programme can be an important sign of its success;
   • Knowledge of other television programmes helps you to appreciate the one you are watching;
   • Viewers like particular actors and wish to watch other programmes which they star in.

2 | Music reviews

These three short reviews of singles appeared in the *New Musical Express*.

(Some words are highlighted in the text. You will find further information about these words at the end of the passages.)

A | WARM JETS
Autopia EP *(This Way Up)*

THE LATEST British hopefuls with **authentic** instruments just like The Beatles used to use. Seeing as this is their debut release, they obviously felt morally obliged to do their homework. And judging from the first 30 seconds of this record, that consisted of a marathon session at home with Blur, Elastica and many more of your knees-up, comedy favourites. Still, while that should have resulted in **generic** tedium with a working-class accent, it hasn't.

So, skip the first bit, and instead discover four unnervingly insistent tunes that could only have been written in 1996. Particularly frisky is the throbbing 'Wires', as that's about the future when we've all got, like, wires in our heads, but we still like music because basically we're human and there's no getting away from it, is there? Know what I mean? Do you? Obviously not, but it's a mark of the Warm Jets' presence that they've got us talking. **Futuristically-retro**, and no mistake.

B | COLLAPSED LUNG
Board Game *(Deceptive)*

RELYING ONLY on a song about football and the backing of a **multinational corporation**, Collapsed Lung somehow managed to fluke a summer hit with 'Eat My Goal'. Never again will these whinging dribblers be so fortunate.

And frankly why should they be? After all, the only redeeming feature of the band is that against every expectation they're not a ranting hardcore act determined to show off their **maverick** muscles. The Collapsed Lung assault, you see, is a far subtler one.

Rapping Cockneys to a man, they record all of their songs in a pot of glue to ensure everything they do is in squelchy, slow motion. Synths burp, beats amble and Collapsed Lung tell you about the time they played Snakes And Ladders for three consecutive years. Or at least, that's what I read into it, after a long time spent pondering the significance of the title.

C | SLEEPER
Statuesque *(Indolent)*

THE DREARIEST band in Britain unexpectedly hit form. Well, what an **unfettered** joy it would have been to write *that* line in all seriousness. Unfortunately though, the dreariest band in **Christendom** continue to plough their traditional furrow of inadequacy without any discernible signs of improvement.

The intensely imaginative process that went into writing and recording this **fetid** piece of **mundane** indiepop (single number 57 from the really rather tremendous 'It Girl' elpee) is reflected in the single's cover design. Yes, having thought long and hard, they've opted for a picture of a statue. And that ties in rather nicely with the song title, don't you think?

J. Oldham, *New Musical Express*, 21 Sept 1996

DICTIONARY

authentic real

generic typical, not unique

Futuristically-retro looking both forwards and backwards

multinational corporation international company

maverick independent, off-beat

unfettered unrestrained

Christendom literally 'all Christian people', but here meaning all the known world

fetid stinking

mundane dull, ordinary

(C)LOSER READING

These three reviews were written in a newspaper aimed at young adults who would be knowledgeable about music and would be looking for advice about which singles to buy. The style and content of the reviews fit this audience well. Copy and complete the table below, finding examples from all three reviews of different uses of language.

Use of language	Warm Jets	Collapsed Lung	Sleeper
insults			
slang			
metaphors			
jargon			
conversational tone			

KEY

slang

Words and phrases that are only used in informal, casual situations and which would not be used, for example, in a formal letter or essay.

metaphor

When something is identified with something else, for example 'He was a tower of strength.' The person is not actually a tower, but is as tough and strong as one.

jargon

Special words used by a particular group of people. For example, a computer programmer will talk about 'interfaces', hardware' and 'modem'. People outside the group may not understand what these words mean.

conversational tone

When someone write as though they are chatting with you. They may ask questions, exclaim things or begin sentences with words like 'well …' or 'so …'.

sarcasm

Putting someone down by saying the opposite of what you mean in order to emphasise it. For example, if a pupil broke a window a teacher might say, sarcastically, 'That was clever.'

3 Film review

The following review is of the film *A Time To Kill*. It appeared in the *Observer* newspaper.

(Some words are highlighted in the text. You will find further information about these words at the end of the passage.)

If the film of John Grisham's first novel, *A Time To Kill*, lasted 90 minutes, you might start thinking about its crudity, **implausibility** and general offensiveness on the way home. At a leisurely two-and-a-half hours, however, there is plenty of slack time to ponder the **manifest inadequacies** while it's going on. In present-day Mississippi a pair of **degenerate rednecks** rape and maim a 10-year-old black girl, whose father Carl Lee (Samuel L. Jackson) acquires a machine gun and kills them on the local courthouse steps as they are being escorted to stand trial.

An inexperienced young white lawyer, Jack Brigance (Matthew McConaughey) undertakes his defence with the intention of pleading not guilty by reason of temporary insanity. A sneering DA (Kevin Spacey) offers to refrain from seeking the death penalty if Jake pleads guilty. The hanging judge, aptly named Omar Noose (Patrick McGoohan), goes even farther and offers a manslaughter verdict in exchange for a guilty plea. But Jake is determined to get his man off, partly because he himself has a 10-year-old daughter, and partly to prove that a history of injustice justifies a black southerner taking the law into his own hands. Apparently, though I find this hard to believe, if a Mississippi jury acquits on an insanity plea, the defendant walks out a free man.

The trial leads to a **recrudescence** of the Ku Klux Klan at its worst, while the National Association for the Advancement of Coloured People tries to hijack the defence (the film **scurrilously** equates the two organisations as troublemakers). But Jake, with the help of his drunken mentor (Donald Sutherland), and another of those brilliant, beautiful female lawyers (Sandra Bullock) that recur in Grisham's novels, defies them all. He gets a little help from the film's producers when it comes to discrediting the state's expert psychiatric witness, for who should turn up in court but the screen's most odious shrink of the Nineties, the smirking Anthony Heald, who played the man Hannibal Lecter proposed to dine on in *The Silence of the Lambs*.

Jake, however, assures the liberal woman lawyer that he isn't 'a card-carrying American Civil Liberties Union radical'. He believes in capital punishment, and it becomes apparent that the movie is solidly committed to **vigilantism**. Although this film would like to be compared with humane works on the operation of Southern justice, such as the movie versions of Faulkner's *Intruder in the Dust* and Harper Lee's *To Kill a Mockingbird*, what it actually resembles is *Anatomy of a Murder*, also based on a crude first novel by a small-town lawyer, in which an attorney and his drunken mentor manage to secure the acquittal of a man who murders a rapist.

P. French, *The Observer*, 15 Sept 1996

implausibility unlikely events and characters
manifest inadequacies obvious weaknesses
degenerate rednecks 'low-life' prejudiced whites
recrudescence breaking out (like a disease)
scurrilously wrongfully (in a shocking way)
vigilantism taking the law into one's own hands

CLOSER READING

1 The first paragraph makes you think one thing about the film and then reverses it. What do you first think and how does this change?

2 Throughout the review the writer gives short 'thumbnail' sketches of each main character. Find and list these. Do they give you a clear picture of the characters?

3 Find examples in the review which show that the writer expects you to have a good knowledge of other films.

4 The third paragraph gives us some of the reasons the reviewer has for disliking the film. Find sentences that show the following opinions:
   • The film is imbalanced in its views of certain political groups.
   • All the heroines in Grisham's novels are the same.
   • The film is cast in such a way as to make it obvious who the 'goodies' and 'baddies' are.

5 Because the review is in a broadsheet newspaper, the focus is on what the film is about as much as what happens. In the final paragraph the reviewer summarises what he thinks the film is about. Describe his opinion in your own words.

4 Book review

The following review is of *Wuthering Heights*, a novel by Emily Brontë published in 1847. The interesting thing about this review is that it was written by author's sister, Charlotte Brontë. She refers to her sister as 'Ellis Bell' – her pen-name.

(Some words are highlighted in the text. You will find further information about these words at the end of the passage.)

I have just read over *Wuthering Heights*, and, for the first time, have obtained a clear glimpse of what are termed (and, perhaps, really are) its faults; have gained a definite notion of how it appears to other people – to strangers who know nothing of the author; who are unacquainted with the locality where the scenes of the story are laid; to whom the inhabitants, the customs. the

natural characteristics of the outlying hills and hamlets in the West Riding of Yorkshire are things alien and unfamiliar.

To all such *Wuthering Heights* must appear a **rude** and strange production. The wild moors of the north of England can for them have no interest; the
10 language, the manners, the very dwellings and household customs of the scattered inhabitants of those districts, must be to such readers in a great measure **unintelligible**, and – where intelligible – repulsive. Men and women who, perhaps, naturally very calm, and with feelings moderate in degree, and little marked in kind, have been trained from their cradle **to observe the utmost evenness of manner and guardedness of language**, will hardly know what to make of the rough, strong utterance, the **harshly manifested passions**, the unbridled aversions, and **headlong partialities of unlettered moorland hinds** and rugged moorland squires, who have grown up untaught and unchecked, except by **mentors** as harsh as themselves …

20 With regard to the **rusticity** of *Wuthering Heights*, I admit the charge, for I feel the quality. It is rustic all through. It is moorish, and wild, and knotty as a root of heath. Nor was it natural that it should be otherwise; the author being herself a native and **nursling** of the moors. Doubtless, had her lot been cast in a town, her writings, if she had written at all, would have possessed another character. Even had chance or taste led her to choose a similar subject, she would have treated it otherwise. Had Ellis Bell been a lady or a gentleman accustomed to what is called 'the world', her view of a remote and **unreclaimed** region, as well as of the dwellers therein, would have differed greatly from that actually taken by the homebred country girl. Doubtless it
30 would have been wider – more comprehensive: whether it would have been more original or more truthful is not so certain. As far as the scenery and locality are concerned, it could scarcely have been so sympathetic: Ellis Bell did not describe as one whose eye and taste alone found pleasure in the prospect, her native hills were far more to her than a spectacle; they were what she lived in, and by, as much as the wild birds, their tenants, or as the heather, their produce. Her descriptions, then, of natural scenery, are what they should be, and all they should be.

Where **delineation** of human character is concerned, the case is different. I am bound to avow that she had scarcely more practical knowledge of the
40 peasantry among whom she lived, than a nun has of the country people who sometimes pass her convent gates. My sister's disposition was not naturally **gregarious**; circumstances favoured and fostered her tendency to seclusion; except to go to church or take a walk on the hills, she rarely crossed the threshold of home. Though her feeling for the people round was benevolent, **intercourse** with them she never sought; nor, with very few exceptions, ever experienced. And yet she knew them; knew their ways, their language, their family histories; she could hear of them with interest and talk of them with detail, minute, graphic, and accurate; but *with* them she rarely exchanged a word. Hence it ensued that what her mind had gathered of the real
50 concerning them, was too exclusively confined to those tragic and terrible traits of which, in listening to the secret **annals of every rude vicinage**, the memory is sometimes compelled to **receive the impress**. Her imagination, which was a spirit more sombre than sunny, more powerful than sportive,

found in such traits material whence it wrought creations like Heathcliff, like Earnshaw, like Catherine. Having formed these beings, she did not know what she had done. If the **auditor** of her work when read in manuscript, shuddered under the grinding influence of natures so relentless and **implacable**, of spirits so lost and fallen; if it was complained that the mere hearing of certain vivid and fearful scenes banished sleep by night, and

60 disturbed mental peace by day, Ellis Bell would wonder what was meant, and suspect the complainant of **affectation**. Had she but lived, her mind would of itself have grown like a strong tree; loftier, straighter, wider-spreading, and its matured fruits would have attained a mellower ripeness and sunnier bloom; but on that mind time and experience alone could work: to the influence of other intellects, it was not **amenable** …

Whether it is right or advisable to create things like Heathcliff, I do not know: I scarcely think it is. But this I know; the writer who possesses the creative gift owns something of which he is not always master – something that, at times, strangely wills and works for itself …

70 *Wuthering Heights* was **hewn** in a wild workshop, with simple tools, out of **homely** materials. The statuary found a granite block on a solitary moor; gazing thereon, he saw how from the crag might be **elicited** the head, savage, **swart**, sinister; a form moulded with at least one element of grandeur – power. He wrought with a rude chisel, and from no model but the vision of his meditations. With time and labour, the crag took human shape; and there it stands colossal, dark, and frowning, half statue, half rock; in the former sense, terrible and goblin-like; in the latter, almost beautiful, for its colouring is of mellow grey, and moorland moss clothes it; and heath, with its blooming bells and balmy fragrance, grows faithfully close to the giant's foot.

From C. Brontë, Preface to E. Brontë, *Wuthering Heights*, 1850 edn

DICTIONARY

rude rough
unintelligible difficult to understand
to observe the utmost evenness of manner and guardedness of language to behave in a moderate and tactful way
harshly manifested passions strong emotions openly displayed
headlong partialities of unlettered moorland hinds the extreme prejudices and habits of uncivilised country peasants
mentors role models
rusticity rough country manner
nursling child
unreclaimed uncivilised
delineation description
gregarious sociable
intercourse conversation
annals of every rude vicinage histories of local people and places
receive the impress retain the image
auditor editor

CLOSER READING

1 Re-read the first two paragraphs (lines 1–19). What reason does Charlotte Brontë give for people disliking *Wuthering Heights*? What is the difference between Emily Brontë and her reviewers?

2 In the third paragraph (lines 20–37) Charlotte explains why her sister set her novel in such a bleak place. Find sentences which make the following points about Emily:
   • she was born and bred on the moors;
   • she would have written about any subject in her own particular way;
   • her writing was no worse for being so distinctive;
   • her relationship with the countryside she described was intense.

3 In the fourth and fifth paragraphs (lines 38–69) Charlotte explains how Emily's relationship with other people affected the way she created characters. Why, according to Charlotte, were her characters so extraordinary?

4 a The final paragraph (lines 70–79) uses two images: the writer is the sculptor and the book is the sculpture. Are these effective images? What impression does it create of the kind of novel *Wuthering Heights* is?

   b There is another image at the end of the fourth paragraph of the way in which Emily Brontë may have developed as a person and as a writer. Explain in your own words the point that is being made.

FURTHER ACTIVITIES

1 People constantly review what they have seen, done or been involved in. In the playground you will discuss television programmes you watched the night before, football or netball matches you took part in or CDs you have just bought.

One thing that you may often talk about, but never write down, is your opinion of a lesson you have just had. Working in pairs, write a review of a lesson that you both remember well and which stands out in your minds. You could describe:

   • the characters (teachers and pupils);

- the plot (what happened);
- the style (how the activities in the lesson were carried out).

Throughout, give your views on what you thought about the lesson. You may need to change the names to protect peoples' identities!

It is important that you write your reviews **separately**, and only when they are finished should you compare them. When you have read each other's review discuss the differences, thinking of the following things:

- which events are recorded;
- which characters are mentioned;
- which views are expressed;
- the overall impression given of the lesson.

Try to account for the differences. What does this tell you about how reliable reviews are?

2 The **type** of review written depends on the 'vehicle' (what it is appearing in) and the audience (who it is aimed at).

Working in groups, gather together different newspapers and magazines, published in the same week, which will have television and film reviews in them. Cut out these reviews, read them and then divide them into two groups:

a those from tabloid newspapers and general magazines;

b those from broadsheet newspapers and specialist magazines.

Paste these two sets of reviews on to two large sheets of paper. Look closely at the differences between the two groups of reviews. Write down on the sheets of paper key words that explain these differences, and underline examples. (Look back at the Closer Reading questions to Text no. 1 on page 156 above for some ideas.)

Now, on your own, write two reviews of a television programme or film that you have seen recently. One review should be for a general magazine or tabloid newspaper which is chatty, informal and focuses on personalities. The other review should be written for a specialist magazine or broadsheet newspaper and should focus on characters, themes and the quality of the programme or film.

3 As Further Activity 1 showed, people with different opinions and tastes may have very different views of the same thing. This can create bias.

Write two views of something of your choice (for example, a film, a book, a computer game, a play or an exhibition). The first review should be very positive, giving lots of examples to support the views.

The second review should be very negative, again using examples to support its argument. In both reviews you could use *slang, metaphor* and *jargon*. In the second one you might also be *sarcastic*, so that you can 'put down' what you are reviewing. (See the Closer Reading questions to Text no. 2 on pages 158–159 above for help.)

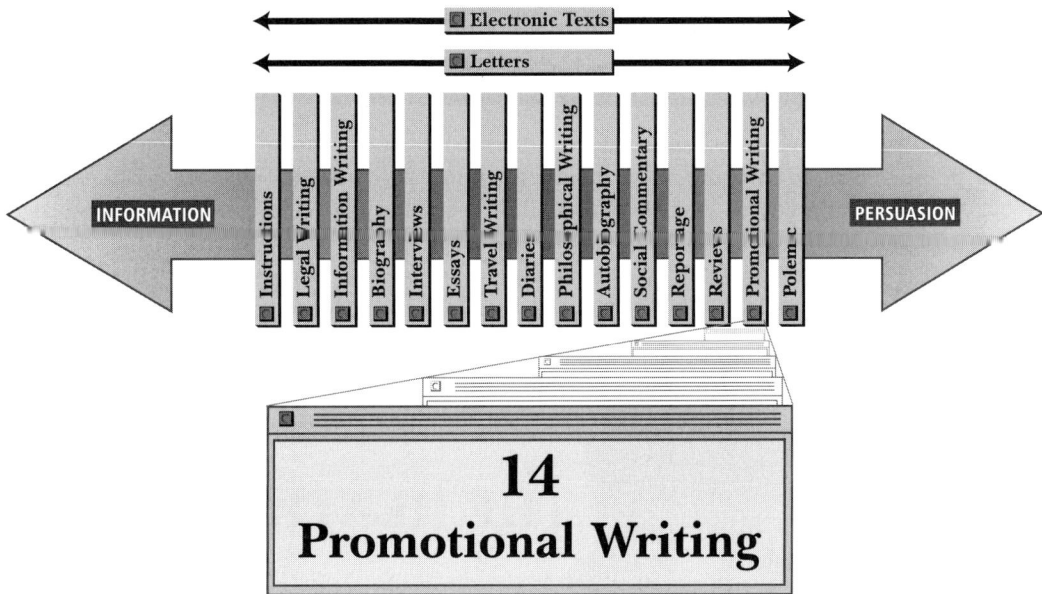

The diagram shows a horizontal axis with a left-pointing arrow labelled **INFORMATION** and a right-pointing arrow labelled **PERSUASION**. Between them, vertical bars are labelled (left to right): Instructions, Legal Writing, Information Writing, Biography, Interviews, Essays, Travel Writing, Diaries, Philosophical Writing, Autobiography, Social Commentary, Reportage, Reviews, Promotional Writing, Polemic. Double-headed arrows above span ranges labelled **Electronic Texts** and **Letters**.

14
Promotional Writing

This type of writing has the clear purpose of persuading its audience to take a course of action. Usually it aims to obtain money from the reader, for example in exchange for a product, in payment for a holiday or in support of a cause. So, advertisements, holiday brochures and charity campaigns can all be considered as examples of promotional writing.

Sometimes, however, promotional writing aims to gain our support and participation. For example, there were many posters published at the beginning of the First World War which used strong language and images to encourage young men to enlist in the army. Likewise, most schools publish a brochure (often called a 'prospectus') which promotes their strong points so that parents and children will 'join up'. Although there are laws which prevent writers from telling complete lies about what they are promoting, each writer will be selective about their subject, praising its positive points while ignoring its less appealing aspects.

The writer of promotional material knows that the organisation or group they are writing for depends on successful promotion for survival. Therefore they attempt to produce a rapid response from their audience with words and pictures which stir it to action. This type of writing often uses powerful, emotional language and striking or attractive images to appeal to deep-seated feelings and beliefs about lifestyles and aspirations.

1   A school prospectus

Most schools now have a glossy brochure, which is given to parents of children who could be joining the school. The brochure not only gives information but also highlights the positive aspects of the school. Below you will find the front covers and first pages of two brochures, for the same school but at different times in its history.

A

THE HEATH SCHOOL

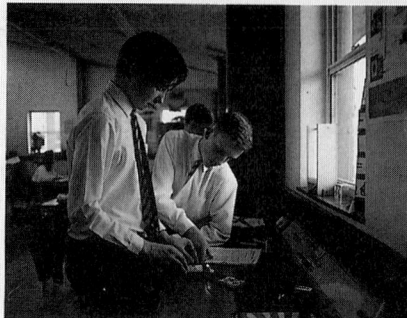

PROSPECTUS

Welcome to the pages of The Heath School Prospectus.

We hope that you will find it useful and informative. From the start there are some issues that I would like to highlight:

Standards
*We are proud of the standards of examination success, sport, discipline, uniform and environment that we have achieved over the last few years but, like this prospectus, we are never content to rest on our laurels - we will **always try to do better.***

Partnership
*We are fully aware that pupils cannot achieve their best unless they, parents, and school work **together in a spirit of positive co-operation.** As parents, you are **a welcome partner** in the process of educating your child; and we will encourage pupils, as they grow older, to take on **more responsibility** for their own work and actions.*

Continuity
*As an 11-18 school based strongly in our local community, we are able to offer pupils and parents the **reassurance of well established links** between ourselves and primary schools with a particularly careful and successful transfer procedure. Added to this are the growing links in areas like Science, Mathematics and English, where we work with our primary colleagues to ensure that there are as few problems as possible - particularly important with the progression of the National Curriculum from primary to secondary stages.*

Care
*Through the school's pastoral system, based in Year and Form Tutor Groups, every pupil is known **personally** and his or her needs can be met by a member of staff with whom your child can feel at ease and whom you can contact to answer any questions you may have.*

*We are proud of the reputation of The Heath, **regarded as the best school in the area in a recent survey of employers,** and with your support, pupils at our school will benefit from that reputation which we are determined will continue to grow.*

Sincerely,

D. H. Davi

Since success depends upon close co-operation between home and school, parents are warmly invited to contact us whenever problems arise or advice is needed, you do not have to wait for a Parents' Evening. We, in turn, will be in touch whenever the need arises.

From *The Heath School Prospectus*, Heath School

B

The Heath School
and Sixth Form Centre

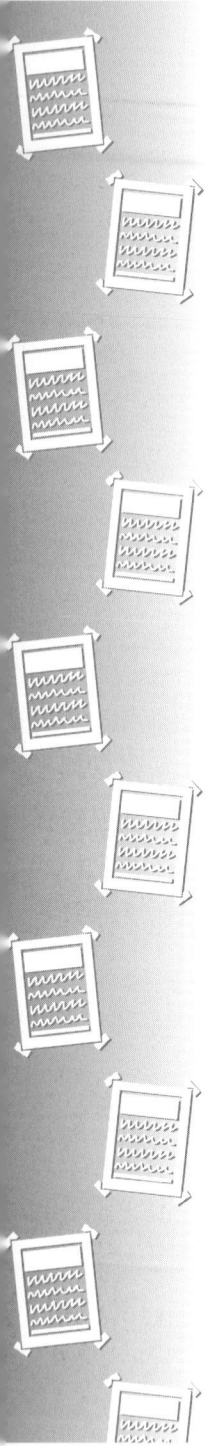

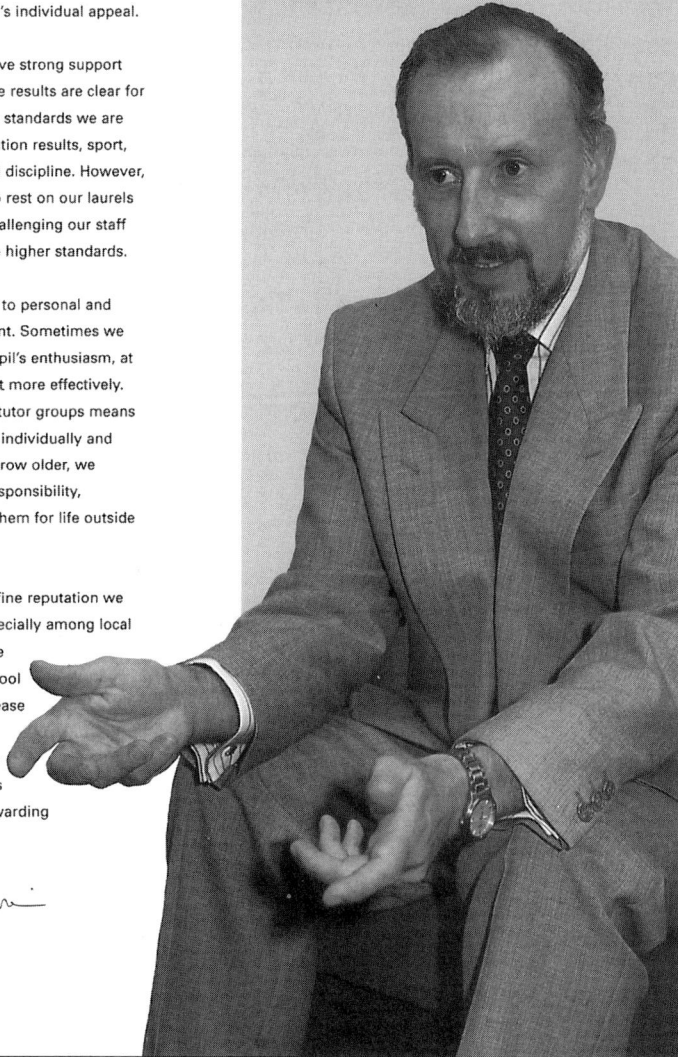

Every school has its own special character and atmosphere, which many parents refer to as its "feel". It is important that pupils attend a school that is right for their personality and ambitions. I hope this prospectus gives you a good "feel" for The Heath School's individual appeal.

At this school, we have strong support from our parents. The results are clear for all to see in the high standards we are achieving in examination results, sport, community work and discipline. However, we are not content to rest on our laurels but are constantly challenging our staff and pupils to achieve higher standards.

Motivation is the key to personal and academic achievement. Sometimes we have to rekindle a pupil's enthusiasm, at other times channel it more effectively. The system of form tutor groups means every pupil is known individually and cared for. As pupils grow older, we encourage greater responsibility, gradually preparing them for life outside school.

We are proud of the fine reputation we have in the area, especially among local employers. I do hope you will visit the school to see it in action. Please come and talk to the staff whose influence will make your child's time here happy, rewarding and successful.

D H Davies

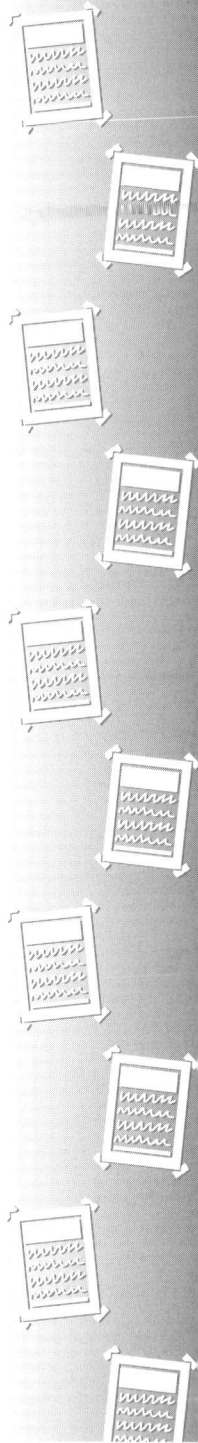

From *The Heath School and Sixth Form Centre*, Heath School

CLOSER READING

1 Pick out the key words in each passage which you think the writers want you to remember. These will be the positive words which show the school in a good light.

2 Both introductions are divided into paragraphs. Copy and complete the grid below, writing down a sentence for each paragraph which summarises the quality of the school being promoted.

Paragraphs	Prospectus A	Prospectus B
1		
2		
3		
4		
5		
6		
7		

3 Look again at the front cover of each prospectus and then at the two pictures of the headteacher. Copy and complete the grid below, describing what you see, and then write what you think these pictures are telling us about what kind of school this is and what kind of man is running it.

Description of front cover	Prospectus A	Prospectus B
What the cover tells us about the school		
Description of the picture of the headteacher		
What the picture tells us about him		

4 Which prospectus do you think is the most successful? Which one appeals most to you? Write down what you think, using the information in your answers to Questions 1–3. Comment on what each prospectus says about the school and the ways in which the writer of each one has conveyed this message. You may also want to look at other aspects of the way the school is presented, such as the use of lettering.

2 | A charity campaign

This extract consists of two pages from a leaflet distributed by Plan International, a charity that invites people to sponsor a child in the developing world.

(You will find further information about some of the words in this extract on page 173.)

YOUR HELPING HAND CAN TURN DESPAIR TO HOPE

It's hard for us, living in a prosperous country, to imagine what it is like to grow up in Africa, Latin America or large parts of Asia.

In many developing countries millions of children die from malnutrition and disease before they even reach adulthood.

For most of those who survive, life is extremely hard.

They live in the most basic kind of hut. Their water for drinking, washing and cooking comes from the local river or stream. They have to work from dawn till dusk, almost from the time they can walk. And for most of the year they go hungry. An average family income is £8 to £10 a month.

Worse still, they lack the opportunity to improve their lives, because there is no education or training in practical skills.

This is what we at PLAN International UK are working to change and we need your help to succeed.

Already we are working in over 30 countries to help children in poor communities raise themselves out of poverty. We know we can change the world if we are prepared to do it one child at a time.

What can you do to help?

Today we are asking you to join our worldwide family and to hold out a helping hand to a child who urgently needs it.

You can do this now, by agreeing to sponsor a child.

It costs no more than £12 a month – 40p a day. To most people in this country, that's an affordable amount. But to a child and family in a poor village, it can be a dream come true.

Your sponsorship can give them some of the things that we take for granted in this country, such as an opportunity to go to school. It can give their families the chance to learn basic skills and health care. And it can start their communities on the long and gradual process of raising their living standards.

The face of poverty that we can change

Because you are sponsoring one particular youngster, you'll have the joy of seeing the difference your help makes. You'll see your sponsored child growing up – learning, developing and gaining in strength and confidence over the years – through letters, photographs and regular progress reports.

CHILDREN LIKE THESE NEED YOUR FRIENDSHIP TODAY!

Name: Diabe Cisse
Age: 11
Place of birth: Dankolo, Senegal, W. Africa

The village where Diabe lives, like thousands in the Third World, lacks even the most basic health care. Neither Diabe nor her brother and two sisters can read or write.

The Cisse family live in a mud compound which they share with relatives. It consists of 20 huts, along with a cookhouse, granary and animal shed.

The Cisses have to rely entirely on their own resources. The soil is poor and, if the rains fail, the crops fail too.

Name: Suresh
Age: 8
Place of birth: Kathmandu, Nepal

Suresh's father is a labourer. His mother works at home. The family do not own any land and the family's total monthly income is about £13.

They live in a house made of mud and stone, roofed with thatch and straw.

A simple woodfire on the floor is all they have for cooking. The house has no water supply or sanitation.

Name: Santos Zacarias
Age: 11
Place of birth: El Divisadero, Guatemala

Santos lives with her family in a one room house made from clay bricks. It has a dirt floor, a single window, and a lavatory in the corner.

Their only source of water is a public well some distance from the house. Santos' father is a farmer who earns barely enough for their most basic needs.

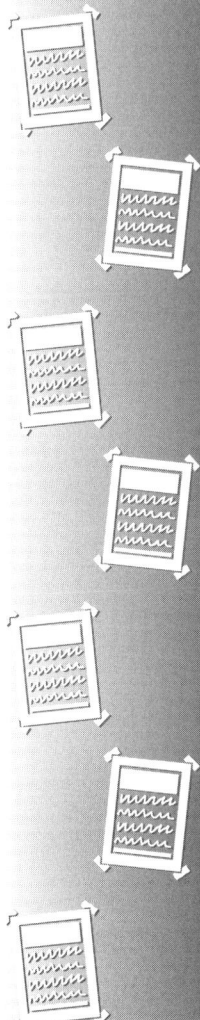

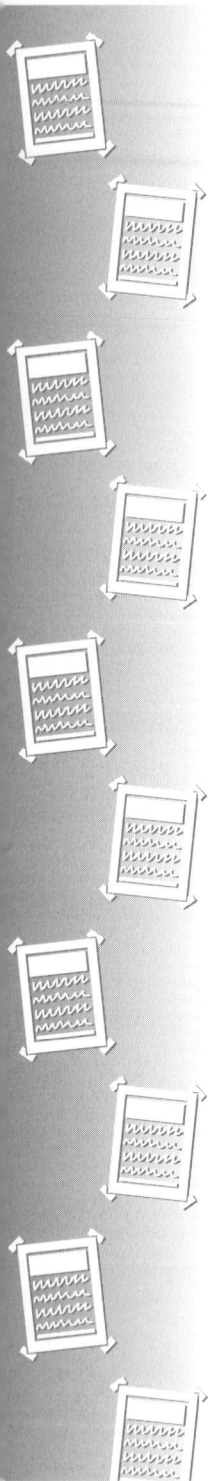

Michael Aspel and Jenny, the child he is sponsoring

Michael Aspel answers your questions about PLAN INTERNATIONAL UK

Q. Can my help really make a difference?

A. Yes, as a sponsor myself I can assure you of that. The proof is in all the schools and clinics, the new supplies of fresh water, and the wells and bridges that PLAN has helped to provide. And the many income-generating projects they've helped families to start.

Q. How can I be sure my money will be well spent?

A. PLAN takes pride in the fact that on average throughout the world, approximately 80p of every £1 contributed goes straight towards development work, with the absolute minimum being spent on administration. Your help will go to the village or area where your child lives – and every year you will receive a report from our local Field Officer to tell you what it has helped to achieve.

Q. How will my Sponsored Child be chosen?

A. When you apply to be a sponsor, you can choose whether you would like to sponsor a girl or a boy, and decide which area of the world you prefer. Your child will live in a village or community where PLAN International is already working and will be chosen by the family to represent them.

Q. How often will I hear from my child?

A. It depends. Some children love writing and send several letters a year, many with drawings of their homes and surroundings. Others are less communicative, and some (especially the younger children) may not be able to write. But PLAN's Field worker will make sure you receive news of your child at least twice a year.

Q. How long should I continue to be a sponsor?

A. Children are normally sponsored until they reach the age of 18, or until they or their family no longer need our help. But becoming a sponsor does not commit you to any fixed period. You can withdraw at any time if your circumstances change.

From 'Thinking of Sponsoring a Child', Plan International UK

CLOSER READING

1 The first section of the leaflet ('Your helping hand can turn despair to hope') aims to appeal to readers by comparing their lives with those in poorer parts of the world. It is essential, as the first paragraph states, that readers imagine what life is like in these places.

- Looking at the first five paragraphs, pick out the details that describe life in developing countries. List these, and next to each one write what your life is like in comparison.
- What emotions do you think the writer is trying to make you feel?

2 Read the remaining paragraphs in the first section (ending with '... regular progress reports.'). This part aims to give you good reasons for choosing this charity. Find evidence for the following things:

- it is already a successful charity;
- it is good value for money;
- you can transform individual lives;
- you can help to rebuild whole communities;
- you will gain a lot yourself by giving.

3 Campaigners need to make their cause stand out amongst many others that are similar. To do this they stress what is distinctive about their charity – their unique selling point. With this charity the unique selling point is the one-to-one contact with a child in another part of the world. To emphasise this, the leaflet includes examples of children who need a sponsor, giving us real individuals with which to identify.

Read the three examples in the leaflet and pick out the details the campaigners have chosen to focus on in order to gain our sympathy.

4 Another tactic used by the campaigners in this leaflet is to include a section written by a famous person, who already sponsors a child.

- **a** Why do you think they have done this?
- **b** Why do you think they have chosen to present this section in a 'question and answer' format?

5 Campaigns like this use pictures to underline what they are saying. Look at each picture in turn and say how it adds to the overall message. You could consider such things as the age, sex and facial expressions of the people in the photographs, or the backgrounds against which some are pictured.

6 There are currently 180,000 charities in the UK. One way in which a charity tries to get itself noticed is through its name. Plan International started in 1937 as Foster Plan for Children in Spain, since its aim at that time was to help orphans from the Spanish Civil War. In 1945 it became Foster Parents Plan for War Children, providing hostels for any children orphaned by the Second World War. The charity then expanded into the developing world, and in 1956 decided to drop the words 'for War Children' from its name, as it was decided that it would now deal with any need.

In 1990 the name was changed again, this time to Plan International, as there were now eight fund-raising countries. However, in Holland, which accounts for a third of the charity's business, they decided to retain the name Foster Parents Plan, as this was recognised and, they felt, contributed to their success.

In the USA there was a proposal to change the name to World Family, but this was rejected by most countries. Since then, the USA has changed the name of the charity in their country to Childreach.

Some who work for Plan International still see problems with the name: it doesn't make clear what the charity does, and it is sometimes mistaken for a family planning organisation!

a Which name do you think is the best one for the charity? Why?

b Suggest an alternative name which you think would describe what the charity does and which would make it sound attractive. Give reasons for your suggestion.

3 | A holiday brochure

The following passage is from a holiday brochure for trips to Australia. This extract is from the introductory pages.

3

'City life, country solitude, soft white sands and soaring surf. Australia has all this and much more besides.'

Whoever said you can't please all of the people all of the time obviously had never visited Australia. There's no doubt about it, Australia is all things to all people. That's hardly surprising when you consider the size - the distance from the east to west coast of this island is greater than the distance between London and Moscow.

It's a unique land of contrasts with a fascinating history. The Aborigines made Australia their home for 50,000 years before the Europeans arrived in 1788. Legends, songs and dances tell the story of how land was created and this 'Dreamtime' period can be seen in Aboriginal rock paintings at Kakadu National Park. White man brought to Australia a different way of life. Cities were built and land was cultivated...but respect has always been preserved.

The 2,000 National Parks and Reserves are evidence of this. Marine, desert, rainforest and tropical wetland ecosystems are all here to be explored. But undoubtedly two of Australia's most visited natural wonders are Uluru (Ayers Rock) and the Great Barrier Reef. In this brochure you'll find the opportunity to visit these sites and many more besides.

"Snorkelling and surfing, koalas and kookaburras, bushwalking and barbies"

NEXT 8 km

Airtours
Going further to make you happy

Where to Travel:...

Sydney
Cosmopolitan Sydney has something for everyone, with art, culture, shops, nightlife and fabulous beaches. It's the gateway to Australia and all Airtours holidays start here.

Melbourne
This is a charming city with fantastic shopping opportunities. Cultural and elegant it is a delight to explore, and of course if you love sports, there's plenty of major action here, including tennis, cricket and golf.

Adelaide
Australian hospitality, southern style. Sandwiched between the hills of the Mount Loft Ranges and the blue waters of Gulf St Vincent, Adelaide is a large modern city, surrounded by parklands and offering a Mediterranean style climate.

Cairns
Surrounded by a wealth of nature, Cairns offers easy access to tropical rainforests and the Great Barrier Reef. You'll find some of the most fascinating natural sights in this part of Australia, together with a 100 year old scenic railway.

Gold Coast
If you want long stretches of sandy beaches and resorts brimming over with theme parks and nightlife, the Gold Coast is your answer. This is pure fun in the sun.

Darwin/Kakadu
Perhaps you'd prefer the Northern Territory, with its relaxed city of Darwin at the 'Top End'. And who could resist an invitation from the Aborigines to experience the World Heritage Site of Kakadu National Park?

Perth
Many visitors fall in love with Perth with its easy going atmosphere and excellent climate. Here you can make the most of the fabulous beaches, swim in the Indian Ocean and explore the bustling Port of Freemantle.

From *Airtours: Australia*, Winter 1966/97

DICTIONARY

ecosystems particular environmental conditions

CLOSER READING

1 The extract is divided into two columns: the left-hand column is a summary of all the reasons for visiting Australia, and the right-hand column is a snapshot of each of the main places to visit.

 Re-read the left-hand column. It is made up of three paragraphs, each underlining the brochure's main theme: Australia is a diverse place with something for everyone. Find a reason in each paragraph which explains this diversity.

2 Look at the two quotations in the left-hand column. These appear to be from satisfied customers, although that is not made clear. They stand out from the main text and act as headlines.

 How do they add to the idea of Australia's diversity?

3 Re-read the right-hand column. The writer of the brochure has chosen to emphasise certain words by choosing to have them in a larger type.

 a Explain why the writer has chosen to emphasise these particular words.

 b Do you agree with the writer's choice? Which words would you choose to highlight if you were editing this extract?

4 List all the adjectives (describing words, such as 'soft') in the extract. These build up in the reader's mind to create a particular feeling about the kind of holiday Australia offers. What feeling(s) do they create in you?

4 | An estate agent's brochure

When a house is put up for sale, the estate agent produces a leaflet which promotes its positive aspects. An example of one is given below.

(Some words are highlighted in the text. You will find further information about these words at the end of the passage.)

4

Superior Three Bedroom Semi Detached

24, Chestnut Road, Donbury, Wiltshire

- Many Attractive Original Features
- Useful Basements
- Superb Family Accommodation
- £84,950

Main Accommodation

This extremely attractive Victorian property possesses many of the charming features associated with this era, including Sash Windows, Period Fireplaces and Stripped Timber Floors. A thorough inspection is essential to appreciate this attractively presented home which **comprises**: a Long Hall; Larger than average Lounge; Separate Dining Room with Built-in Original **Pantry** Cupboards; Large Kitchen; Three Good Bedrooms; Period style Bathroom; Good Sized Useful Basements. There is Off-The-Road Parking and there are **Well Stocked Gardens** to Front and Rear.

Accommodation Details

Ground Floor

Hall	26′ × 5′ 6″ maximum. An **immaculate** reception area which sets the theme for the period character throughout the property.
Lounge	16′ × 14′. An excellent main reception room featuring an interesting Victorian timber fireplace.
Dining Room	15′ × 13′ 6″. An unusual room which has a large window offering a most appealing view of the rear garden.
Kitchen	12′ × 11′. A stylish room offering a full range of storage units, work surfaces and connections for electric and gas appliances. The decor helps to retain the distinctive qualities of this house.

First Floor

Bedroom 1	14′ × 8″. Again, decorated to an attractive scheme. Ample space for fitted or free-standing furniture.
Bedroom 2	13′ × 8′ 6″. An excellent guest bedroom containing antique wash basin with gold-coloured fittings.
Bedroom 3	9′ × 6″. A useful additional room.
Bathroom	Fitted in a period style with many unique and individual features. White four piece bathroom suite with gold coloured fittings.

Basements

With immense potential for conversion into additional living space.

Outside

Pleasant, mature gardens to the front and rear with the garden to the rear of the property offering considerable privacy. Shaped lawns and useful patio area.

Location

Donbury is a much sought after location in easy reach of a number of towns which offer a range of excellent shopping and recreational facilities. The nearest motorway link is only 15 minutes by car.

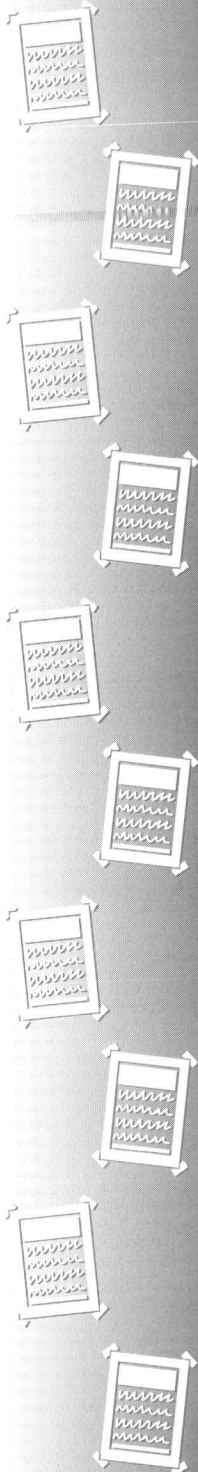

comprises includes
Pantry walk-in food cupboard
Well Stocked Gardens gardens full of plants or shrubs
immaculate in perfect condition

CLOSER READING

1 This brochure uses the same language tactic as the travel brochure: it uses a lot of positive adjectives to promote its product. Find all the adjectives in the leaflet.
   • What have they got in common?
   • How would the brochure read without these words?

2 One aspect of this house is being promoted as its unique selling point – what makes it different from or better than other houses. Write down what you think it is, and then find all the occasions this 'uniqueness' is stressed.

3 Look at the layout of the brochure. It is set out like this for two reasons:
   • to make the house as attractive as possible;
   • to communicate its attractiveness in a clear and user-friendly way.

   Do you think it succeeds? In your answer, comment on some or all of the following:
   • the choice of picture
   • the use of 'headlines'
   • the unusual use of capital letters
   • the use of italics and underlining
   • the separation of information into small sections
   • the level of the language.

4 Sometimes, if an aspect of a house is not a strong point, the estate agent will try to put a positive 'spin' on it. For instance, if a house is described as being 'handy for the town centre' it might mean that it is right next to a noisy and polluted bus station!

   Can you find any phrases in this brochure that could be interpreted in a negative way?

FURTHER ACTIVITIES

1 You should work in groups for this activity. Imagine that you are a team hired by your school to produce a prospectus. You will need to:
   • design the front cover;
   • write the introduction;

- give details of the school's achievements;
- provide information on the school's facilities, for example the library, sports hall, drama studio;
- explain the school's discipline policy;
- describe the school uniform.

You should divide these tasks between you. For some of these areas you will need to do some research: ask your teacher where you can get hold of the information you need.

Remember, your aim is to attract as many parents as possible, so you must try to present your school in the most positive way. Although you can't lie, you can focus on what your school does best. This will mean drawing your parents' attention to the school's values, achievements and strengths in an interesting and eye-catching way. Consider the following things:

- the values your school believes in (those things the school considers important);
- positive words to communicate those values;
- images and colours that convey those values;
- the layout of the prospectus, which should make your ideas clear and eye-catching.

2 Imagine that you have been on a holiday, which was a great disappointment. All the good things that the brochure claimed about the place where you were staying turned out to be half-truths. It had also failed to mention a number of bad points.

a This task should be done in pairs. Firstly, each of you should write and design an entry for a holiday brochure.

You should use as many positive words as possible in your writing, making the holiday destination sound like the fulfilment of a dream. The pictures should also give a very positive image of the place.

b Now swap your brochure entry with your partner and read what they have written. Imagine that you went on this holiday and it was a total disaster. Write your own version of what happened. You aim to send your version to a consumer magazine which advises people on the truth behind brochures.

You should explain how the brochure failed to mention all the negative sides of your holiday destination. Also, you should say how some of the things stated in the advertisement were misleading. For example, 'in walking distance of the beach' may not have been a lie as long as you were prepared to walk five miles! Similarly, 'a lively atmosphere' may, in reality, have been describing a disco where there are continual fights …

3 Choose a cause that you really believe in. It could, for example, be concerned with vulnerable people or animals, treatment for illnesses or an environmental issue.

Design a leaflet which promotes this cause. (You could write one for a charity that already exists or invent your own.) Look back at Text no. 2 in this chapter (pages 171–172), which features a campaign by Plan International. If your campaign is to be successful you should:

- stress the urgency of your campaign;
- make the reader feel certain emotions, such as guilt, sympathy, anger;
- use emotive words to help encourage these feelings – in particular, strong adjectives;
- include a dramatic and memorable headline;
- explain how the reader will not have to give up much, but will receive great satisfaction;
- include examples that the reader can identify with;
- set out the writing in short, punchy paragraphs, each of which gives a clear reason for supporting the charity.

The layout and pictures in the leaflet are as important as the text. Make sure you:

- underline the emotions you want to encourage in the reader in your choice of photographs, drawings or charts;
- emphasise words by different lettering, using bold or underlining
- use colour to help create the right feeling (even if you choose to stick to black and white).

4 Imagine that you had to write the estate agent's leaflet for your own house. You need to make it sound as attractive as possible so that you can get a quick sale and the best price. Look back at the example in Text no. 4 (page 177) to see how you should set your leaflet out. You could also visit your local estate agents and get hold of a range of brochures, which would give you further ideas about language and layout.

Remember the following points:

- use as many positive words as you can;
- stress the unique aspects of your house;
- either ignore any problems or make them sound minor;
- describe its location and outlook positively;
- make it sound as though it is a bargain;
- make sure the layout is user-friendly;
- turn any limitations into good points, for example 'small' could become 'cosy'.

When you have finished your leaflet, get into groups and read through each other's. You could then vote on whose house you would most like to buy!

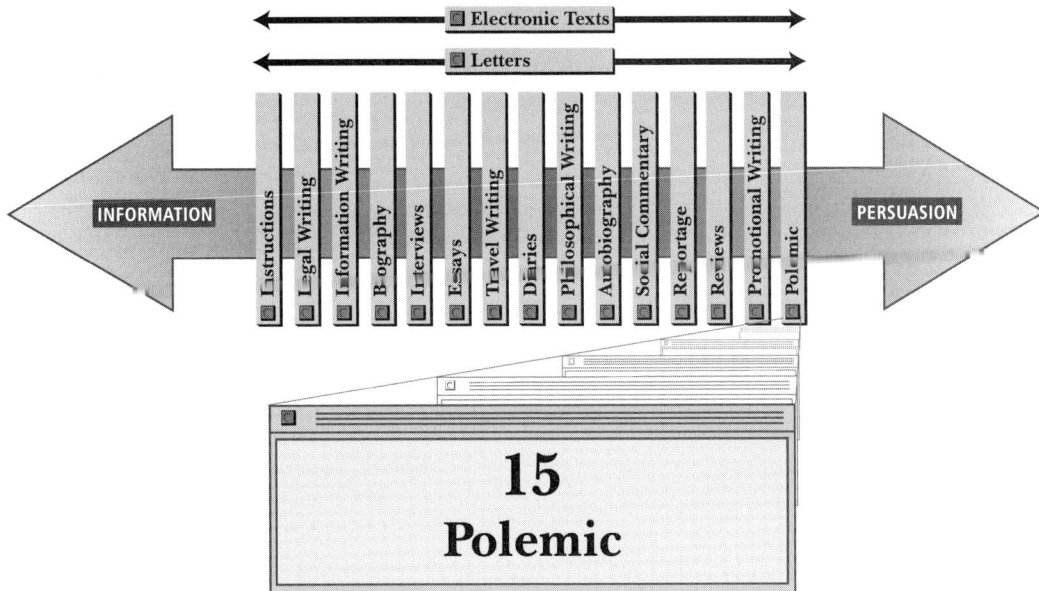

The diagram shows an arrow spectrum ranging from INFORMATION on the left to PERSUASION on the right, with the following categories labelled: Instructions, Legal Writing, Information Writing, Biography, Interviews, Essays, Travel Writing, Diaries, Philosophical Writing, Autobiography, Social Commentary, Reportage, Reviews, Promotional Writing, Polemic. Above these are two double-headed arrows labelled Electronic Texts and Letters.

15
Polemic

Polemic is writing from a committed point of view, and is aimed at persuading its readers of the complete rightness of some cause, and the utter wrongness of another. One example of polemical writing which you may already be familiar with is Mark Antony's speech from Shakespeare's *Julius Caesar*, in which Shakespeare has Mark Antony incite the crowd to attack Caesar's murderers, while apparently speaking in support of the murderers himself.

In the passages that follow, you will be asked to identify the point of view being expressed, and to assess the effectiveness of the way in which it is expressed in terms of persuading its readers of the rightness of its cause.

1 | I have a dream …

This is an extract from a speech by Martin Luther King, an African-American Baptist pastor and activist. He was a leading figure in the American Civil Rights Movement in the 1960s, a movement concerned with finally achieving equal voting, schooling and employment rights for African-Americans. 'I Have a Dream', which was his most famous speech, was given in Washington in 1963. He was assassinated in 1968.

(Some words are highlighted in the text. You will find further information about these words at the end of the passage.)

I have a dream that my four little children will one day live in a nation where they will not be judged by the colour of their skin but by the content of their character.

I have a dream today.

I have a dream that one day the state of **Alabama**, whose governor's lips are presently dripping with the words of **interposition** and **nullification**, will be transformed into a situation where little black boys and black girls will be able to join hands with little white boys and white girls and walk together as sisters and brothers.

10   I have a dream today.

I have a dream that one day **every valley shall be exalted**, every hill and mountain shall be made low, the rough places will be made plain, and the crooked places will be made straight, and the glory of the Lord will be revealed, and all flesh shall see it together.

This is our hope. This is the faith with which I return to the South. With this faith we will be able to **hew** out of the mountain of despair a stone of hope. With this faith we will be able to transform the jangling discords of our nation into a beautiful symphony of brotherhood. With this faith we will be able to work together, to pray together, to struggle together, to go to jail
20   together, to stand up for freedom together, knowing that we will be free one day.

This will be the day when all of God's children will be able to sing with new meaning 'My country 'tis of thee, sweet land of liberty, of thee I sing. Land where my fathers died, land of the pilgrim's pride, from every mountainside, let freedom ring.'

And if America is to be a great nation this must become true. So let freedom ring from the prodigious hilltops of New Hampshire! Let freedom ring from the mighty mountains of New York! Let freedom ring from the heightening Alleghenies of Pennsylvania!

30 Let freedom ring from the snowcapped Rockies of Colorado!

Let freedom ring from the curvaceous peaks of California!

But not only that; let freedom ring from the Stone Mountain of Georgia!

Let freedom ring from every hill and mole hill of Mississippi. From every mountainside, let freedom ring.

When we let freedom ring, when we let it ring from every village and every **hamlet**, from every state and every city, we will be able to speed up that day when all of God's children, black men and white men, Jews and Gentiles, Protestants and Catholics, will be able to join hands and sing in the words of that old Negro spiritual, 'Free at last! Free at last! Thank God almighty, we **40** are free at last!'

> **DICTIONARY**
>
> **Alabama** a state in the southern United States, where slave-owning had been commonplace until it was outlawed in the 19th century, and where assumptions of white people's superiority over African-Americans were still strong in the 1960s
>
> **interposition** intervention
>
> **nullification** the action, on the part of a State legislature, of refusing to allow a general law to be enforced within the State
>
> **every valley shall be exalted ...** this and the rest of the paragraph is a reference to, and quotation from, the Bible
>
> **hew** dig
>
> **hamlet** tiny village

CLOSER READING

1 There are four stages to Martin Luther King's speech in this extract. Re-read the whole passage carefully, and decide where each of these stages begins and ends.

2 In your own words, summarise each of the four stages in two or three sentences.

3 Re-write the sentences that you have written, making any changes necessary, to make them into a continuous summary of the passage.

4 Re-read your summary, and then look at the original extract again. Note down the differences in style between your summary and the original.

5 In a few sentences, with examples from the text, explain the characteristics of Martin Luther King's style in this extract, and try to explain why it is written as it is.

2 | The battle for personal freedom

This is an extract from *Why Vote Conservative?* by David Willetts. At the time of writing this passage, David Willetts was a Conservative Member of Parliament who had been active for some time in formulating the policy of the Conservative Party. The book from which this extract was taken was published in the spring of 1997, just before a General Election in which the Conservatives were hoping to be returned to power, but were in fact massively defeated.

(Some words are highlighted in the text. You will find further information about these words at the end of the passage.)

Conservatives have spent this century fighting the battle for personal freedom with energy and with **relish**. Our opponents, first the New Liberals at the turn of the century, then **command-economy** socialists, and now Tony Blair's Labour Party, all share a belief in interventionist, intrusive government. Conservatives by contrast trust the people.

Since 1979 Conservative Governments have moved forward like ice-breakers, ploughing their way through the frozen wastes of state control. Back then the state tried to fix the price of goods in the shops. It tried to fix the pay which people received and threatened to blacklist and withhold contracts from

10 firms which did not pay the rates which government thought right. It controlled the amount of money which companies could distribute in dividends to put into our pension funds. It controlled how many pounds we could take abroad. Now all that seems incredible. Anybody who tried to argue for such policies would be laughed out of court. We have won a great victory.

There are several reasons for our victory. One is the sheer intellectual creativity of **free-market economics** over the past twenty years. Great excitement and energy has been generated by applying elementary economic tools (supply and demand, cost–benefit analysis, the price mechanism) to

20 areas which are wrongly thought to be somehow **immune from** rational economic appraisal. A rich and ambitious policy agenda has developed – including privatization, tax reform, and internal markets within the public sector. Free marketeers have generated the ideas and ideas matter in politics.

Technology and industrial change have also been on our side, promoting individualism both in production and in consumption. For most of this century the dominant industrial model was large-scale manufacturing, with hundreds of workers carrying out virtually identical tasks on long production lines. Now large firms are a declining proportion of total national output and employment. We see the rise of small firms and larger enterprises

30 **restructuring** so that people work in smaller groups. Rewards are increasingly not fixed on some standardized basis but individually determined (and our left-wing **egalitarians**, so preoccupied with explaining

greater dispersion of income in terms of the tax and benefits system, completely fail to understand that the crucial explanation is greater tailoring of pay to personal skills). Technology also makes market solutions practical in areas where they were just theoretical curiosities in the past ...

Above all, the appeal to personal freedom has a moral authority which it is almost impossible to challenge. As Margaret Thatcher so powerfully showed, people respond to the message that they are free to choose, can seize
40 opportunities, can make their own way in the world and can take responsibility for their own actions.

The power of free-market thinking, the drive of technology, the collapse of Marxism, the moral authority of the appeal to personal freedom, all mean that modern Conservatives ought to feel that the tide of ideas and events is in our favour. The main problem facing Conservatism in Britain should be triumphalism and complacency. That vigorous, exhilarating battle over the past twenty years should have left us enjoying the same domination of the political scene as Liberalism enjoyed in the middle of the last century.

By and large, parties which win the battle so comprehensively stay in office
50 for a generation. It is wrong to think of British policies as somehow delivering frequent and regular changes of government. In practice in Britain, as in many other advanced Western countries, the tendency has been for a dominant party to emerge which captures the spirit of the age and carries it forward. Modern Conservatives occupy precisely such a position in Britain today.

On some measures that dominance is clear – nearly eighteen years in government is no mean feat. But in other ways Conservatives can still feel like an **embattled** minority: the media, the Church, academia, are still largely uncomprehending and the conventional wisdom hostile. Despite all
60 the advances we have made since 1979, the collapse of the socialist Left has not given the Conservatives the intellectual dominance which we deserve.

From D. Willetts, *Why Vote Conservative?*, Penguin Books, 1997

DICTIONARY

relish eagerness, enjoyment

command-economy a system in which the economy of a country is managed by the State rather than through individuals and companies

free-market economics a system which allows the laws of supply and demand to dictate the economy

immune from untouched by

restructuring changing the organisation of

egalitarians people who believe in equality

embattled surrounded by enemies

©LOSER READING

1 Re-read the third and fourth paragraphs of the extract (lines 16–36) and list in your own words all the reasons David Willetts puts forward for the triumph of Conservatism.

2 Look again through the passage as a whole, and draw up two lists, one for all the things that Willetts sees as positive, the other for all those that he sees as negative. Your lists might begin like this.

Positive	Negative
Trusting the people	Interventionist, intrusive government

3 Re-read the final paragraph of the extract (lines 56–61).
  • Summarise in your own words the point that Willetts is making here.
  • Say how the use of the word 'deserve' links to the rest of the extract.

3 The work ethic

This is an article entitled 'The Haunted House' by Zygmunt Bauman, Professor of Sociology at Leeds University in England. His main concerns are with the nature of society today, and how we meet changing demands in the workplace.

(Some words are highlighted in the text. You will find further information about these words at the end of the passage.)

Whenever you hear talk about '**ethics**' you can be pretty sure that someone somewhere is dissatisfied with the way other people are behaving and would rather they behaved differently. This is especially true in the case of the notorious '**work ethic**'.

Since its emergence in the early days of the Industrial Revolution, the work ethic has served politicians, philosophers and preachers by removing the obstacles to the brave new world they envisaged.

The main obstacle was the basic human inclination to do no more than satisfy one's needs. Why work more than necessary? the individual might ask.
10   For more money? There are so many other worthwhile things to do of which you might lose sight if you spent all your time running after money.

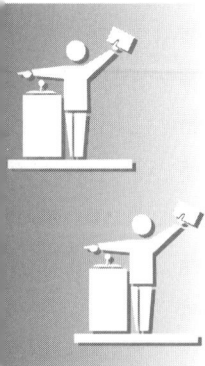

The early **entrepreneurs** had different plans, though. **Shiftless** and **laggard** factory hands were to be taught – or forced if need be – to wish for a better life, to desire more, and to improve themselves by desiring more.

The moral crusade for the work ethic was presented as trying to recapture – within the factory – the commitment and pride that came naturally to the craftsperson. The trouble was that it was the factory system itself which had destroyed these in the first place.

So under the guise of a work ethic a *discipline* ethic had to be promoted. As
20 Werner Sombart commented, the factory system needed part-humans: soulless little wheels of a complex mechanism – and war was waged against the other, now useless, emotional 'human parts'. No wonder critics of that time such as Ferdinand Lasselle spoke in support of the 'right to laziness'.

Finally, for the first time in history, the work ethic prioritized 'what can be done' over 'what needs to be done'. The satisfaction of human needs became irrelevant to the logic of production – and cleared the way for the modern **paradox** of 'growth for growth's sake'.

Since then, however, something has happened which neither the industrialists nor the critics of capitalism imagined. A century ago Rosa
30 Luxemburg predicted that capitalist modernization could not survive without devouring the ever-shrinking **enclaves** of non-industrialized life. The tendency of capital to move from already 'modernized' areas and into the 'under-developed' territories of the Third World seems to have proved her right.

But what she did not predict was that Modernism (or industrialism) would create expanding enclaves of 'post-modern' existence in which people are consumers first – and workers only a very distant second. The work ethic has been replaced by the consumer ethic; the savings-book culture of delayed **gratification** has been replaced by the credit-card culture that 'takes the
40 waiting out of wanting'. The inhabitants of these enclaves are kept in place not be coercion but by seduction, by the creation of new desires rather than by normative regulation.

Inside these post-modern enclaves the work ethic has lost its obvious and crucial usefulness. There is simply not enough paid employment any more to support the model of full-time jobs for life.

It is tempting to applaud the **demise** of the work ethic and to rejoice in the post-modern way's recognition of the multiplicity of human existence. The learned classes are always the first to wax lyrical about the blessings of new life. Now they praise liberation from the **stultifying** monotony of assembly
50 lines with as much **ardour** as their predecessors a century ago brought to their songs about the glory of factory chimneys. What the songs of praise stifle, however, are the voices of the victims: the new poor, denied the opportunity to follow the rules of the work ethic in a world in which the only access to the resources needed to exercise one's freedom is still through the door marked 'work'.

The idea that the poor – and the rich – will always be with us is not new. But never before has the split been so unambiguous, so unequivocal. The reason

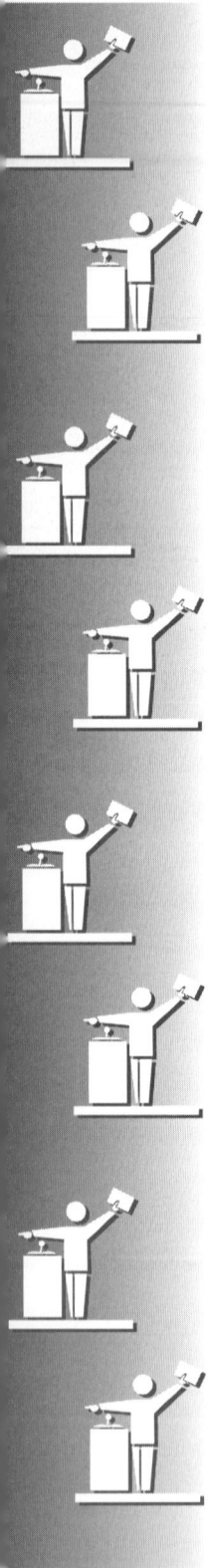

is simple. The rich – who happen also to be the most politically powerful – no longer need the poor. They do not need the poor for the salvation of their souls – which they do not believe they have and which at any rate they would not consider worthy of care. Nor do the rich need the poor for staying rich or getting richer – in fact they reckon they would be better off if the poor weren't there at all, making claims on their riches.

The poor are not a reserve army of labour which needs to be groomed back into wealth-production. Neither are they consumers who must be tempted and cajoled into 'giving the lead to economic recovery'. Whichever way you look at it, the poor are of no use. This is a real novelty in a world undergoing perhaps the deepest transformation in the long history of humankind.

So the mutual dependency between rich and poor has gone. No wonder the US pollsters of both competing camps informed their respective candidates for the Presidency that the voters wanted cuts in benefits to the poor and lower taxes on the rich. Both rivals did their best to outspit each other in their proposals to cut down welfare assistance and to lavish the saved funds on building new prisons and employing more police. As Pastor John Steinbruck, the minister at Luther Place Memorial Church in Washington, recently summed it up: 'This nation has as its symbol the Statue of Liberty, with the message carved at its base "Give me your poor, your homeless, your huddled masses". But here we are now in this damn country, the richest in history, and we've forgotten all that.'

To a growing number of people the demise of the work ethic comes too early and in too malformed a fashion to be experienced as a liberation. What such people know for sure is that there is not enough work for them in a society that can easily obtain all the goods it needs – and more – without calling on their labour power. But at the same time they are told that in order to get access to those goods they have to sell their labour. They are reminded, day by day, that without 'being available for work' they are not entitled to any part of the social riches, however meagre and pitiable their share might be. In the US they were told recently that they would be allowed to stay out of work for no more than two years during their entire life. Regardless of the reasons for their unemployment, they are derided as misfits, reproached for **sloth**, dubbed anti-social and **stigmatized** as spongers.

The fact is that the house of post-modernity is haunted by the ghost of the work ethic, no less sinister in its posthumous life than it was in its **halcyon days**.

We have two worlds, at opposite poles, which are becoming increasingly out of touch with each other – much as the no-go areas of contemporary cities are carefully fenced off and bypassed by the traffic lines used for the mobility of well-off residents. The inhabitants of the First World, the relatively affluent and employed, live in a perpetual present. These people are constantly busy and always 'short of time'. People marooned in the opposite world are crushed under the burden of abundant, redundant and useless time they can fill with nothing. In their time 'nothing ever happens'. They do not 'control' time – but neither are they controlled by it, unlike their clocking-in, clocking-out ancestors, subject to the faceless rhythm of factory time. They can only kill time, as they are slowly killed by it.

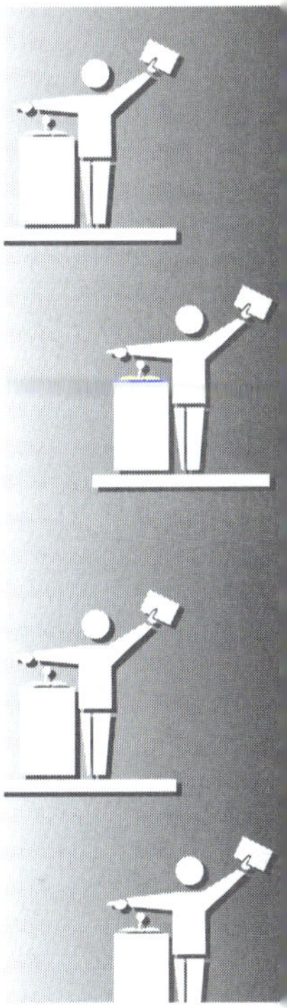

For the residents of the first world, abiding by the rules of the work ethic and sacrificing their lives to professional success is the supreme test of freedom. They wear the badge 'workaholic' with pride. For the inhabitants of the second, not being able to follow their example is the symptom of failure and carries a stigma of shame.

Those who have the capacity to act out the principles of the work ethic at will are sceptical and ironic about its virtues. But those who can only dream of their share of a chance bitterly complain of their deprivation. If their ancestors rightly saw the work-ethics preachers as the enemies of their freedom, today's unemployed see those who criticize the work ethic as members of a worldwide conspiracy against their right to humanity.

And this will remain the case unless, as Claus Offe suggests, the proper conclusions from the great social transformation are drawn and *all* lifestyles are treated equally, including lifestyles that do not involve employment or do so only in a very fragmentary fashion. The old distinction between 'anomalous' and 'normal' life situations and modes of conduct needs to be abolished. Not just in word, but in deed: through breaking the link between employment and living resources and establishing material entitlements to all citizens – a 'minimum wage' that is not tied to work.

Exorcising the spectre of the work ethic will take no less than that.

Z. Bauman, 'The Haunted House', *New Internationalist*, April 1997

DICTIONARY

ethics morality
work ethic the belief that moral goodness is achieved through work
entrepreneurs businessmen
Shiftless lazy
laggard slow
paradox apparent contradiction
enclaves small areas
gratification pleasure
demise death
stultifying numbing and boring
ardour passion
sloth laziness
stigmatized unpleasantly labelled
halcyon days prime of life

CLOSER READING

1 Look again at the first seven paragraphs of the passage (lines 1–27). In your own words, summarise the reasons that Bauman gives for the rise of the 'work ethic'.

2 Re-read paragraphs eight and nine (lines 28–42). What does Bauman say has happened to the work ethic in recent years?

3 Look again at the rest of the passage apart from the last two paragraphs (lines 43–116) and summarise in your own words, in two or three sentences, the main point that Bauman is making.

4 Re-read the last three paragraphs of the passage (lines 111–125). Say in your own words what is the course of action that Bauman is recommending.

---

4 A Modest Proposal for Preventing the Children of Poor People from Being a Burthen to their Parents, or the Country, and for Making them Beneficial to the Publick

This is an extract from a pamphlet published in 1729 by Jonathan Swift. Swift, best known as the author of *Gulliver's Travels*, was born in Ireland and, although of English parentage, was deeply concerned with the Irish cause and with the difficulties endured by the Irish through the English conquest of Ireland. In particular, laws passed by the English in favour of England and of English landlords had reduced the Irish peasant community to a state of profound poverty by the end of the 17th century. It was this situation against which Swift was protesting in his pamphlet.

(Some words are highlighted in the text. You will find further information about these words at the end of the passage.)

It is a melancholly Object to those, who walk through this great Town, or travel in the Country, when they see the Streets, the Roads, and Cabbin-Doors, crowded with Beggars of the female Sex, followed by three, four, or six Children, all in Rags, and **importuning** every **Passenger** for an **Alms**. These Mothers instead of being able to work for their honest livelyhood, are forced to employ all their time in Stroling, to beg **Sustenance** for their helpless Infants, who, as they grow up, either turn Thieves for want of work, or leave their dear native Country to fight for the **Pretender** in Spain, or sell themselves to the **Barbadoes**.

10   I think it is agreed by all Parties, that this prodigious number of Children, in the Arms, or on the Backs, or at the heels of their Mothers, and frequently of their Fathers, is in the present deplorable state of the Kingdom, a very great additional grievance; and therefore whoever could find out a fair, cheap and easy method of making these Children sound and useful Members of the common-wealth would deserve so well of the publick, as to have his Statue set up for a preserver of the Nation …

The number of Souls in this Kingdom being usually reckoned one Million and a half, of these I calculate there may be about two hundred thousand Couples whose Wives are Breeders, from which number I Substract thirty
20   Thousand Couples, who are able to maintain their own Children, although I apprehend there cannot be so many under the present distresses of the Kingdom, but this being granted, there will remain an hundred and seventy

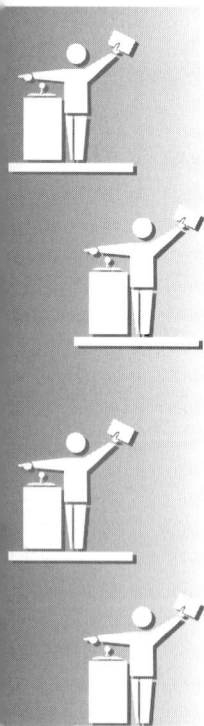

thousand Breeders. I again Substract fifty Thousand for those Women who miscarry, or whose Children dye by accident, or disease within the Year. There only remain an hundred and twenty thousand Children of poor Parents annually born: The question therefore is, how this number shall be reared, and provided for, which, as I have already said, under the present Situation of Affairs, is utterly impossible by all the methods hitherto proposed, for we can neither employ them in Handicraft, or Agriculture; we

30 neither build Houses, (I mean in the Country) nor cultivate Land: They can very seldom pick up a Livelihood by Stealing till they arrive at six years Old, except where they are of towardly parts, although, I confess they learn the Rudiments much earlier, during which time, they can however be properly looked upon only as Probationers, as I have been informed by a principal Gentleman in the County of Cavan, who protested to me, that he never knew above one or two Instances under the Age of six, even in a part of the Kingdom so renowned for the quickest proficiency in that Art.

I am assured by our Merchants, that a Boy or Girl, before twelve years Old, is no saleable Commodity, and even when they come to this Age, they will not

40 yield above three Pounds, or three Pounds and half a Crown at most on the Exchange, which cannot turn to Account either to the Parents or the Kingdom, the Charge of Nutriment and Rags having been at least four times that Value.

I shall now therefore humbly propose my own thoughts, which I hope will not be lyable to the least Objection.

I have been assured by a very knowing American of my acquaintance in London, that a young healthy Child well Nursed is at a year Old a most delicious, nourishing, and wholesome Food, whether Stewed, Roasted, Baked, or Boyled, and I make no doubt that it will equally serve in a **Fricasie**,

50 or a **Ragoust**.

I do therefore humbly offer it to publick consideration, that of the hundred and twenty thousand Children, already computed, twenty thousand may be reserved for Breed, whereof only one fourth part to be Males, which is more than we allow to Sheep, black Cattle, or Swine, and my reason is that these Children are seldom the Fruits of Marriage, a Circumstance not much regarded by our Savages, therefore one Male will be sufficient to serve four Females. That the remaining hundred thousand may at a year Old be offered in Sale to the persons of Quality, and Fortune, through the Kingdom, always advising the Mother to let them Suck plentifully in the last Month, so as to

60 render them Plump, and Fat for a good Table. A Child will make two Dishes at an Entertainment for Friends, and when the Family dines alone, the fore or hind Quarter will make a reasonable Dish, and seasoned with a little Pepper or Salt will be very good Boiled on the fourth Day, especially in Winter.

I have reckoned upon a Medium, that a Child just born will weigh 12 pounds, and in a solar Year if tollerably nursed encreaseth to 28 Pound.

I grant this food will be somewhat dear, and therefore very proper for Landlords, who, as they have already devoured most of the Parents, seem to have the best Title to the Children.

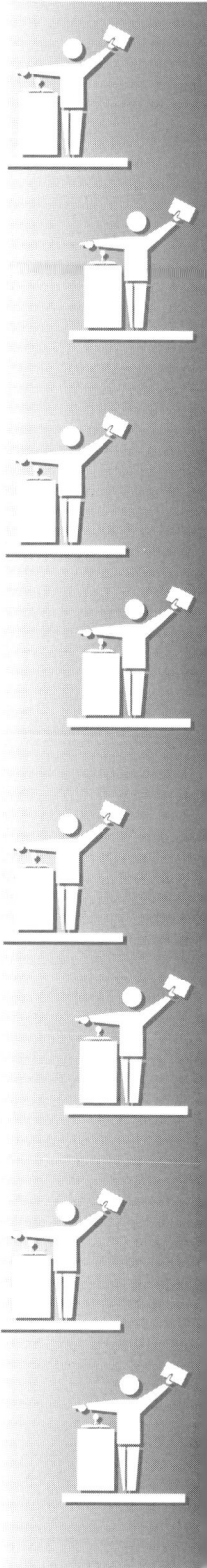

From J. Swift, 'A Modest Proposal', ed. J. Hayward, Nonesuch Press, 1939

DICTIONARY

importuning bothering

Passenger passer-by

Alms handout

Sustenance food

Pretender claimant to the English throne

Barbadoes West Indies, where people could sell their labour on long-term contract

Fricasie fried dish

Ragoust stew

CLOSER READING

1 Look again at the first two paragraphs of the passage (lines 1–16). Summarise in your own words the situation that Swift is describing here.

2 Re-read the third paragraph (lines 17–37) and say in your own words which part of the problem Swift says he is going to address.

3 Look again at the rest of the passage except for the last paragraph (lines 38–65). What is the solution that Swift is putting forward? Summarise it in your own words in two or three sentences.

4 Re-read the final paragraph of the passage (lines 66–68). Say in your own words what point Swift is making here, and how it links with the passage as a whole.

FURTHER ACTIVITIES

1 On your own, re-read Text no. 2 and Text no. 3 (pages 184–185 and 186–189 above).

- Make notes on the general position that each of the authors is taking up.
- With a partner, imagine a conversation between Willetts and Bauman, in which each is trying to convince the other of their own point of view.
- Write up your conversation as a playscript and perform it to the rest of the class.

2 On your own, re-read Text no. 1 and Text no. 4 (pages 182–183 and 190–191 above).

- Rewrite Text no. 4, saying directly what Swift wishes to change and why, modelling your style on that used by Martin Luther King.
- Write a short review of your version of 'A Modest Proposal', comparing it with the original, and saying which you feel would be more effective in putting forward a point of view, and why. Use quotations to back up your argument.

3 On your own, choose a topic about which you feel strongly.

- Use whatever books and other sources of information you can find to research the topic thoroughly, so that you have a solid base of facts on which to base your case.
- Choose any one of the four texts in this section as a model, and write an argument for your point of view, in the style of your chosen text.

4 Working in groups of four, divide into two pairs.

- One pair in the group must research the arguments in favour of abolishing experiments of animals, while the other pair researches the arguments in favour of continuing animal experiments.
- Using Martin Luther King's speech (Text no. 1) as your model, work with your partner to compose an exciting speech supporting your side of the argument.
- Listen to each other's speeches, and make notes on the main points that your opponents are making.
- On your own, write an argumentative essay on animal experiments, using the information you have gathered to make a balanced case before arguing your own point of view.

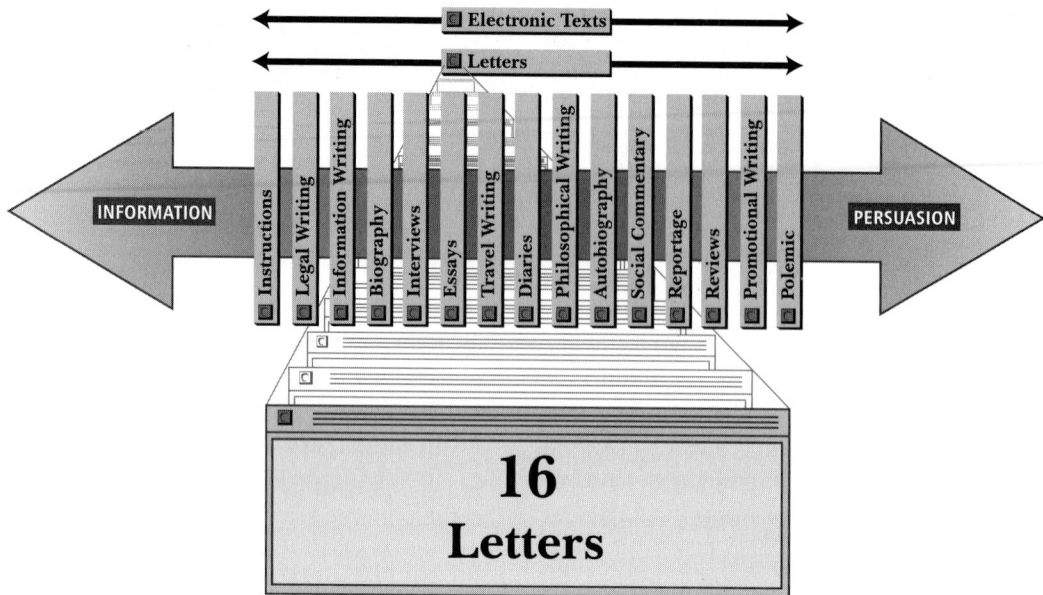

INFORMATION ← → PERSUASION

Electronic Texts

Letters

Instructions · Legal Writing · Information Writing · Biography · Interviews · Essays · Travel Writing · Diaries · Philosophical Writing · Autobiography · Social Commentary · Reportage · Reviews · Promotional Writing · Polemic

16
Letters

Letters can be anything – persuasive, informational, autobiographical, instructional, intimate, formal and even, on occasions, fictional. The important thing is that the language and layout fit the purpose for which the letter is being written.

In the section that follows you will find a range of different letters, written for different kinds of audience, with different aims in view. While you are reading them, think about the way in which the purpose for which the letter is written affects the tone and choice of language of the letter-writer.

1 │ Life sucks

Advice columns in newspapers and magazines are a modern invention. They provide a way of asking for and getting advice on topics that are sometimes too intimate and embarrassing to share with friends and family. The tone of voice they adopt tends to be one of friendly conversation, although with an awareness that, while the subject may be personal, it will be read by thousands of people.

Below is a selection of letters to Life Sucks, the advice column of *J-17*, a magazine aimed at young teenage girls. The replies are from Anita Naik, the 'agony aunt' for the column.

Your letters

A

Mum's so embarrassing

My mum's quite young compared to my mates' mums and is always showing me up. Once, my friends and I came home to find her getting off with her boyfriend on the sofa. I nearly died, but she just laughed it off. Another time she picked me up from school in tight leather trousers and once she asked my friends what they thought of Wonderbras. She thinks it's funny, but I don't.

Boyzone Fan (14), Kent

Cringey parents are more common than you think. But what's mortifying to you isn't to an outsider. You're sensitive about your mum's antics, simply because she's your mum. In some people's eyes, she's probably pretty cool! While you'll never change her completely (would you want to?), I'm sure she'd be open to suggestions about how she can be less embarrassing. So tell her how you feel (nicely!) and see how things go.

B

I can't trust him any more

I've been going out with my boyfriend for three months and thought he was sweet, shy and kind – a perfect boyfriend. But now he's told me things about his past which have changed my opinion. He said he lost his virginity when he was 12, and two weeks before I met him he slept with his best mate's sister and dumped her two days later. I feel a bit funny about all this and it's putting me off him. It's like he lied to me about who he really was. My friends think I'm overreacting. Am I?

Tanya (16), Devon

Your boyfriend's still the same person he was before he told you all these things. What's changed is your *view* of him. In your mind you made him 'perfect' and now you're annoyed with him. You have to remember he didn't have to tell you these things, he obviously chose to because he trusted you. However, if you feel funny, don't keep quiet about it. The only way you're going to feel better about all this is by discussing it with him.

From 'Life Sucks', *J-17*, May 1997

CLOSER READING

1 Look again at passage A. Draw up two columns. In one, headed Negative, list all the things that the girl writing in finds embarrassing about her mother. In the other, headed Positive, list all the different points made by Anita Naik. Your list may start something like this.

Negative	Positive
Turned up at school wearing tight leather trousers	She's pretty cool!

2 Re-read passage B, and draw up the same kind of Positive/Negative lists that you have already made for passage A.

3 In your own words, summarise each of the four letters. Try to do this in one sentence for each letter.

4 Look again at the two letters from Anita Naik. Is there anything in common between them in the kind of advice she is giving? In your own words, write two or three sentences describing Anita Naik's approach to giving advice.

2 A formal business letter

Business letters can come in all forms, written for all sorts of occasions, ranging from the informative to the persuasive. The one thing they have in common, though, is that they are written in formal Standard English, and that the writers avoid any use of slang or colloquial expressions.

The letter below is an example of a letter from a company handling insurance policies, reminding somebody that their insurance policy on the contents of their house is about to fall due for renewal.

(Some words are highlighted in the text. You will find further information about these words at the end of the passage.)

Mid-County Insurance Services
Insurance Brokers & Independent Financial Advisors
240A The High Street, Upper Stanton, Oxon OX15 9PQ

Broker **Ref:** SMSM01HC01
09/10/97

Mr Jones
3 Levellers Cottages
Upper Stanton
Oxon
OX15 8PZ

Dear Mr Jones,

Re: *Householders Comp. Policy No. 87611d27925*

Risk Address	*Sum Insured*	
3 Levellers Cottages	Buildings	£Nil
Upper Stanton	Contents	£17881
Oxon		

We have to inform you that the above policy expires on 06/11/1997 and we request that the renewal **premium** of £151.87 is paid at least one week prior to this date as no further reminder will be sent.

New policies are now available which may be more suitable for your needs. If you would like to discuss your policy please do not hesitate to contact us. Values have changed considerably during the last few years, and it is **imperative** that the sums insured are **maintained** in line with current replacement costs, otherwise difficulties will arise in the event of a claim.

If you wish to pay by Visa, Access or instalments, please complete the attached sheet. We look forward to hearing from you shortly.

Yours sincerely

Mid-County Insurance Services

Enc.

DICTIONARY

Ref reference, the title under which this document is filed

Re with reference to, about

premium in an insurance policy, the agreed amount to be paid to the insurers

imperative crucially important

maintained kept up

Enc. further documents are enclosed with this letter

◉ CLOSER READING

1 There are four main items of information in the letter. Note them down.

2 Sort the items of information into two categories: information that *must* be acted upon and information that *may* be acted upon.

3 Re-write the letter in your own words, using less formal language, but making sure that all the information you have listed is included.

---

3 Letter from No Man's Land

Wilfred Owen was a poet who, as young man at the beginning of the First World War (1914–1918), was living and working in France. He joined the British army and served as an officer during the war, writing some of the hardest-hitting and best-known poetry dealing with the experiences of war. He was killed in 1918, two weeks before the war came to an end. The passage below is an extract from a letter which he sent to his mother early in 1917.

(Some words are highlighted in the text. You will find further information about these words at the end of the passage.)

Tues. 16 January 1917   [2nd Manchester Regt., **B.E.F.**]

My own sweet Mother,

I am sorry you have had about 5 days letterless. I hope you have had my two letters 'posted' since you wrote your last, which I received tonight. I am bitterly disappointed that I never got one of yours.

I can see no excuse for deceiving you about these last 4 days. I have suffered seventh hell.

I have not been at the front.

I have been in front of it.

10   I held an advanced post, that is, a '**dug-out**' in the middle of **No Man's Land**.

We had a march of 3 miles over shelled road then nearly 3 along a flooded **trench**. After that we came to where the trenches had been blown flat out and had to go over the top. It was of course dark, too dark, and the ground was not mud, not sloppy mud, but an octopus of sucking clay, 3, 4, and 5 feet deep, relieved only by craters full of water. Men have been known to drown in them. Many stuck in the mud & only got on by leaving their waders, equipment, and in some cases their clothes.

High explosives were dropping all around out[side], and machine guns
spluttered every few minutes. But it was so dark that even the German flares
20   did not reveal us.

Three quarters dead, I mean each of us $\frac{3}{4}$ dead, we reached the dug-out and
relieved the wretches therein. I then had to go forth and find another dug-
out for a still more advanced post where I left 18 bombers. I was responsible
for other posts on the left but there was a junior officer in charge.

My dug-out held 25 men tight packed. Water filled it to a depth of 1 or 2
feet, leaving say 4 feet of air.

One entrance had been blown in & blocked.

So far, the other remained.

The Germans knew we were staying there and decided we shouldn't.

30   Those fifty hours were the agony of my happy life.

Every ten minutes on Sunday afternoon seemed an hour.

I nearly broke down and let myself drown in the water that was now slowly
rising over my knees.

Towards 6 o'clock, when, I suppose, you would be going to church, the
shelling grew less intense and less accurate: so that I was mercifully helped to
do my duty and crawl, wade, climb and flounder over No Man's Land to visit
my other post. It took me half an hour to move about 150 yards.

I was chiefly annoyed by our own machine guns from behind. The seeng-
seeng-seeng of the bullets reminded me of Mary's canary. On the whole I can
40   support the canary better.

In the Platoon on my left the sentries over the dug-out were blown to
nothing. One of these poor fellows was my first **servant** whom I rejected. If I
had kept him he would have lived, for servants don't do Sentry Duty. I kept
my own sentries half way down the stairs during the more terrific
bombardment. In spite of this one lad was blown down and, I am afraid,
blinded.

This was my only casualty …

Your very own Wilfred

From W. Owen, *Collected Letters*, ed. H. Owen and J. Bell, OUP, 1967

DICTIONARY

B.E.F. British Expeditionary Force, the title given to that part of the British Army which was fighting on the Western Front, in northern France and Belgium

dug-out a shelter literally dug out of the ground

No Man's Land the area between the two opposing armies

trench a deep ditch along and in which the soldiers moved and lived

servant officers had ordinary soldiers assigned to them as servants, to help look after their equipment and to see to their general welfare

CLOSER READING

1 In your own words, describe what Wilfred Owen's job was during the time he talks about in his letter.

2 How many men was Owen responsible for, and what jobs did he give them to do?

3 Draw a sketch map of the area of trenches and No Man's Land which Owen describes. Label it with all the information that you can gather from the letter.

4 What happened to the sentries guarding the dug-out to the left of Owen's position? What did Owen do to ensure that his own sentries did not suffer in the same way?

5 Using the information provided in the letter, write Owen's report to his senior officer setting out what happened during the four days he was stationed in No Man's Land. Remember that your account will be straightforward, formal and factual, and will be written in Standard English.

4 | Advice to his son

This is an extract from a letter of Philip Dormer Stanhope, Earl of Chesterfield (1694–1773). Chesterfield was an active politician, and knew many of the influential people of his day. He published a number of volumes of letters, including a set of letters which he wrote to his son, in which he advised him on his education and behaviour. In the passage below, addressed to his son while he was travelling in Europe, Chesterfield talks to him about what to look out for in others, and how to model himself on what he admires in other people.

(Some words are highlighted in the text. You will find further information about these words at the end of the passage.)

DEAR BOY,

Whatever I see, or whatever I hear, my first **consideration** is, whether it can in any way be useful to you. As a proof of this, I went accidentally the other day into a print-shop, where, among many others, I found one print from a famous design of Carlo Maratti, who died about thirty years ago, and was the last eminent painter in Europe; the subject is *il Studio del Disegno*, or the School of Drawing. An old man, supposed to be the master, points to his scholars, who are **variously employed** in perspective, geometry, and the observation of the statues of **antiquity**. With regard to perspective, of which
10 there are some little specimens, he wrote, *Tanto che basti*, that is, *As much as is sufficient*; with regard to Geometry, *Tanto che basti*, again; with regard to the contemplation of the ancient statues, there is written, *Non mai a bastanza*; *There never can be enough*. But in the clouds, at the top of the piece, are

represented **the three Graces**, with this just sentence written over them, *Senza di noi agni fatica è vana*; that is, *Without us all labour is vain*.

This everybody allows to be true in painting; but all people do not seem to consider, as I hope you will, that this truth is full as applicable to every other art or science; indeed to everything that is to be said and done ... It must be owned, that the Graces do not seem to be natives of Great Britain; and, I

20   doubt, the best of us here have more of the rough than polished diamond. Since barbarism drove them out of Greece and Rome, they seem to have taken refuge in France, where their temples are numerous, and their worship the established one.

Examine yourself seriously, why such and such people please and engage you, more than such and such others of equal merit; and you will always find that it is because the former have the Graces and the latter not. I have known many a woman, with an exact shape, and a **symmetrical assemblage** of beautiful features, please nobody; while others, with very moderate shapes and features, have charmed everybody. Why? because Venus will not charm

30   so much, without her attendant Graces, as they will without her. Among men, how often have I seen the most solid merit and knowledge neglected, unwelcome, or even rejected, for want of them! While flimsy parts, little knowledge, and less merit, introduced by the Graces, have been received, cherished, and admired. Even virtue, which is moral beauty, wants some of its charms if unaccompanied by them.

If you ask me how you shall acquire what neither you nor I can define or ascertain, I can only answer, *by observation*. Form yourself, with regard to others, upon what you feel pleases you in them. I can tell the importance, the advantage, of having the Graces; but I cannot give them you; I heartily wish I

40   could, and I certainly would; for I do not know a better present that I could make you.

To show you that a very wise, **philosophical**, and **retired** man thinks upon that subject as I do, who have always lived in the world, I send you ... the famous Mr Locke's book upon education; in which you will find the stress which he lays upon the Graces, which he calls (and very truly) good breeding. I have marked all the parts of that book which are worth your attention; for as he begins with the child, almost from its birth, the parts relative to its infancy would be useless to you. Germany is, still less than England, the seat of the Graces; however, you had as good not say so while you are there.

From Earl of Chesterfield, *Letters*, 1774 edition

DICTIONARY

consideration thought

variously employed doing different things

antiquity from classical Greece and Rome

the three Graces three ancient Greek sister-goddesses regarded as the givers of beauty and charm, and portrayed as women of exquisite beauty.

symmetrical assemblage well-ordered arrangement

philosophical learned

retired living a private rather than a public life

CLOSER READING

1 Re-read the whole letter, numbering the paragraphs 1 to 5. In your own words, write five sentences, one sentence summarising the essential meaning of each paragraph.

2 Chesterfield wrote these letters to give his son information and advice. Draw up two columns, one headed Information and the other headed Advice. Note down in each column all the information and advice contained in this letter. Your chart might begin a little like this one.

Information	Advice
Description of Maratti's print	Look at why you like some people more than others

3 In your own words, summarise the advice that Chesterfield is giving his son here, then write a brief paragraph saying whether you agree or disagree with what he is saying. Give reasons drawn from your own experience and observation to back up your point of view.

FURTHER ACTIVITIES

1 Working on your own, look back over the continuum diagram on page vi and its explanation on page vii.

- Re-read all four texts in the section above.

- Draw your own continuum, going from Information to Polemic, and place each of the four texts where you think they would best fit.

- Compare your findings with a partner, and discuss any differences there are between your two diagrams. What clues in the texts did you use to come up with your findings?

- On your own, write an advice leaflet for Year 7 students on the language and layout of different kinds of letter.

2 On your own, look again at Text no. 1 (page 195) and Text no. 4 (pages 200–201).

- Imagine that Chesterfield's son writes to an agony column about his father and the advice he is giving him. Think about the way the young man would feel, and the worries he might have about measuring up to his father's expectations of him, and write the letter he might have written. Model your letter on the style and tone of the letters in Text no. 1.

- With a partner, swap your letters, and each write the kind of reply Anita Naik might have written. You may find it useful to refer back to your notes to Question 4 in the Closer Reading exercises on Text no. 1.
- Use the pairs of letters to mount a class display.

3 On your own, look through all four texts.

- Make sure you are clear about the different kinds of tone and language used for different audiences and purposes.
- Imagine that you are a householder who has had a flood in your house because the neighbours have left the sink blocked and a tap running all over the weekend. Write a series of letters to:

  a Your insurance company, making a claim for all the damage that has been caused. You will need to give the insurance company clear details about what has been damaged and what the replacement costs are likely to be.

  b Your mother, letting her know what has happened without worrying her too much.

  c Your best friend, telling the story of the flood and giving them a good idea of just how you are really feeling, and what you would like to do.

Make sure your letters show in their tone, language and layout the different audiences and purposes for which they are written.

INFORMATION ◄──► PERSUASION

Electronic Texts

Letters

Instructions · Legal Writing · Information Writing · Biography · Interviews · Essays · Travel Writing · Diaries · Philosophical Writing · Autobiography · Social Commentary · Reportage · Reviews · Promotional Writing · Polemic

17
Electronic Texts

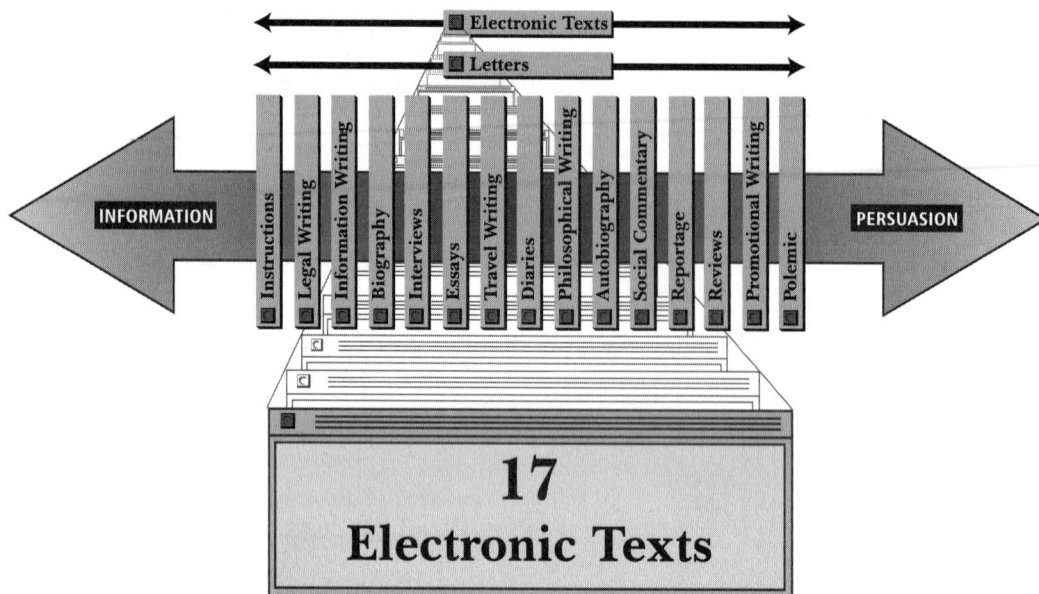

Electronic texts are becoming more and more part of our lives. Some, such as Ceefax and Teletext, already appear to us perfectly ordinary; others, such as CD-ROMs and the Internet, are only just beginning to reach a mass readership. All of these different kinds of text are beginning to affect not only our way of life, but also our ways of reading and writing.

The texts in this chapter have been taken from a CD-ROM and from a book on designing CD-ROMs, from Teletext, and two texts from a 'Making Friends' web page on the Internet. In the following activities, we will be looking less at the content of the texts, since electronic texts can be about anything, and more at the ways in which that content is conveyed to the reader. You will be asked to consider different kinds of electronic text, to examine the different audiences they are addressing and to assess the different reading and writing skills that they demand.

1 CD-ROM

Hypermedia texts, the technical name for texts that are published on CD-ROM, seem to be almost limitless in their potential. All that restrains their scope is the amount of memory available on disk and the cost of production. Both of these factors are constantly being improved, with disks able to store more and more information, and with production costs coming down as techniques become slicker and more sophisticated.

What, then, makes a hypermedia text distinctive and different from any other kind of text you may read in conventional printed form?

The most obvious difference is that implied in its name – it uses a variety of media, text, sound and graphics to create an experience and to impart information. At the same time, the different 'pages' of a hypermedia text are linked in a different way from the pages in a printed book. Books such as the one you are reading now are usually read in a *linear* way, with the reader travelling through the text along a sequence of pages from first to last. In a hypermedia text there is no set sequence – the reader can choose which path to follow along all the routes available to them. This is known as 'random access'. The only limit to the reader's choice is the number of different 'pages' and links between them available on the CD. In practice, the limit is that of the current technology, so that the reader's choice is made only from those areas that have already been selected by the text designers. One question you will be asked to consider later is just this notion of the reader's freedom when operating a hypermedia text.

Below you will find two hypermedia passages, one a selection of screens from a CD-ROM on Shakespeare's *Twelfth Night*, the other a working drawing for a hypermedia educational quiz game called Grand Tour.

A SHAKESPEARE'S *TWELFTH NIGHT*

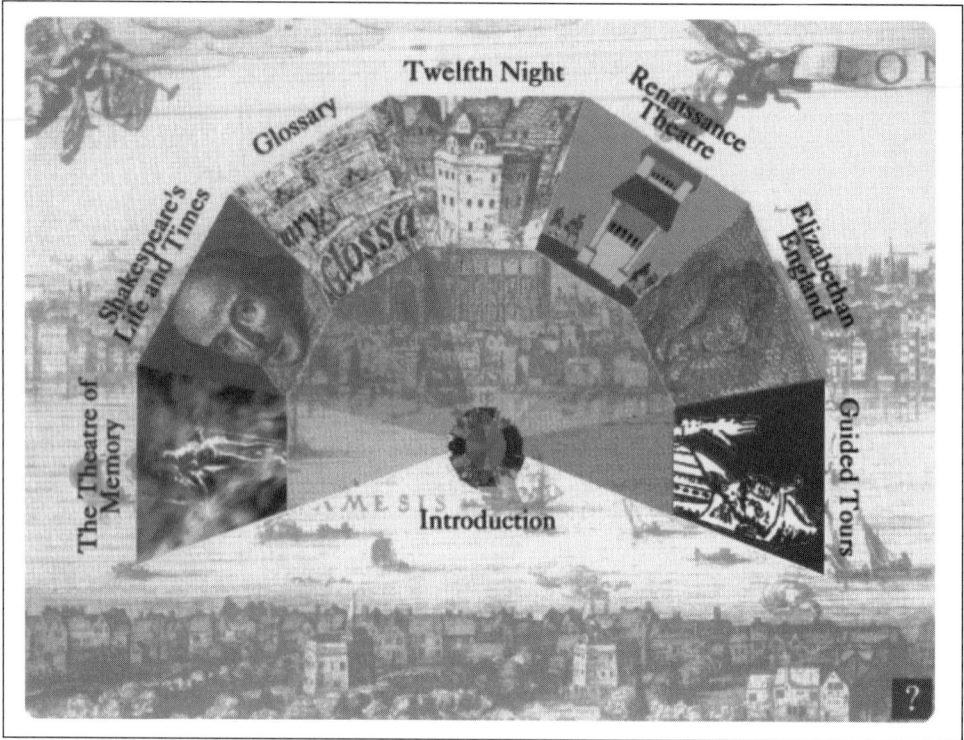

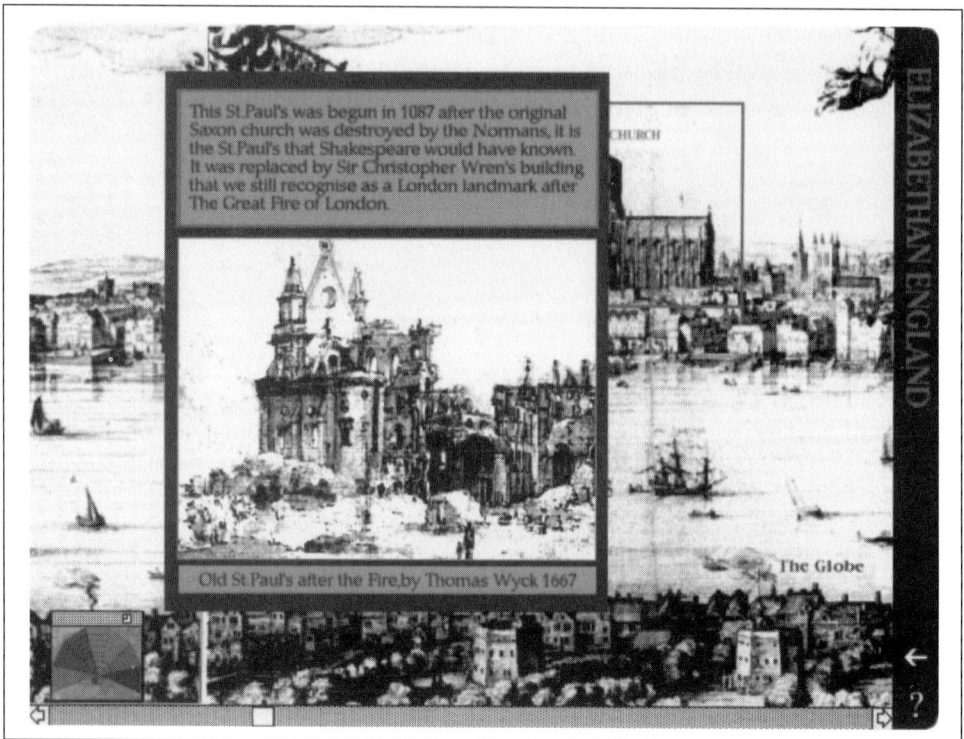

This St.Paul's was begun in 1087 after the original Saxon church was destroyed by the Normans, it is the St.Paul's that Shakespeare would have known. It was replaced by Sir Christopher Wren's building that we still recognise as a London landmark after The Great Fire of London.

Old St.Paul's after the Fire, by Thomas Wyck 1667

From *Twelfth Night* CD-ROM, Art of Memory (Interactive)

B THE GRAND TOUR

'Grand Tour' was designed by the authors as a European cultural quiz game. Users can choose from a variety of subjects and have to answer questions related to the country or city they have selected. Answering correctly allows them to choose another venue. The winner is the first to complete the Grand Tour, linking all the European Community countries together. This working drawing shows how the structure of the game was developed.

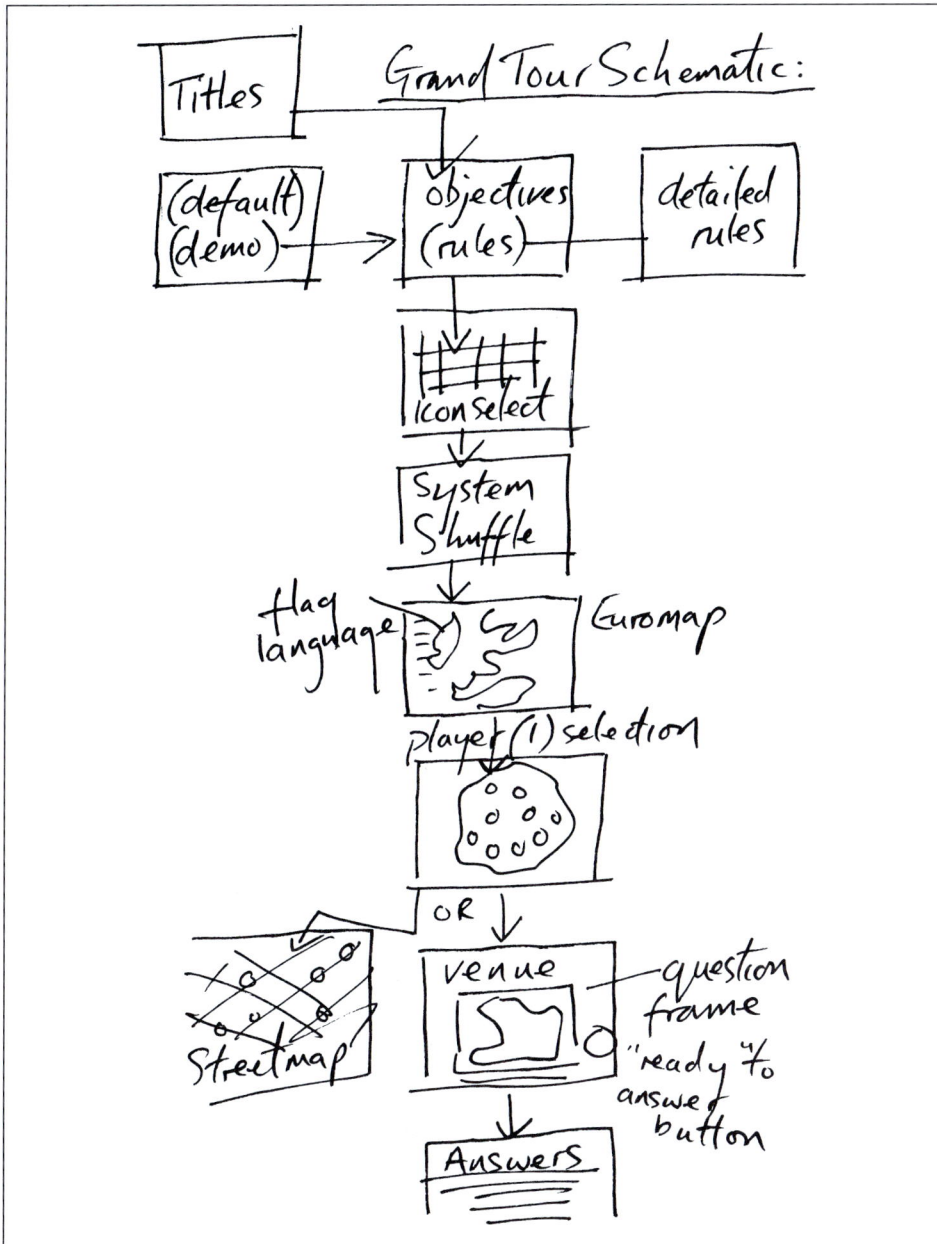

Adapted from B. Cotton and R. Oliver, *Understanding Hypermedia*, Phaidon, 1992

CLOSER READING

1 Look again at passage A, then note down all the information that the two screens give you.

2 Now draw two columns, one headed Text, and the other headed Graphics. In the Text column, list all the written information you are given on each screen; in the Graphics column, list all the pictures. Your columns may start off like this.

Text	Graphics
1. Introduction	1. Picture of London at the time of Shakespeare
2. Guided Tours	

3 Choose **one** item from your list about which you are given both text and graphic information. In your own words, write two or three sentences summarising the information you are given in both sources.

4 Write a short paragraph giving your view as to the value of the different kinds of information given to you in Passage A. Say which you find most interesting, and which you find most useful (they may not always be the same thing …). Use examples from the passage to back up your point of view.

5 Look again at Passage B. This is a script for part of a hypermedia quiz game called Grand Tour. In your own words, summarise how the designer is expecting the user to respond to the material offered. You might like to do this in the kind of language the designer would use in writing a proposal to the manufacturer.

2 Ceefax

Ceefax and its rival Teletext are like a mixture of magazines and newspapers. They provide up-to-the-minute information of changing situations in the news, weather and sport, as well being an easily accessed database of information about topics as diverse as holidays for sale or astrological readings.

The passage below is an extract from five pages of music reviews on Ceefax. As you read it, you might like to think about the tone and language of the reviews, and about how much information you are being given.

———— **new album** ————

**PAUL McCARTNEY FLAMING PIE
(Parlophone) WATCH OUT, BEATLE'S ABOUT!**

Macca's got his knighthood, his wife is thankfully on the mend and he's finally remembered he used to be in a half-decent little band.

Fab Four links are scattered throughout the album. The title itself, Ringo's appearance on Really Love You and Beautiful Night and George Martin's influence on Somedays and Calico Skies.

For good measure, Linda, son James and Steve Millar also figure on what's a bluesy, Beatly affair – suits you, sir!

———————— by Chris Charles ————————

———— **new singles** ————

SINEAD O'CONNOR GOSPEL OAK EP

(Chrysalis) A quartet of ballads from the woman with the golden tonsils who has forgotten how to get angry.

This is to Mother You tells the sad tale of her lover's unhappy childhood and how she has kissed it better.

All sweetly sung by the voice of a contented woman. It'd be good to see her have a rant now and again though.

MY LIFE STORY STRUMPET (Parlophone)

Strumpets, trumpets, 'Queen Medusa serial seducer,' AND a choir. Extremely busy but never really goes anywhere.

———————— by Chris Charles ————————

CLOSER READING

1 Read through the whole of the passage above and note down all the items of information that you are given. You should end up with about twenty items.

2 Sort your list into two categories, one containing 'hard' information, the other containing opinion. Which list is the longer?

3 Re-write the reviews in your own words. Make sure you include all the information and opinions that you have noted down.

4 Count the total number of words in your version, and the total number of words in the original reviews. Which is the longer? Look in detail at the differences between the two versions, and write a brief account of what they are, and why the original is written in the way that it is. Use examples from the text to illustrate what you are saying.

3 | The Internet

There are as many different kinds of texts on the Internet as there are throughout the domain of printed material. There are letters, magazines, advertisements, shopping catalogues ... anything that anybody wants to communicate is there. What, then, makes it different from printed material?

There are two main important differences, one to do with *what* is read, and the other to do with the *way* it is read.

So long as you have access to the appropriate hardware, the Net provides you not only with text, but with colour graphics, video graphics and even sound. In terms of the whole experience provided, it appears much more exciting than a printed page.

As for the readership, readers of material on the Net tend to be on their own when reading, and so form a one-to-one relationship with the text. In this way the medium is both very public – anybody can access the Net at any time from anywhere in the world – and very private – only one person is likely to be reading their screen.

In the passage that follows, from a 'dating agency ' on the Net called Cupid's Network, you will be asked to think about the language, tone, presentation and layout of the text, as well as the actual content.

(Note: the spelling has been left exactly as it was in the original, even when incorrect.)

Get Hitched on This Net!

http://www.get-met.com

No hype! Get Met is a very well put together singles site with a great layout and tons of fields for you to search on. They carry lots of photos with even a photo viewing section so you can look at individuals and choose instead of searching. As with any good site, your identity is Secure with Get Met as all communications take place within the site.

American SINGLES

American Singles is the largest non-profit dating service in the US. Over 65,000 active members online. There are extensive profiles written by each of the members and many photos. Real people that want to meet you!

Your Chance for Romance!!

Free Trial   Click Here

MatchMaker

Trying to find romance on the internet can be like finding a needle in a haystack.... come use our magnet!! MatchMaker, the only place you will ever have to go to to find quality people! With over 75,000 users on-line from every walk of life and advanced features like chat, personal e-mail and postcards finding your mate will be a cinch.

Single Search

Matches Guaranteed -- Local Bases in All Areas

Single Search is based upon University Research and Surveys of what singles value most in relationships. Its proven technology enhances the opportunity for romance and saves time for busy singles. Single Search is NOT a dating service nor a 900 service. It is a highly successful method of searching for soulmates.

ANASTASIA
FIND YOUR HAPPINESS

Cupid's Network ™
Cool Sites

These sites have been selected as the best of Cupid's Network. Each of *Cupid's Cool Sites* has a large member base, many services and many happy customers. Although *Cupid's Cool Sites* may not have the breadth or depth of some of our regional or special interest sites, we think they come the closest to "ALL things for all people". Look for more of Cupid's Featured sites with a triple heart ♥♥♥ graphic. The sites listed below are NOT in any particular order. We shuffle them regularly to give each equal time.

match.com

Just leave your bags behind. Those blind dates, bar scenes, hang-ups, mixed messages and lost moments that make you wonder, "Is there a right person for me?" Match.Com is where you meet new people in the most popular, comfortable, engaging place around. Discover how thousands have found relationship bliss thanks to Match.Com online and off.

Romance Online

Tired of blind dates? Check out Romance Online, where every single's profile has a photo. With singles from all over the world, our search engine allows you to quickly find that special someone. You can also submit your photo-profile for free! Let Romance Online help you find the love of your life.

mix'n match

mix 'n match

the online dating 'n mating

Members Respond

You *Have* Been a Fool For Love!

We asked for your stories about playing the fool for love, and some whoppers. All names have been removed to protect the potentially embarrassed!

- Going All Out
- Taking a Leap for Love
- Older Woman, Younger Man
- Romancing a Gorgeous Stranger
- Does Hitting on a "Taken" Person Ever Work?
- Are You a Single Parent? Send us Your Stories!

Going All Out

My college has an annual girls ask guys dance. I wanted to ask this guy I had been crushing on for a while. We never seemed to be alone together, so I made a HUGE banner asking him to go with me to the dance. I hung it in the lobby of his dorm. When he saw the banner, he called me up and quickly agreed. We had a great time!!

Worth it? Yes. We like your style!

Taking a Leap for Love

I was Airborne in the military and loved to jump. My (now ex) me teach her and she became a most accomplished jumper. On had been talking about trust and she held she never knew if a actually trusted her or how they really felt since any statem merely words and there was no real way to evidince it.

Our discussion contiued into the air and I was standing in the about to jump when it hit me that there WAS something one c

to prove their feelings. I unhooked my harness, turned to her . "Well, I trust you." With that I handed her my chute and steppe gate.

Needless to say she did not let me down. She wept for joy fi knowing that someone did love and trust her, something she h always wanted but was never sure of. It may have been crazy foolish, but I have never regretted my impulsive act. I guess a little of the romantic in me.

A little bit?! Wow! We're impressed!

Older Woman, Younger Man

Oh yes, was I ever a fool. At age 49 I met a young man over h and fell madly in love. We went on a wild and crazy ride for 2 years. But sadly and finally, I got really tired of braking for games and a steady diet of Bart Simpson. I missed the maturi conversation of someone my own age. I kept trying to stretch boy-man into a husband, but he was just too little and inexpe And of course, I was "mom" and made most of the household n did get tired of the heavy fiscal responsibility.

We learned so much though. Being different ages can be fun s His youth and energy were contagious so that now I have mor and look much, much younger than my years. I still find young attractive, but would be careful not to get too involved since well the pitfalls of age differences. I don't want to be "mom" for anybody. My own children are grown up and now I want to some fun, date, and meet all kinds of different men.

It was always unsettling to introduce my sweetie to relative friends who have known me a long time. He was shorter than about three inches and looked so boyish. Walking hand in hand sidewalks of the city I couldn't help feeling in some way like robber.

Who knows, now I'm making room in my heart for someone my and maybe the last is best!

This is a bittersweet story. But it goes to show that no matt an experience was like, you can learn from it.

CLOSER READING

1 Look through the extract as a whole, and then, in two or three sentences, note down your initial impression of it. Comment not only on the content, but also on the layout and graphics.

2 Re-read the 'Cool Sites' section (page 211). Make two lists, one noting all the similarities in information being offered in each of the sites, the other noting any similarities in language, tone, punctuation etc. in the advertisements for each site.

3 Write a brief (200 word) guide for those wishing to advertise in the 'Cool Sites' section of Cupid's Network, giving clear advice on the kind of product being advertised, and the recommended language and layout.

4 Look again at the 'Mix 'n match' section (pages 211–212). In your own words, summarise:
   - each of the readers' letters
   - the responses from Cupid's Network.

5 Write two or three sentences describing the tone and language used in this section (formal, chatty, etc.). Use examples from the text to illustrate your comments.

6 Play the detective. On the basis of the notes that you have made above, write a 'profile' of the typical reader of Cupid's Network. Include details of age, gender, the kind of job they do and the place and time in which they visit the website.

FURTHER ACTIVITIES

1
- With a partner, turn to chapter 3 of this book (Information Writing) and look at **either** Text 1 **or** Text 2 on health advice (pages 22–24).
- Note down in two columns the similarities and differences between this text and the texts you have been looking at in this chapter. Consider layout, formality/informality and reader involvement.
- On your own, read the extract that follows (pages 214–215), which is taken from a book on hypermedia texts.

HYPERMEDIA TEXTS

Tiger Media: Production Sketches for "Murder makes strange Deadfellows"

Tiger Media are in the vanguard of companies developing hypermedia programmes that utilize the work of top-grade illustrators and animators. Cartoon-style animations use only a restricted number of colours and this makes them ideal for systems with a limited capacity for data transfer as images can be compressed without loss of quality.

animation

"autoplay" condition, where a specific animation is looped as a "trailer" or come-on for the programme if no user interaction has taken place for some minutes. This default condition can be driven by software that selects parts of the programme at random, providing an ever-changing montage of features, or more simply a sequence of slow "dissolves" between graphic frames, or even a specially designed screen saver. The default condition instantly responds to any new action taken by the user, with some sort of "Continue?" or "Start again?" prompt.

Transitional effects are a form of feedback, letting users know that the system is responding to a command such as selecting the required section of the programme, or progressing forward through that section. Most hypermedia

programmes, for example, involve some sort of information hierarchy. The user selects the required section, then the sub-section and eventually the frame that is of interest. This frame may link to other frames in other parts of the programme. The transitional effects that signal these frame changes can identify which level of the programme is currently in use, and can give the user a sense of "place" within the programme. Simple animations can also give important feedback to the user in "wait states", where the action taken by the user cannot be performed within the time it takes for the system to display a new screen. The conventional options here are a ticking clock, emptying egg timer, moving bar chart, flashing "alert" icon, animated cursor or highlight changing colour.

Video Games

Videogames use a variety of animation techniques to provide both 2d and 3d moving images. Typically, 2d games use animated "sprites", small graphics which are manipulated by the user and move around over a 2d backdrop. Animations in 3d can involve constructing complete environments using vector graphics, or using variable-size sprites on top of drawn backgrounds.

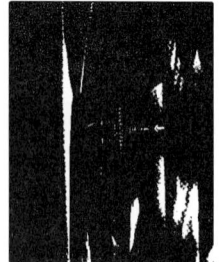

Flight simulators

Videogame flight simulators use vector models, computer graphic models from which images are computed in realtime in response to the user's actions. The user is in direct control of the animations, moving a joystick or mouse to determine the flight path of the aircraft through the virtual space of the game.

animation

take a LETTER

EXTRUDE

it into Hyperspace

and it becomes a

FRAGMENTED

PIXELLATED

and dispa rte set of s a

RANDOM
RANDOM DATA.

Computer Graphics Workshop: High Bandwidth Panning

Even within the restricted format of Hypercard 1.0, it is possible to produce lively animation sequences, either by displaying illustrated cards in quick succession (as though they were frames of a film), or by scripting actions to take place on the card itself, such as moving objects around, resizing them or instructing Hypercard to use its painting tools, and specifying the necessary X, Y coordinates to create an image that appears to draw itself.

A ten second essay on "hypertypography" in the Computer Graphics Workshop's hypermagazine. Words are flashed staccato fashion at a speed that borders on the subliminal, synchronized with a digital-audio metronome and punctuated with distinct spoken words. The sense of the essay is only acquired through time. This technique was first explored by Michael Snow, the Canadian avant garde film-maker in the 70s.

HyperTypography

"Music Plus is now the

Authoring "In a
vision Mixmaster

HARD DISK:HBP:Bandwidth Panic
HARD DISK:HBP:hypertypo2

From B. Cotton and R. Oliver, *Understanding Hypermedia*, Phaidon, 1992

- On your own, list three different elements in the way the information is presented in the text you have just read and the way in which it is presented in the information text on health advice which you have just been working on with your partner.

- In two or three short sentences, suggest why the authors of the hypermedia text chose to present their information in the way that they have.

- Write a short paragraph comparing the ways in which the information is presented in the two texts. Which seems to you to be the more successful? Use quotations and references to back up your comments.

2
- On your own, turn to chapter 3 (Information Writing) and re-read Text no. 4 on the 'Space Race' (page 26).

- In a short paragraph, summarise the main items of information contained in that text.

- Look again at the script for a hypermedia text on page 207 (the Grand Tour working drawing).

- Design a hypermedia text for a CD-ROM on the 'Space Race', using the information from the Space Race text that you have noted down.

- Write a brief assessment of your script, comparing it with the original text. Say which you think conveys more information, which conveys it successfully and why. Use quotations and references to back up your argument.

3
- In a small group, brainstorm all the different forms in which information is available (such as encyclopaedias, dictionaries, leaflets, CD-ROMs …).

- In the same group, brainstorm all the different places in which information is available (such as bookshops, post offices, libraries …).

- Discuss together which are the easiest and most reliable sources of information, and put your list in a rank order from the easiest to the most difficult to consult. Consider both ease of access and ease of extracting information.

- On your own, write an argumentative essay in response to the statement below, giving your own point of view, and using specific references to back it up.

'For all the apparent freedoms of CD-ROMs and the Internet, printed books and libraries continue to offer the reader a greater range of reliable information.'